Those Vintage Years of Radio

Those Vintage Years of Radio

John Snagge & Michael Barsley

PN
1991.3
G7
S6

Pitman Publishing

First published 1972

SIR ISAAC PITMAN AND SONS LTD
Pitman House, Parker Street, Kingsway, London WC2B 5PB
PO Box 46038, Portal Street, Nairobi, Kenya

SIR ISAAC PITMAN (AUST) PTY LTD
Pitman House, 158 Bouverie Street, Carlton, Victoria 3053, Australia

PITMAN PUBLISHING COMPANY SA LTD
PO Box No 11231, Johannesburg, South Africa

PITMAN PUBLISHING CORPORATION
6 East 43rd Street, New York, NY 10017, USA

SIR ISAAC PITMAN (CANADA) LTD
495 Wellington Street West, Toronto 135, Canada

THE COPP CLARK PUBLISHING COMPANY
517 Wellington Street West, Toronto 135, Canada

© John Snagge and Michael Barsley, 1972

ISBN: 0 273 31663 X

Text set in 11/12 pt. Monotype Ehrhardt, printed by letterpress, and bound in Great Britain at The Pitman Press, Bath

G.93:11

to Eileen and Jenny

without whose help this book
would never have been rewritten

Preface

We have chosen 1935 to 1953 as the Vintage Years of Radio, for within those years the BBC, faced by events of world-wide importance, each of which threw down a gauntlet, as it were, accepted the challenges, and produced the greatest achievement in broadcasting the world has ever known.

Having said this, we would like to add that this collection of reminiscences about people and programmes is in no way an official BBC history of those years.

The series of Royal occasions (the Silver Jubilee of King George V, his death, the Abdication of King Edward VIII, the Coronation of King George VI, all within two years), the Munich crisis, and the Second World War—each and every one posed new problems, and was a "first-ever" radio experience.

The vintage was not therefore a mellow one. It was sparkling, heady and exciting for anyone in the BBC, and for the listener it had an equally exciting flavour, for the connoisseur and the newcomer alike.

During these years, too, the BBC offered a unique realm of entertainment—the world of Tommy Handley's *ITMA*, the *Brains Trust* of Joad, Huxley and Campbell, John Watt's infinite Variety, Val Gielgud's plays and Laurence Gilliam's Features—and reflected the country and people at war.

This is the radio world in which we worked. These are the people we met. These, and many others, are the programmes in which we had a hand. To those who tasted the vintage of those years, we offer a host of memories of our own choosing: to those accustomed to a new, colour television age, it may come as a surprise that such talent and tomfoolery were to be had for the listening.

Acknowledgements

It is usual, in a book like this, to have the assistance of researchers. But since this is a volume of joint reminiscences rather than a history of a period in radio, we have done most of the research ourselves. We would, however, like to thank Mr Peter Carrick for invaluable help in the early stages, when the book was taking shape.

We may seem to have regarded "Auntie" (as it was once the fashion to call the BBC) as a cross between a game old girl and a pernickety old prune. All the more reason for us, in our independent attitude, to thank those ex-colleagues and others who have given up valuable time to let us have their contributions and stories at first hand (this being a radio book, it owes much to that admirable standby of radio, the tape-recorder).

We have been given every support by various BBC Departments, where we have met many old friends. Particular thanks are due to Mr George Campey, Head of BBC Publicity, Miss Joan Houlgate of BBC Library, Broadcasting House, Mr John Lane of BBC Archives, and for special enthusiasm and vivid memory Mr Howard Thomas of Thames Television and Mr Ronnie Waldman of Vis-News.

Our thanks are also due to Mrs Bruce Wyndham and Miss Joan Wilson, not only for typing the manuscript, but often for correcting us on finer points of detail.

A final word of thanks to a body which does not always come in for its meed of praise: British Rail. Many of our discussions and recordings took place in a room in the Great Western Royal Hotel at Paddington, a convenient meeting-place for authors who live in Stoke Poges and Oxford respectively. We hope that this room will hereafter be known as the SNAGBAR.

Most of the material in this book that is not our own reminiscences was obtained at first hand. In addition, many books were consulted and the most important are listed below, arranged under publishers:

BBC Publications: *Muggeridge Through the Microphone* by Malcolm Muggeridge; *Persons from Porlock and Other Plays for Radio* by Louis MacNeice.

ACKNOWLEDGEMENTS

Bodley Head Ltd: *Years in a Mirror* by Val Gielgud; *The Third Floor Back* by Hugh Greene.
André Deutsch Ltd: *Behind the Screen* by Michael Barsley.
Evans Brothers Ltd: *BBC Features* edited by Laurence Gilliam.
Faber & Faber Ltd: *The Dark Tower* (Introduction).
Heinemann Ltd: *Both Sides of the Hill* by Lord Hill of Luton.
Hodder & Stoughton Ltd: *Into the Wind* by Lord Reith, and *One Man in His Time* by Bruce Belfrage.
Hutchinson & Co Ltd: *In Show Business Tonight* by Peter Duncan, and *"Good Evening, Everyone!"* by A. J. Alan.
Herbert Jenkins Ltd: *No Chip on my Shoulder* by Eric Maschwitz.
Michael Joseph Ltd: *The Wolf at the Door* and *Tape Recording* by Michael Barsley; *Number One Boy* by Edward Ward.
T. Werner Laurie Ltd: *TommyHandley* by Ted Kavanagh.
Lawson & Dunn Ltd: *Shreds and Patches* by Mabel Constanduros.
Macdonald Ltd: *Quizzically Yours* by Kenneth Horne and John Ellison.
Macdonald & Evans Ltd: *This is London . . .* by Stuart Hibberd.
Odhams Press Ltd: *Here's to the Next Time* by Henry Hall; *Up and Down the Line* by Jack Train.
Peter Owen Ltd: *Portrait of the Artist as a Professional Man* by Rayner Heppenstall; *One Thing at a Time* by Harmon Grisewood.
Oxford University Press: *War Report—a record of despatches*, *The Birth of Broadcasting*, *The Golden Age of Wireless* and *War of Words* by Professor Asa Briggs.
Pan Books Ltd: *Anzio* by Wynford Vaughan Thomas.
Sampson Low, Marston & Co Ltd: *The BBC and All That* by P. P. Eckersley.

A large number of radio personalities have written their own personal story, and occasional odd remarks may come from these. We have tried to check this list thoroughly, but apologize in advance for any inadvertent errors or omissions.

J. S.
M. B.

Contents

	Preface	*page*	vii
	Acknowledgements		ix
	Illustrations		xiii
1	"The Chummy Place"		1
2	Life in the BBC		10
3	Corridors of Power		48
4	The BBC Comes of Age		65
5	Royal Broadcasts		84
6	Drama and Variety		106
7	Talk, Talk, Talk		156
8	The Organized Jungle		171
9	The BBC Faces War		179
10	Some Radio Personalities		204
11	The BBC's Jubilee		229
	Index		243

Illustrations

Between pages 16 and 17

A dramatic photograph of Broadcasting House after the bombing of December 1940
John Snagge's first BBC job
Sir William Haley
John Snagge with Lord Reith
Sir Lindsay Wellington CBE
Charles Hill seen as "The Radio Doctor"
Charles Curran
King George V, the first royal broadcaster
King Edward VIII
King George VI
HRH Princess Elizabeth
Barsley's first programme: Christmas Day 1943

Between pages 80 and 81

Stuart Hibberd and John Snagge celebrate twenty-five years' service
ITMA
Children's Hour
Dylan Thomas
Louis MacNeice
Howard Thomas coping with Brains Trust questions
Val Gielgud and Stephen Potter
Laurence Gilliam with Alan Burgess
Ronnie Waldman and Gordon Crier
"Lobby" (Seymour Joly de Lotbinière)
John Watt in discussion with Eric Maschwitz
Harassed BBC Secretary

Between pages 144 and 145

Vintage '47: line-up for the BBC's 25th Birthday Programme
John Snagge commentating at Henley
Oxford Sinks! The 1951 Boat Race
Christmas Day Round the World
Barsley interviews Trevor Howard in Ceylon
Two Barsley drawings
BBC cricket team travelling in style 1946
On location on the Norfolk Broads 1946
D Day Announcement read by John Snagge, 6th June 1944

ILLUSTRATIONS

Between pages 208 and 209

Jack Payne
Henry Hall says goodbye
Richard Dimbleby training with the BBC War Reporting Unit
Alistair Cooke
Franklin Engelmann in *Brains of Britain*
"Tommy" Woodrooffe
Marjorie Anderson with the crew of HMS *Roebuck*
Godfrey Basely of *The Archers*
Godfrey Talbot and Wynford Vaughan Thomas
Michael Barsley at the production panel
Bernard Braden discussing his radio script
Stewart Macpherson

"To work. To my own office, my own job,
Not matching pictures but inventing sound,
Precalculating microphone and knob

In homage to the human voice. To found
A castle in the air requires a mint
Of golden intonations and a mound

Of typescript in the trays. What was in print
Must take on breath and what was thought be said.
In the end there was the Word, at first a glint,

Then an illumination overhead
Where the high towers are lit. Such was our aim. . ."

LOUIS MACNEICE   *Autumn Sequel*[1]

---

[1] Reprinted by permission of Faber & Faber Ltd from *The Collected Poems of Louis MacNeice*.

1 "The Chummy Place"

ON Tuesday, 14th November 1922, the British Broadcasting Company first went on the air, as a public service, from Marconi House in Aldwych. Very shortly, the Company moved its headquarters to No. 2 Savoy Hill, a building on the Embankment behind the Savoy Hotel. Here the Company was dissolved, and became a Corporation, in 1927, and here broadcasting went on until 1932, when the BBC moved to its present headquarters, built and designed for the purpose, in Portland Place.

So much for the facts. What was life at Savoy Hill really like?

It was, as Jack Payne called it, a "chummy place." You wandered into it: it appeared just like an office building, not being very much used. The studios (we've forgotten if they had red lights outside or not) were just like one office after another. Going in was so easy. There was a commissionaire sitting at a little desk, and you might go up and say "My name's so-and-so, and I'm supposed to give a talk...." "Oh yes," the commissionaire would say kindly, as if he was at a gentleman's club, "would you come along to the drawing-room?" and there Colonel Brand, who looked after all visitors, would come in, perhaps in a dinner-jacket, would greet you, and say "Will you have a drink?" and, having properly installed you, he'd say "I'll go along to the announcer and tell him you're here." It was all done with such ease and informality.

Once inside the studio, you found quite a different aspect. The atmosphere was dead, the walls heavily shrouded with drapes and curtains, and in front of you stood that strange object, the microphone, perhaps with a red cyclopean eye on it. Remember that the BBC then had a monopoly of microphones. There weren't any mikes for handholding. Stage singers didn't use them, they were unknown things to the public, and because speakers on the wireless were some distance away, they felt they had to shout. Hence the reason for the terrifying little notice on the table, printed in almost Victorian type, which said "If you cough or rustle your papers, you will deafen millions of listeners." Sounds absurd today, but it's true.

Listeners in those early days used headphones, not loudspeakers, and a cough could have a much more devastating effect. But it was enough to make any nervous speaker hesitate even to breathe. Announcers usually remained standing with their scripts on a music-stand; guest speakers were allowed a chair and table. Yes, they were dismal places, those studios with their draperies, and with no ventilation except a couple of punkahs which merely stirred the air. The cubicles were a telephone-box—literally the same size—and the producer wore headphones. There was no manual control, no knob to turn. This was done by control-room. The original microphones were known as the meat-safe, four-legged machines with a great blue silk topping, about two foot by one, and a whacking great microphone in the middle which the engineers used to come and prod every now and again, because the coil had got stuck. If you took a watch near it, the watch would be paralysed, because the mike had such a heavy magnet. Meat-safes were on wheels, which might squeak when moved, and then the engineers would have to come in with an oil-can, perhaps in the middle of a concert.

People would say it was casual, and by later standards perhaps it *was* casual, but it was serious; serious in intention, though there was a lot of gaiety and laughter. There was a time when a studio caught fire, and firemen came in among everybody, making it like a scene from a Marx Brothers film. You might go down a corridor and find a Talks Director like Lionel Fielden, leaning against the wall and talking to, say, Tommy Handley or G. K. Chesterton. Everybody knew everyone else. Control-room staff mingled with everyone else.

To take an example of informality. Say you'd announced a concert in a studio near the drawing-room, and had nothing else immediately to do, you might go and meet Brand, that splendid character who looked like a colonel and *was* a colonel, with white moustache, hair and big athletic frame—he was very keen on sport—and with two others you might sit down and begin a game of bridge, while the music went round and round, and if it stopped you might look up and say "I wonder, is that the end of a movement or the end of the whole thing?" and, if it went on, "Two hearts." If the pause was long, you'd get up and go and make the appropriate announcement, and then return to the game. This sounds terribly casual, and it was in Reith's time, but it worked, because there was no panic, no rush, no stampede of people dashing by with scripts in their hands. The announcer of the evening introduced all the programmes, news, a talk, a symphony concert, an epilogue—the lot. This meant, of course, leaving time to go from one studio to another, so as to be in time for the next programme. When a programme ended, it was "buzzed out" by the announcer, but if he couldn't be there, he'd tell an office-boy to do it, to wait till the speaker looked up after he'd finished, then buzz him out. Many regular speakers buzzed themselves out—probably with a sense of relief!

It was a friendly atmosphere, with the shadow of Reith towering over all—and Carpendale.[1] When something went wrong, one of them would be on the phone at once—those phones you took off the hook. In a way, it was a sort of fantasy, a fairyland if you like. Nobody complained about the hours of work they had to do. John Snagge remembers, in the very early days, coming back to Savoy Hill one Christmas time because he'd forgotten his umbrella. He met Rex Palmer in the corridor, who said "Oh, John, I'm so glad you're here, because I've got to go off to a party. You might do that Savoy Hotel thing for me, would you?" So you did it—rather fun in a way, because you hadn't got to prepare anything. In that ghastly phrase of the modern young generation, you did your own thing. But it was with a good orchestra, like the Savoy Orpheans or the Havana Dance Band.

Rex Palmer, one of the indomitable, cheerful, versatile figures of those days, became the Company's first station director of 2LO. Like others, such as Gladstone Murray, he had a fine war record, being in the Royal Flying Corps and at Gallipolli (with Uncle Mac), and he was to become Uncle Rex of the Children's Hour. Rex had a beautiful singing voice, too, as did Frank Phillips and Alvar Lidell, and he set the whole pattern for announcers. Under him worked Dan Godfrey Junior as Station Musical Director: Stanford Robinson, Lindsay Wellington, Stanton Jeffries, and the enthusiastic newcomer Stuart Hibberd. In 1946 John Glyn-Jones produced an illuminating programme called *Over Ten Million* (listeners) in which A. R. Burrows was heard to say "we worked like lunatics in a pandemonium such as I hope may never fall to anyone else's experience." Snagge pointed out the difficulties of expansion in such a building.

The main staff lived cheek by jowl, in sort of loose-boxes, all the way along. There was only a glass partition between the Station Director and the Chief Accountant, and it didn't even reach the ceiling. The Cashier was a Miss Mallinson, who worked for a man called Wallage. She was important to people like announcers, who only got

[1] Admiral Charles Carpendale was then Controller BBC.

about £5 a week and had to be sociable, and were frequently broke before the end of the month. It was an old friend, that great character, the late Godfrey Adams who, when he needed a couple of quid for beer money to last him out, would address her as "Lady Mallinson of Wallage." Flattery? Ah, but it always worked.

In general, you found you enjoyed being on duty, which is more than can be said of the harassed BBC types of today. You were never overwhelmed by it; never overawed, and never in fear of your director or boss. That was the great change which later took place: the bosses became the bosses, and let you know it. At that time, they were with you, all involved in the same job. Carpendale and Lindsay Wellington, for instance, used to take part in radio plays—not in the BBC Amateur Dramatic Society, like Reith on a famous occasion—but on the air itself. Cecil Lewis was the first director of programmes, and soon found himself faced with a big problem: how to feed that "voracious monster," as he used to call the microphone, with enough material. Asa Briggs quotes a typical reply by Reith, when Lewis, who was working his twelve-hour day like everyone else, went to him and said he was likely to have a breakdown if things went on much longer: "Let me know when you're going to have it," said Mr J. C. W. Reith, "then we can arrange to have it in turns."[1]

But by contrast, the friendly feeling made up for it. The whole thing was done in an atmosphere of "what d'you think, old boy—d'you think this will be all right—d'you think Reith would approve of this?—we've got to work out these programmes, because we've got these stations outside London—there's this chap Percy Edgar in Birmingham, we'd better tell him he's got to take that programme, because it's going to cost us money—put a *phi* on his schedule...."

This needs explanation. Each region received a list of programmes, and the Greek letter *phi* against any item meant that, like it or not, it had got to be taken, rather like ITV network programmes today, which are supposed to be accepted by all companies. Typical of the BBC to choose a classical letter, which might be—well, not Greek but gibberish to any messenger boy.

The atmosphere was also a strange one. The building wasn't like a theatre, a place of entertainment: it wasn't like a film studio: it was an office building, from which this curious blend of information, education and entertainment was going out. They added bits here and there,

---

[1] *The Birth of Broadcasting*; Lewis's own book, *Broadcasting from Within*, was published as early as 1924.

"The Chummy Place" 5

and devised strange décor—there was a Chinese studio down below, and I suppose these designs would be very popular today as a sort of Art Nouveau.

More experiments were made, with an effects studio and echo chambers. The former came under Bryan Michie, later the gargantuan figure who put out *Housewives' Choice*—a sort of Fred Emney disc-jockey—and George Inns, who became, with George Mitchell, the power behind the *Black and White Minstrels*, a show which has triumphed over both box-office and apartheid. There the hardware gathered: the tank of water, the coconuts for horses' hooves, the doors which opened, the letter-boxes which clanged, the knockers, the bells—all of them live, with no recordings. The door in *ITMA* was perhaps the most famous effect sound in BBC history. It had that frantic double-rattle, which could lead so obviously to, say, Sidney Keith crying "Boss, boss, something terrible's happened!" It was most expertly opened, that door, and among the radio tributes paid to Tommy Handley after his death was a talk by the two effects boys who were on the last show—Brian Begg and Johnnie Ammonds. They chatted together about *ITMA* effects, and how Tommy loved them, and they demonstrated them in *Mirror of the Month*, a Light Programme magazine Barsley produced. The short item ended with one of them saying "Shall we close the door for the last time?" and they did; and there was a five second pause afterwards. One of the radio critics said it was the most poignant tribute of them all.

To add echo was an experiment carried on in a bare room in 2LO, without any artificial aid. This could give, for instance, added effect to the voice of the Ghost in *Hamlet*, but there were more up-to-date uses in what one might describe as the early "workshop" side of production, pioneered by Lance Sieveking and Tyrone Guthrie, and later developed by Val Gielgud. In his introduction to the published edition of *The Squirrel's Cage*, that remarkable landmark of 1929,[1] the late Sir Tyrone Guthrie wrote:

"The BBC has subordinated the question of popular appeal to Principles of Moral Philosophy; but has, none the less, been moderately adventurous and quite encouraging to technical experiment."

Lance Sieveking began as a member of the news staff, with topical talks added. When the BBC had partially settled its initial running fight with the press and the agencies (to whom the Company gave the

[1] See page 117.

copyright in the bulletins) it formed a news branch of its own, with Sieveking working first for J. C. Stobart of the lyrical "Grand Goodnight," which was part of the euphoria of the times. But Sieveking had a mind of his own, and soon developed his personal style, making full use of the control-panel, and becoming one of the first major figures in the Features side of the Drama department, as Gilliam acknowledges.

Gladstone Murray—a Canadian, an Oxford Rhodes scholar, a Major in the Royal Flying Corps—was a picturesque choice as the Company's first Director of Publicity. Peter Eckersley, Chief Engineer, had been given considerable freedom in personal broadcasts about how radio worked (the rest of the staff were tied down, under Reith's fatal fiat, to a ban on writing books or articles except with permission, and to the avoidance of personal publicity, resulting in the withdrawn, aloof, frightened image of the BBC "type") but the moment had come for the Company to have an Official Organ, most appropriately named in honour of *The Times*. This was to become a mammoth production, with, at one time, the largest circulation in the world, some nine million copies, and a very valuable source of revenue. It was not so much a newspaper, more a goosepaper, laying the golden eggs.

Asa Briggs writes: "Reith's concern for the right kind of publicity was as profound as his distaste for the wrong." Therefore, the Director must be a man with the record of a Gladstone Murray. Therefore, the editor of the paper (though he, Leonard Crocombe, had been editor of *Titbits*) must act in a dignified and responsible way. Editorial control lay in the hands of Newnes Ltd, who published it—and thereby hung a tale (if one may be allowed to pun) which nearly wagged the dog, for the editorial policy disappointed and even disgusted the Savoy Hill men, who had seen in it an outlet for their own articles and the self-advertisement otherwise denied them. Their attitude might, in fact, have killed the paper, or relegated it to the category of a highbrow weekly.

Crocombe set to work entirely differently. He began by being mainly concerned with two things: the programme details supplied by the BBC, and the advertising, which was eventually to command fabulous rates. The editorial matter of the *Radio Times*, the layout, the make-up, was, is, and apparently, always will be a question of opinion. Well-known BBC men worked on it, and made great improvements—Maschwitz, Maurice Gorham (who held the editorship from 1933 to 1941) and Laurence Gilliam, all forthright characters. The aims were all right, but we do not believe that the end product ever lived up to their expectations. The publication of *The Listener* hived off a lot of the articles which Maschwitz wanted and Gorham didn't, but this was small fry compared with the mass circulation the *Radio Times* was achieving, and frankly didn't deserve, on editorial grounds, to achieve. Obviously radio producers, that breed of men and women perpetually frustrated behind the scenes (only when the public hears your voice, and see your face, do you really exist and become well-known and recognized in the fish queue or on buses), wanted to write about their productions, but writing and producing are two different things, and not everyone is a Louis MacNeice. Rates for members of staff have always been lower than for outside contributors, which is true in journalism, but a staff journalist is paid to write and doesn't have to produce radio or television programmes. Ultimately, the wide circulation of their names nearly always won contributors round.

The magic formula of the *Radio Times* (and now the *TV Times*) is simply that it can't be thrown away for a week. No wonder it has always been such a magnet for advertisers, whose offerings may be looked at, not once but many times. The cry "Where's the *Radio Times*?" goes out daily in thousands of homes. It is *wanted* and, though the days of gigantic circulation are over, the free plugs are still there on radio and television. The new "facial" recently given to it is a compromise, with attempts at trendy type faces and illustrations, but this in our opinion will make little difference to its readers who, as in the original concept, take it primarily as a guide to programmes.

A. J. ALAN

The name—or more properly, pseudonym—A. J. Alan, is one to be remembered from the early years of broadcasting. His was one of the voices recalled by Sir Harold Nicolson in the BBC's Silver Jubilee programme in 1947, and as one listened it was the voice and the style which mattered as much as the stories themselves: a voice entirely distinctive, defying imitation, with an urbanity which reflected the appearance of the real man.

A. J. Alan—Captain L. H. Lambert—held a job in the Admiralty, which was thought to be in that select and secret branch, Naval Intelligence. The suggestion to attempt broadcasting came from him, after listening to one Sir William Bull on the wireless, lamenting the neglect of story-telling. The honour of engaging him, at the first meeting, goes to Rex Palmer, who gave him an audition and signed him immediately as a result. Lambert was always immaculately dressed in civil service garb, and would arrive at the studio carrying a rolled umbrella and a small dispatch-case. He always used to carry with him a candle and matches in case the lighting failed during a broadcast, which on one occasion it did. When he broadcast, he used to sit on a high stool close to the microphone: his script, which sounded quite informal, was in fact pasted on to sheets of cardboard in a pile on his knees. Thereby he avoided all sounds of rustling of paper. At intervals in the script there would be notes reading "cough here," "pause," "sigh," etc.

What seemed so informal was in fact carefully contrived. Alan would never smoke or drink for at least a week before broadcasting, and everything that he said—and the way that he said it—was meticulously rehearsed: moreover, he carefully maintained the "mystery" of his reputation by broadcasting only a few times each year.

A. J. Alan's "Good evening, everyone!" given in his light, almost surprised, voice, became a great favourite with a devoted section of the public. His was entirely a radio discovery, though his first talks, given in 1924, were collected in volume form four years later,[1] with an introduction by J. C. W. Reith himself, who wrote:

"An old-time story-teller has found his way into the twentieth century from those days before the invention of printing, when the art of story-telling was honoured by court, castle and cotter's ben.... As printing became established in the fifteenth and sixteenth centuries, the art gradually died out, and several centuries have had to pass before Broadcasting has afforded the long-delayed opportunity for a revival. It is no exaggeration to say that A. J. Alan has been a pioneer. No story-teller before him ever had so many listeners: no listeners a better story-teller."

Reith goes on to speak of the enjoyment given by the genial cynicism, the gentle satire, the ridiculous, but convincing yarns of burglary and adventure told by A. J. Alan, "and all in such a blasé manner, too." Another intriguing quality of the stories is that, right

---

[1] "*Good Evening, Everyone!*" (Hutchinson, 1928).

from the first one, "An Adventure in Jermyn Street," they tend to have no real solution, almost like ghost stories—and indeed, the mysterious Captain Lambert, candle and all, has almost a ghost-like quality himself, but it was an easy and, as Reith noted, blasé ghost.

We have, alas, to add an epilogue—or should it be epitaph?—to the A. J. Alan story. In 1971, an attempt was made, by the ever-acquisitive people in television, to transfer some of Lambert's stories on to the screen—not, mercifully, by making up someone to look like him (though one would not put it past some television people) but with two well-known actors. But the television critic of *The Times* reported: "With him (Alan) the voice and the tale were always sufficient. . . . Any bits and pieces that television chose to add could only be a distraction."

When will they ever learn?

2 Life in the BBC

REITH shut the door of Savoy Hill in 1932, and the "Chummy Place" was locked inside it.

The new headquarters brought about a sudden change of atmosphere as well as activity. What somebody said about "BH," as it has always been called is that when he went in and went up to the desk he always felt as if he ought to ask for a towel as well as a bathing-dress, because there's something very open and something very austere about the building, and one felt rather cowed with the solemn notice about Reith at the top, and commissionaires all over the place, and the huge desk, and that makes a good first impression. True, they'd put Eric Gill's Prospero and Ariel over those massive swing-doors, as a civilized gesture, and there were window-boxes outside the third-floor Council Chamber, but all that echoing stone and marble: yes, one saw where the towel came in.

The Latin phrase carved underneath Eric Gill's statue of a Sower in the entrance hall is DEUS INCREMENTUM DAT—to the staff a perpetual reminder that a rise in salary came from God alone![1]

As for activities, it became clear to the Savoy Hill staff that here was a new order of things. The lift system had its own apartheid: the lifts in the main hall for staff and visitors, those behind for studio performers. New Departments sprang up overnight. The new Empire Service under Sir Cecil Graves was broadcast from the same building. Though Val Gielgud described BH as "an architectural disaster," it was awe-inspiring to many, like a great battleship towering about the graceful pencil-point of All Souls' steeple.

In attempting to describe life in the BBC as we knew it, we are obviously covering only a fraction of the multitude of activities that made up the many-headed Corporation. We make no apology for ground uncovered and people not mentioned. We can only reply, if blamed for omitting anything or anyone, by paraphrasing Colonel Chinstrap's immortal phrase—we don't mind if we do, because this is

---

[1] Eric Gill, of course, also carved the famous figures of Prospero and Ariel above the main doors. When the group was exposed to view "adjustments" were hurriedly made, at Reith's request, to conceal Ariel's genitals. A "full frontal" was only permitted later on.

only one facet of radio life and work, and many BBC personalities and listeners have written down their own recollections.

BBC TYPES

How much importance can be attached to someone's saying "I'm from the BBC"? There's a fascinating speculation about this in the public mind. Its significance is often lost on the more conventional BBC types—and they run into some thousands. It may have the authority of someone saying "I'm a doctor," as the crowd peers uncertainly at a body on the pavement. It may have the unwelcome ring of someone saying "I'm from the Inland Revenue," or the comforting sound (to those adoring ladies listening to Stuart Hibberd) of someone saying "I'm your friend"—or the patriarchal sound of "I'm your father." The variations are endless. Perhaps they end with the inevitable impression, in some minds, that "I'm a sort of superior being, educated at a public school, and talking down to you."

But in each case, the implication is "I am someone special." A symbol of mirth, magic, or majesty—which is the BBC?

Admiration and envy may be instilled by the words "He's Someone in the BBC," more alluring in its way than if he were Something in the City. One thing is certain: the further away from Britain's shores, the more important—or dastardly—the implication is, depending whose side you are on, since there is an unshakeable conviction among foreigners that the BBC is a government department. It is also likely that, with the proliferation of television, the shrinking of the British Empire, and the general lack of the spirit of awe about anything, even landing on the moon, the initials have lost the significance they once had in the Golden Days of Radio.

An entire book could be compiled, citing genuine cases where the use of the name BBC won the battle or saved the day. Stuart Hibberd's diary records how by saying "I'm BBC," he once had a special train commanded for him and his fellow passengers stranded through a fault of British railways.

Michael Barsley remembers the floods in January 1953, when tremendous storms hit both Britain and the Netherlands. "The Dutch crisis was by far the worse of the two. In one small town alone—Oude Tonge—more people were drowned in twenty minutes than in the whole of south-eastern England. With the BBC, it was the Features Department, as often before, which rose to this occasion, almost as fast as the waters themselves. Since he realized I knew Holland well, Laurence Gilliam packed me off at once. I flew by night in a freight plane, filled with sandbags for the Dutch, and contacted a friend of mine in Amsterdam, a dentist called Jacques Lioni, who'd been in the Dutch Irene Brigade in England during the war. He spoke impeccable English, and even owned an Austin with right-hand drive. He also knew the way down to the flooded area, which we covered at breakneck speed. Jacques was a Monte Carlo and Tulip Rally driver.

"As we were leaving Bergen op Zoom, we were told there was strict security over the danger zone. Our news man, stuck in Rotterdam, had only flown over the stricken dykes; Laurence had told me 'Get your feet wet.' I had no press pass and no documents, only a portable tape recorder. So I stuck a large card on the windscreen with the letters 'BBC' on it, and we raced off. Whenever we were checked by guards, and they saw the card, they waved us on, shouting 'BBC! Home Service!' and one soldier cried 'Frank Phillips!' So we reached the edge of the terrible waters, and the helicopter field at Woensdrecht. The officer commanding twenty-four machines from five nations belonged to our own Fleet Air Arm. 'Well, it's good to see the BBC so soon,' he said. 'How did you make it?' I pointed to the card on the windscreen."

Snagge's memory is of the Royal Tour in 1951 with Princess Elizabeth and Prince Philip in Canada. "I was with Bing Whitaker of Canadian Broadcasting at an airport, awaiting the arrival of the royal plane. He had to make the commentary: I was just there with him, on the rooftop. About half-an-hour before the commentary was due, Bing said to me 'I hear there's some story about the driver of the royal car. I don't know who he is—I think he's a sergeant or something—anyway they've selected him as driver for some reason. I can't get the story from anyone: I've tried to make the airfield, but they won't let me on.' So I said 'Well, I've got nothing to do. I don't mind having a shot, though I'll probably get the brush-off as well.' I went down to the gate where the red-coats stood, and they stopped me, of course—where did I think I was going, and so on, and I said, 'I want, if I may, to go over there, because the royal car's waiting for the plane, and I'm anxious to have a word with the driver.' But they said 'Oh, no. Nobody's allowed past here, no one at all.' I pointed out I'd got an accreditation card, and added 'I'm BBC, London. My name doesn't matter at all, but I'm BBC.' 'Oh well,' came the reply, 'BBC? That's O.K., then. Go ahead.' So I got to the car, and spoke to the chap, who turned out to have served with Prince Philip in the Royal Navy—he was a Petty Officer—and that's why he was chosen. I got in the car and we talked together for about ten minutes. When I returned to the rooftop, I was able to tell Bing Whitaker I could give him the whole story, and Bing said, 'I saw it! I saw you stopped, and then go on. How did you do it?' I simply said 'I used the words BBC,' and he replied, 'You bastard! So that's it.'"

Experiences like these are gratifying. The BBC had indeed earned an enviable reputation in some countries, among people who knew that the organization was independent and non-commercial. On the other side of the coin, the Corporation has often been associated with aloofness, obtuseness, and a "holier-than-thou" attitude—impressions which some of its members, unfortunately, have failed to dissipate, particularly with bodies such as local councils, mayoral worthies and, in general, people-who-ought-to-have-been-consulted, but weren't. This is where a supreme diplomat like Dimbleby never let the side down, doing his homework and suffering local fools, if not gladly, at least tactfully, as in the early days of *Down Your Way*. John Shuter, who first produced him in the series, puts this down to his being a trained journalist with a genuine interest in meeting people.

In other cases, a disastrous visit by a BBC team would be remembered for years, and brought up in full force for the next team when, in all innocence, they arrived. It was once said, by a producer, "Always check up, before you go to a place, whether *Country Magazine* has been there first." But this is to malign Francis Dillon and his magnificent series, which added such a splash of colour to BBC programmes. The fault there would probably be that "Jack" Dillon had so set the village at a roar, and been such a good host, that any subsequent visit would be an anticlimax. One story of Jack which must be recalled is the occasion when his expense-sheets were queried after one broadcast. The Admin. type of his department pointed to one item which ran "Lunch for five farm labourers, ten shillings." The Admin. type pointed out that the Corporation allowance for lunch in such cases was (at that time) about six shillings per "actuality" speaker. "Ah," said Jack, "but you haven't turned over the page." Page two began "Refreshment for five farm labourers, four pounds sixteen shillings."

For expenses incurred abroad on BBC business, there were some strange anomalies. Men who failed to spend their entire allowance, and brought foreign currency back, were despised by their colleagues.

The cheers went up for those who got away with it. Sometimes it was legitimate. When much-travelled producer Leonard Cotterell put in an item from a remote part of Africa "To purchase of One Cow, for bribing Chieftain, £40," the item was rightly approved. The neatest bit of work is credited to equally well-travelled reporter Rene Cutforth. At one period he was making frequent visits to Paris, and on every expense sheet there was an item for lunch with Monsieur X, an attaché at the Polish Embassy, at Maxim's. The meals continued so regularly that an Admin. type checked up with Paris, and summoned Cutforth, who was told that there was not, apparently, anyone with the name of X working at the Polish Embassy. Rene replied, unabashed; "I always thought the fellow was an impostor."

ANNOUNCERS

Today we accept on both radio and television that announcers and news-readers shall be named, and, within limits, shall be allowed, even encouraged, to express some sort of personality. The personality cult, though hinted at in pre-war radio, first came into prominence on Independent Television News in 1955, when Geoffrey Cox, the Editor, fielded a team consisting of Chris Chataway, Robin Day, Ludovic Kennedy and Hugh Thomas. Not only did the picture give them an image—Robin's spotted bow-tie, Hugh Thomas's sympathetic look at any moment of tragedy (and in real life, being a warm-hearted man, he really felt that sympathy) Ludo's serious mien, and Chataway's wry closing smile—they were also allowed to alter their scripts to suit their style, provided the meaning wasn't altered, or the facts. Within the BBC, the script, as provided by the news-room, had always been the authorized version, and not one jot or tittle of the scriptural script could be changed by the reader.

Any informality on the part of BBC announcers was also forbidden, just as any additions, interpolations or opinions were "out." The approach gradually became a little bit more permissive, and with the public this proved popular. Announcers were remote but admired figures—in the case of Stuart Hibberd, adored figures—so that any relaxing of the Iron Curtain of the impersonal voice became welcome. For example, when Frank Phillips read the shipping forecast late at night, he would end, off his own bat, by saying "Good night, gentlemen, and good sailing"—an immensely popular gesture. Alvar Lidell broke the rule severely, but successfully, when the battle of Alamein was won. He began "I'm going to read you the news—and there's some cracking good news coming." No memo of rebuke fluttered on to Alvar's desk that day (if he had a desk at that time, which is unlikely). As to the tone in reading bad news, no declared policy was made: the emphasis could be left to the judgement of an experienced announcer. In television, the task became more difficult, because facial as well as vocal expression became involved. Perhaps some viewers remember the anger caused when an ITN newscaster inadvertently smiled after announcing the death of Mr Smith, the man who invented the Potato Crisp. Big Brother viewer was watching. In radio, there was no suggestion that the announcer should use a "death" voice, edged in black, or powdered. News is news, and must be treated without undue sentiment. The news editor will have a say in the responsibility of describing an item as being given with regret, or deep regret, or whether, say, an air-crash was "tragic" or just an air-crash. It must, in any case, be read straight, though the intonation may be levelled out. The professional trick which Snagge advised was the use of a pause. Perhaps one had a cheerful but nationally important piece of news, followed by an air-crash involving British passengers. By allowing just two or three seconds pause, the announcer could alert listeners to think "What's coming now?" (to believe, in other words, that something different was to come). They might know of relatives who were on that plane, or were perhaps about to fly to the place concerned, in which case such an item would come as a shock to them. The "pause" trick seems to have been forgotten now, particularly in the brief news summaries on Radios 1 and 2, which are followed with knife-edge swiftness by a slick programme engineer, who may put on a racy hullabaloo of pop noise, even though it follows a tale of tragedy. The harsh contrast may come about because the news is prepared by a different department, and usually put out from a different studio, and there's unlikely to be any close liaison between the two. It is all, alas, part of the hurrying, let's-get-on-with-it attitude of today, in which patter replaces style.

Once upon a time, when introducing programmes with speakers in the studio, the announcer embodied the BBC, as their brief ambassador to the air. The late John Morris, when Controller of the Third Programme, when asked whether the announcer's job could merely be described as that of a waiter, who brings the food he hasn't prepared and mustn't partake of, replied: "Not so much a waiter, more a butler." The subtle difference explained the often-derided dinner-jackets announcers used to wear in the evenings, the neat and tidy clothes generally, and the avoidance of personally taking alcohol in any quantity beforehand—all this to put the speakers at their ease. Most BBC announcers have invariably played this role well: it goes with the job. They know all about "butterflies" before a broadcast, and are used to giving nervous speakers reassurance when there is no producer present. It is probable, in any case, that the appearance as well as the manners of the average announcer would be more acceptable to strangers than those of some producers, often tousled and distrait and caught up in the toils of a last-minute crisis. From the producer's end, of course, it is often necessary to make script cuts immediately before transmission, and doing this literally before the anguished gaze of a new speaker demands a well-balanced blend of apology and firmness. Local officials on their dignity are often the most difficult customers!

Before the war, all announcers and news-readers remained anonymous, although some of them became so well known, both by repetition and reputation, that we reached the stage when the *Daily Express* had "The Secret Six Revealed?" and printed their pictures and put their names underneath, as if letting the cat out of the bag. Certainly it was the war, and reasons for security, which clinched the matter. But Snagge had raised the matter before this. "When I was in the OB Department, I'd have my name printed and publicized for commentaries—such as the Boat Race—also when I played the part of a stunt man (believe it or not). Then with the outbreak of war, I moved across and became Head of Presentation, and at about the same time my previous boss, Lotbinière, was made Assistant Controller of Programmes. I said to him one day 'It seems to me ridiculous, Lobby, that if OB people can get their names mentioned, why shouldn't these announcers chosen to read the news also give their names?' This was in 1940, and Lobby thought it a sensible idea, so I said 'Well, what do I do about it?' and his reply was 'Go ahead and do it.' We agreed on such a wording as 'Here is the News, read by Alvar Lidell.' To my surprise the powers that be accepted it with one rephrasing, thus: 'Here is the News, and this is Alvar Lidell reading it.' This to my surprise was the only comment made by the Board of Management. When it came out afterwards, and a reason was asked for it, Lobby and I said it was for security reasons. After the invasion of Poland, there had been a number of false announcers put up by the Germans—in fact, after the Battle of Britain and the calling-off of the

A dramatic photograph of Broadcasting House taken after one of the two bombings survived by Admiral Carpendale's "battleship" in December 1940

Radio Times Hulton Picture Library

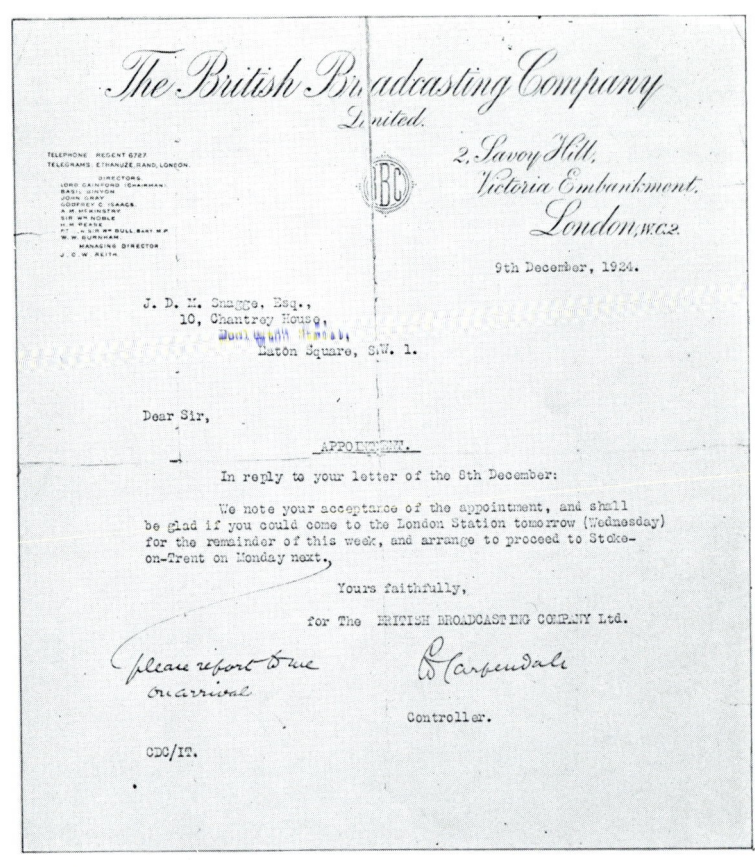

John Snagge's first BBC job

Photostat of letter of acceptance from Admiral Carpendale, for appointment to a post at BBC station, Stoke-on-Trent (9 December 1924)

Sir William Haley relaxes
The DG with French officials on the Eiffel Tower in 1950

Radio Times Hulton Picture Library

John Snagge with Lord Reith at Henley in 1949 (Lady Reith at far right)

Radio Times Hulton Picture Library

Sir Lindsay Wellington CBE
A BBC man who went from the rough-and-tumble of Savoy Hill to a room at the top in Broadcasting House, as Director of Broadcasting

BBC Copyright Photograph

Doctor at Large
Charles Hill, here seen as "The Radio Doctor," who as Lord Hill of Luton became Chairman of ITV and BBC consecutively (1948)
Radio Times Hulton Picture Library

The man who resigned—and changed his mind
Charles Curran, Director-General, BBC
BBC Copyright Photograph

King George V
First Royal Broadcaster (Opening India Conference, 1930)
Radio Times Hulton Picture Library

King Edward VIII at Broadcasting House
Introduced as "His Royal Highness, the Prince Edward" at his Abdication Broadcast (March, 1936)
BBC Copyright Photograph

King George VI
3 p.m. Christmas Day 1944

BBC Copyright Photograph

HRH Princess Elizabeth broadcasts on her 21st Birthday during the Royal Tour of South Africa (21 April 1947)

BBC Copyright Photograph

CHRISTMAS DAY Home Service
DECEMBER 25

203.5 m. 1474 kc/s   391.1 m. 767 kc/s
449.1 m. 668 kc/s   48.54 m. 6.18 Mc/s

BLACK-OUT
	p.m.	a.m.
London	5.26 to	8.35
Plymouth	5.47 to	8.46
Cardiff	5.37 to	8.48
Leeds	6.18 to	8.64
Edinburgh	5.11 to	9.14
Aberdeen	4.58 to	9.18
Belfast	5.31 to	9.17

7.0 a.m. Time, Big Ben
' O come, all ye faithful '
NEWS
and summary of Forces programmes

7.15 This Week's Composer
RIMSKY-KORSAKOV
Gramophone records of excerpts from
' Scheherazade '

7.45 CHRISTMAS GREETINGS
from Uncle Mac, with verse and
carols to start the day. Carols sung
by Derek Barsham, the Boys' Brigade
boy soprano (recording)

8.0 CAROLS
sung by the BBC Chorus: conductor, Leslie Woodgate
A Child this day is born...............arr. Geoffrey Shaw
God rest you merry, gentlemen........trad.
I saw three ships..................arr. Geoffrey Shaw
The Holly and the Ivy
.................arr. Rutland Boughton
Good King Wenceslas..arr. Geoffrey Shaw
(BBC recording)

8.15 RICHARD CREAN ORCHESTRA
March of the Toys (Babes in Toyland)
.........................Victor Herbert
Waltz (The Sleeping Beauty)..Tchaikovsky
Selection: Snow White and the Seven
Dwarfs..........................Churchill
Entry of the Little Fauns..........Pierné
All on a Christmas morning..H. G. Amers
Gingerbread Waltz (Hansel and Gretel)
......................Humperdinck
(BBC recording)

8.40 'THE POSTMAN'S KNOCK'
In a London street—in a country
village—town and country folk welcome the postman on his Christmas
morning ' walk ', accompanied in
London by Michael Standing, and in
Grantchester by Gilbert Harding

9.0 Time, Greenwich
' O come, all ye faithful '
NEWS
and Programme Parade

9.15 THE KITCHEN FRONT

9.20 CHRISTMAS BELLS
from the four corners of the British
Isles. A message of greeting from the
bells of Westminster Abbey; St.
Cuthbert's, Edinburgh; Armagh
Cathedral; St. John's, Cardiff; and
St. Mary's, Lowdham, Nottinghamshire

9.30 FODEN'S MOTOR WORKS BAND
Conductor, Fred Mortimer
Idyll: All on a Christmas morning..Amers
Extracts from The Royal Water Music
..................................Handel
Trombone Solo: Down the Vale....Moir
(Soloist, Ellis Westwood)
Selection: A Southern Maid..Fraser-Simson
Minuet and Galop (Orpheus in the Underworld).......................Offenbach

10.0 'MESSIAH'
Selections from Handel's oratorio, on gramophone records

10.45 GUERNSEY CHILDREN SINGING
Choir of the States Intermediary
School, of Guernsey, conducted by
Winifred Roughton
Now once again our hearts we raise: Jean
Grosjean; Le jour du lavage (Washing-Day)...........................anon.
Minuit chrétien (The Watch-Service Carol)
...........................arr. Rodney Bennet
Voici Noël................arr. Weckerlin
Lift your heads, rejoice..arr. Martin Shaw
(BBC recording)

11.0 Time, Big Ben
CHRISTMAS MORNING SERVICE
from St. Mary's, Lowdham, Nottinghamshire, conducted by Canon
Anthony Otter
O come, all ye faithful (S.P. 78: C.H. 55)
Sentence
General Thanksgiving
The Lord's Prayer
Versicles and Responses
Venite
Psalm 8
Lesson: St. Luke 2, vv. 1-20
While shepherds watched their flocks
(S.P. 82: C.H. 42)
Creed and Collects
Carols: Little Jesus, sweetly sleep
(S.P. 383); Angels from the realms of
glory (S.P. 71: C.H. 65)
Address
Behold, the great Creator (S.P. 72)
Prayers
Hark! the herald angels sing (S.P. 74)
Blessing
Organist, Arthur Cowen

P.M.

12.0 WORKS WONDERS
Munition-workers entertain their colleagues in a Christmas Day concert
at a factory in Scotland

12.30 'CHRISTMAS CHARIVARIA'
A 'hubbub' of recorded music and
song, prose and poetry for today, contrasted and introduced by Raymond
Raikes, with Bransby Williams,
Joseph Macleod, and Geoffrey
Wincott, and the recorded voices of
Harry Hemsley, Peter Dawson,
Ernest Lough, and Paul Robeson.
Programme edited by Peter Eton

1.0 Time, Greenwich: NEWS

1.15 THE ARCHBISHOP OF CANTERBURY
gives a Christmas message

1.30 VIOLIN MUSIC
played by Eda Kersey (violin)
Sonata in D..................Vivaldi—Respighi
Sonatina in G, Op. 100..............Dvořák

2.0 'WE ARE ADVANCING'
towards Victory, towards Understanding
A Christmas reunion of the peoples
of the British Commonwealth and of
the United Nations, linked by radio
from all parts of the world to exchange greetings on the fifth wartime Christmas Day
Christmas in the British Isles: at home—
with the workers—with British and Allied
Forces
Christmas with the Imperial Forces Overseas: Italy—New Guinea—India
Christmas in Occupied Europe
Christmas in the United Nations: Russia
—China—Brazil—U.S.A.
Christmas in the Holy Land
Narrator, Howard Marshall. Music
by Victor Hely-Hutchinson, played
and sung by the London Symphony
Orchestra and Alexander Choir, conducted by Muir Mathieson. Written
and produced by Laurence Gilliam
and Leonard Cottrell
(Full details will be found in the article on page 3)

3.15 NATIONAL ANTHEMS OF THE ALLIES

3.30 BBC SCOTTISH ORCHESTRA
Conductor, Ian Whyte. Janette
Sclanders (soprano)
Overture: Iolanthe...................Sullivan
Four Scots Songs: O whistle and I'll come
to ye, my lad; Flora MacDonald's
Lament; Robin Adair; Comin' thro' the
rye......................................trad.
Berceuse: Praeludium..............Järnefelt
Waltz: The Skaters...............Waldteufel

4.0 'WHAT ELSE DO THEY DO?'
with C. H. Middleton, Mary Ferguson, 'The Radio Doctor', C. A.
Lejeune, and Douglas Houghton
(recording)
Five radio 'regulars' take a brief holiday from their regular subjects

4.20 'IS YOUR GENIE REALLY NECESSARY?'
A satirical pantomime for a wartime Christmas, written by Michael
Barsley. Produced by John Glyn-Jones
Fairy Godmother........Mabel Constanduros
Cinderella.................Marjorie Westbury
Aladdin.......................Stephen Manton
Ali Baba.......................Antony Holles
Man in off-licence...............Roy Emerton
Tax-men, thieves, Ministry officials
played by members of the BBC Drama
Repertory Company

5.0 Time, Greenwich
NEWYDDION (News in Welsh)

5.5 'CYFARCHION NADOLIG'
Oddi wrth fechgyn a merched Cymru yn
y lluoedd arfog, a wledydd tramor yn
ogystal ag o wersyllocdd ym Mhrydain.
(Recorded Christmas greetings in Welsh)

5.20 CHILDREN'S HOUR
Tommy Handley in 'Well, for
Santa Claus': a Christmas Day
Unfairy Story, by Dorothy Worsley.
Cast includes Dorothy Summers,
Fred Yule, Sydney Keith, Bryan
Herbert, Ronald Chesney, and
Barrett and Max Field. BBC Variety
Orchestra conducted by Charles

Shadwell. Story-Teller, Derek McCulloch. Produced by Francis Worsley. (BBC recording)

6.0 Time, Greenwich: NEWS
National and Regional announcements

6.30 'SNOW WHITE AND THE SEVEN DWARFS'
Excerpts from the sound-track of
Walt Disney's fantasy

6.45 CAROLS OF THE ALLIES
sung by the BBC Chorus, conducted by Sir Adrian Boult
All rejoice now (Russian)
..........................arr. David Stanley Smith
Lord Jesus hath a garden (Dutch)
..........................arr. Geoffrey Shaw
Rocking (Czech).........arr. Martin Shaw
O leave your sheep (French)
...........................arr. Cecil Hazlehurst
I hasten early (Polish)
..........................arr. David Stanley Smith
A Merry Christmas (English)
..........................arr. Arthur Warrell

7.0 BBC SYMPHONY ORCHESTRA
Conductor, Sir Adrian Boult
Overture: Leonora, No. 3......Beethoven
Scherzo: L'Apprenti Sorcier (The Sorcerer's Apprentice).................Dukas
Pictures from an Exhibition
....................Mussorgsky—Ravel

8.0 'VAUDEVILLE OF 1943'
A Saturday-night entertainment
featuring famous stars of Variety,
music, and drama. Randolph
Sutton, Mr. Murgatroyd and Mr.
Winterbottom, Robert Donat, Anne
Ziegler and Webster Booth, and
Elsie and Doris Waters. Revue
Chorus and augmented BBC Revue
Orchestra, conducted by Leighton
Groves. Producers, John Sharman
and Harry S. Pepper. (BBC recording)

8.55 'WIRELESS FOR THE BLIND'
Appeal on behalf of the British
'Wireless for the Blind' Fund (registered under the Blind Persons Act
1920), by the Rt. Hon. the Lord
Woolton, C.H.
Contributions will be gratefully acknowledged, and should be addressed to Lord
Woolton, British 'Wireless for the Blind'
Fund, 224, Gt. Portland Place, W.1.

9.0 BIG BEN MINUTE NEWS

9.20 'ALICE'S ADVENTURES IN WONDERLAND'
by Lewis Carroll, dramatised by
Herbert M. Prentice. Radio adaptation by Cynthia Pughe. Produced
by Howard Rose

10.10 SCHUBERT
Sonata in D, Op. 53
played by Clifford Curzon (piano)

10.45 'THE CRADLE'
Verse and carols for Christmas

11.0 CHRISTMAS CABARET
Carroll Gibbons, at the piano, invites
you to join the party at the Merchant Navy Club. You meet Bill
Kent, Esther Coleman, 'Hutch',
Billy Mayerl, Jack Jackson, Paul
Debroy Somers, and—recorded for
the U.S.A.—Rudy Vallee. Dance
music played by Carroll Gibbons
and his Orchestra. Produced by
Alick Hayes. (BBC recording)

12.0 midnight-12.20 a.m.
Time, Greenwich: NEWS

A page from the *Radio Times* showing, among other things, Michael Barsley's first
radio programme at 4.20 p.m. (Christmas Day 1943)

German invasion, we learned that the Nazis had trained speakers to imitate the BBC voices. Security, therefore, became the accepted reason and then the official one, but it was in fact I, not normally the inventive type, who first suggested it, for a different reason.

"After a post-war period of anonymity again, the names were brought back with my original intention. Now, every Tom, Dick and Harry seems to call himself and his colleagues Tom, Dick and Harry at the slightest opportunity, which is pushing it a bit far, and has put announcing and continuity into its present parlous, third-rate state."

WILFRED PICKLES

One news-reader's voice during the war came as a surprise to the listeners, as well as to the man himself—Wilfred Pickles. Already, in the North Region, Pickles was well known for his casual, friendly, meet-the-people series called *Billy Welcome*, a predecessor to the more widely known *Have a Go!* The idea of using him to read BBC's news bulletins came, not from within the Corporation, but from outside, from the Ministry of Information, where it was felt, quite erroneously, that the "southerner" was having too much say on the air for the northern listeners' liking. Wilfred's definite but not obtrusive northern accent could redress the balance. An additional, and to the BBC very puzzling, reason was again security. "His accent," said a Memo from the Ministry, "might not so easily be copied by the Germans." The reaction at Broadcasting House was less than lukewarm, and Pickles had a feeling in advance that he might not be as welcome as his character Billy was.

However, he acknowledges the friendly reception by the staff at BH, apart from Bruce Belfrage, who had to take his place in Manchester, and didn't want to go. He went to Snagge, and admits that it was made clear to him that the choice had been made from outside. However, he was given freedom, within the rules, to present the news in his fashion. Wilfred admits in his book: "If Snagge had not been so human and fair, he might well have told me to go ahead and make a mess of it, to prove how wrong some people were, and how right he was!"

To sweeten the experience, the BBC immediately raised his salary from £480 to £800 a year, which convinced even his wife Mabel, who had had her doubts, that the Corporation neant business. Wilfred watched the regular announcers at work with something like awe. He noted how Alan Howland joked with the engineers to within seconds of transmission, and how Alvar Lidell loosened the top of his trousers when the red light went on, apparently "gently massaging his stomach while reading." Stuart Hibberd he appreciated immensely: "not a bit parsonical and prudish." From Freddie Allen, he heard a new story about the BBC Bomb. Freddie had been standing by a lift, just about to get out his pass-card for the Home Guard man on duty when the blast of the bomb, coming down the shaft, blew him forward. He declared it was the first time he'd got through without showing his pass!

Pickles was already a known name in Variety. The newspapers took up the story of his new role in anticipation, but Wilfred, used to applause and success, had fears of a disastrous slip. He gladly accepted the help of Elizabeth Miller, the BBC's own expert in pronunciation, who retired in 1971. Mabel said "Never mind, if you make a mess of it, we can always go back to the North!" and went to their hotel to listen. Bus conductors were supposed to have been shouting "All alight for Wilfred Pickles!" in the neighbourhood of Broadcasting House.

Was Wilfred secretly enjoying it all? We don't think so. The Moment of Truth came. It was a fairly long bulletin: twenty minutes. "A new tank battle near Sidi Omar in the Western Desert.... Germans making some progress in Russia.... Air attacks on Brest and Cherbourg...." Then it was over, with Franklin ("Jingle") Engelmann on continuity, entering into the spirit of things by saying into the microphone "As we've got a minute or two to spare, here's something appropriate," and put on a record of *Ilkley Moor Baht' At*. Joseph Macleod came in with fifty telegrams. On the midnight news, emboldened, Wilfred added to his good night "And to all Northerners, wherever you may be, good neet!"

That touch of friendly hospitality by Franklin Engelmann was typical of a man universally admired, not only by his colleagues, but later by a vast, nation-wide public. During the war, "Jingle" was not allowed to read the News, because his name had a German-sounding ring. This panic BBC prohibition affected him not a whit. When he died, tragically and at the height of his fame, in March 1972, John Snagge's radio tribute referred to one of his supreme qualities—that he never showed the slightest hint of jealousy, a characteristic only too rife in the realms of the BBC. That any man should be able to take on two prodigiously successful series—Dimbleby's *Down Your Way* and Freddie Grisewood's *Gardeners' Question Time*—at one and the same moment, and make them his own, is one of the supreme individual feats in the history of radio. In all his other programmes, chairing *Brain of Britain*, compèring *Mirror of the Month*, he remained the same urbane yet sympathetic voice, always enlivening, always professional. He undoubtedly deserves to be classed as one of the Vintage men.

The Pickles experiment failed, but through no fault of Wilfred's. He enjoyed getting a big mail for doing an apparently simple job, even though there were letters of complaint, even abuse. More to the point was his own very valid objection, that the news bulletin was written by a southerner for a southerner to read, which could make a lot of difference in the actual choice or order of words.

The Listener Research Department made a special door-to-door survey, which was much more favourable to the Pickles voice than the correspondence had been, and R. J. Silvey, Head of the department, assured him "people mainly write when they're annoyed." The surprising revelation lay in that the Pickles accent was apparently more popular in the South than in the North.

Mabel encouraged him in asking for his return to Manchester. Wilfred ends his account of this minor saga as follows: "John Snagge readily agreed for me to go. He did more: he promised to secure my release, asking me not to say anything to the Press, as 'there could be a bit of trouble over it!' "

THE HIBBERD DIARIES

Of all BBC announcers, Stuart Hibberd has probably been the most revered, the most often parodied, and the most generally accepted as the kindly voice which told you nothing but the truth. Of one famous announcer it was said that he didn't so much read the news as break it. Hibberd at least broke it gently, and if he had said no other words, he would have gone down to history as the man who made the announcement on George V, orginated by Lord Dawson of Penn:

"The King's life is moving peacefully towards its close."

Apart from being written up—almost every book by a radio personality has some reference to him—his was the most assiduous and detailed writing-up of himself and the BBC way of life.[1] No detail

---

[1] *"This is London . . ."* (Macdonald & Evans, 1950).

escapes him—not even the fly which once buzzed round him while reading the news, "attracted no doubt by the heat of the studio," and to which he devoted almost a page. There is not an unkind word in the book: Hibberd wouldn't, in fact, have hurt that fly, but he undertook his announcing job with tremendous devotion and energy and attention to detail, particularly the pitfalls of pronunciation and stress. He is equally serious about the tools of his trade. Using one of the new ribbon microphones is an event: "It does not overload, or 'blast' as it is called; it is sensitive on two sides—a great advantage in broadcast discussions—and is of robust construction." He then adds, in perfect character, "crooners will adore it and fondle it lovingly."

In his diary of 1932, remarkably, he does not mention that most dramatic moment in radio history, the first Christmas Day message by King George V. But the death of the King he covers in full, noting that on the night before, Reith replaced him by Dr Iremonger for the Epilogue, saying somewhat incongruously "It must not be done by a layman." This, surely, was as much a misreading of the public mind by Reith as his peremptory closing down of all services until 8 p.m. the following day.

Jubilee week in 1935 Hibberd found, as most BBC staff did, a hot and tiring time, ending with a train breakdown—Stuart was often inveighing against his particular railway line. A paragraph in August begins, surprisingly like Commander Campbell: "I remember that when I was serving in Waziristan in 1920, one of our sentries shot a porcupine...." But this was serious: he had just met Gypsy Petulengro in the studio, and been told that hedgehog pie was a Romany delicacy. Hibberd—Cambridge and Indian Army—would have made good casting as an average member of the BBC, but he also noted many Hindustani words Petulengro used, adding "strong evidence of the Eastern origin of the gypsies."

Slow to anger as Hibberd may have been, he was very shocked at the departure of his colleague Harmon Grisewood that year to take up a desk job, and protests about it. "If he is so good—and I maintain he is—why not reward him with a salary commensurate with his worth—pay him twice the salary I am receiving, if you like, as long as you keep him at the microphone—rather than let him go to become a backroom boy? But it was of no avail: I was over-ruled and we lost him." That again, was typical of Hibberd: the quality of programmes and their contributors was what mattered most.

He became only mildly involved over the Abdication of Edward

VIII. In the train the day after the Crystal Palace fire (and Lotbinière's famous outside broadcast) he saw a newspaper headline: THE KING WANTS TO MARRY MRS SIMPSON. "This," writes Hibberd, "was the first time I had seen that lady's name mentioned in print in this country." Having visited the US earlier in the year, he must no doubt have read what *Time* magazine had been printing. The sale of relevant copies had been banned in Britain for months. He read the special bulletin at 4.45, giving Baldwin's speech and the King's statement, a bulletin lasting nearly thirty minutes. The 7 p.m. bulletin lasted over forty minutes, and the nine o'clock news went on for nearly an hour. Listeners—and announcers—were made of sterner stuff in those days!

Hibberd often refers to comments about announcers, as if they were regarded as a special breed, particularly when they receive adoring letters from doting females. "You are admirable substitutes for husbands," one letter to him ran, "in fact models; never late, never worrying if dinner is late, always at home in the evening, never bad-tempered, generally fairly cheerful and delightfully Victorian. Anyway you have two quite devoted and grateful friends whom you can never hear. We always say 'Good night, good night!' to you. Wish I could sign my name, but after this frankness . . . excuse me!"

As for the inevitable *faux pas*, one was particularly excruciating for Stuart, even though he was not responsible for it. It occurred when Sir Kingsley Wood, then Minister of Health, was finishing a broadcast on Pensions, and Lionel Marson, the announcer who had, strangely enough, introduced Tommy Woodrooffe's "Fleet's Lit Up" commentary, was discussing with the News Editor what extra items should be included in the bulletin to follow. The News Editor had mentioned an item about the notorious, womanizing Rector of Stiffkey. Marson protested, saying "What, that bloody man?" at the precise moment when Sir Kingsley's talk ended and the engineer faded up the News Studio, forgetting to flash the red warning light. This apparent description of a Minister went out loud and clear—and how the telephones rang! The BBC was obliged to put out an official statement and apology, but the story has a happy ending. When Sir Kingsley heard about the incident, he seemed, so Hibberd reports, "highly amused."

Stuart does not spare himself over mistakes like these. Years later, in 1946, he remembers the Terrible Occasion when, after reading the News, he went on to announce a talk. But the red light flickered violently in front of him, and he exclaimed "What the hell is happening now?" The first three fatal words went out on the air—and not only did listeners ring up, but reporters too, recognizing the Voice. It seemed awful that this respectable Uncle-figure of Auntie should use such words. There were "hundreds of calls," the Press Officer told Hibberd, almost in awe. The next day one paper had a photograph of him with the semi-banner headline, "Oh, Mr Hibberd!" A French paper went one better, and used the phrase "Révolution à la BBC." There must have been a fellow-feeling when Stuart heard, or heard about, the occasion when the equally exalted voice of Richard Dimbleby, in a harassed moment on a royal occasion, muttered "Jesus wept!"

The departure of Reith brought many tributes from his colleagues, and we are sure that Stuart, now in retirement in Devon (where he still makes sprightly appearances, to open local fêtes and gymkhanas) still agrees with what he wrote of him in 1938.

"A man of vision, a fair man, a man who knew what he wanted and knew how to get it, a statesman of the first order, a disciplinarian with a sense of humour, a shy man, who combined a stern expression with a leaven of sweet reasonableness, a much-misunderstood man, a born leader of men, a doughty fighter, a man with an iron will, but a lonely man—at least that was my impression—but a human being and a most loyal friend."

With the Munich crisis impending, and Queen Elizabeth launching the ship which bore her name with the message from the King, asking his people to have "cool heads and brave hearts," Stuart smilingly notes that Lord Aberconway launched the ship himself by accidentally touching the press-button.

The death of his friend B. Walton O'Donnell, who had raised the Wireless Military Band in 1927 aroused his memory:

"In the old days King George V often listened to 'Bandy's Band,' as we used to call it. When he visited Broadcasting House, and the Senior members of the Staff were being presented to him, lined up in the entrance-hall, he looked at them, and then, turning to the Director-General, inquired 'Where is that fellow Walton O'Donnell?'"

When war came, Hibberd, like his colleagues, stood by for days. It was, in fact, Alvar Lidell who made the announcement of the ultimatum from Downing Street, leading an hour and a quarter later to Chamberlain's broadcast—followed, as many of us remember, by the first, mistaken air-raid Alert. A few days later, Hibberd is on early morning duty, musing as he stands on the roof of the building to see the dawn. The top of Broadcasting House, he decided "was like the boat-deck of a ship; only the funnels were missing to complete the picture." Then he adds the only unkind remark in all his diaries: "I cannot help thinking what a hideous place St Pancras is."

These extracts are only a fraction of an immense diary output, but they may reveal something of the rare and kindly nature of the BBC's most steadfast announcer—a man, in fact, who seems never to have wanted to be anything else, which is perhaps why he is, in the best sense, a perfectionist.

"I'LL RING UP THE BBC!"

In Broadcasting House there has always been a room called the Duty Room, on the ground floor. At one time it was a small, cramped, cut-off place. Now it is pleasantly furnished in modern style and is capable of entertaining several people. It is staffed by the two busiest people in the whole BBC: the Duty Officer and his assistant. They handle all calls passed on to them by the switchboard; only a fraction of the callers know that there is such a person as a Duty Officer, or ask for him by name. The majority are people simply ringing "The BBC" to protest about something, or perhaps to inquire. Each station of the Corporation has, of course, its own Ombudsman to handle local complaints or queries.

These vary so widely that only a man with a quick mind, great patience, and a tremendous sense of humour can handle them properly. So Duty Officers need special qualifications, but over the years they have varied in personality, so that callers do not necessarily get their answers in a standardized formula. One famous human target, the late "G.P." (John Graves-Pierce), used to say he thoroughly enjoyed the experience: whether it was a compliment, or something vicious, or somebody drunk, or a crank, or a religious maniac—he loved them all, and would write up his logbook with relish. Two wartime Duty Officers, Forte and Baxter, were somewhat alike: very gentle, always polite, sometimes conveying an air of being bored when someone needlessly complained, but never annoyed.

The annoyance is almost invariably on the caller's side, and takes many forms. Once a Duty Officer was upbraided because the eleven o'clock time signal had been suppressed since a quartet hadn't finished. The caller had waited for that exact moment to release his racing pigeons, and now he had to bed them all down till next morning. "Big Ben was wrong today!" another caller would shout down the line. "I know it was, because I missed my train." But besides these inconsequential interruptions, there will always be the expected deluge after any obvious mistake has been made on the air, any controversial remark uttered, or any programme having caused offence. If the volume gets too great, evasive action can be taken by the PBX girl or the Duty Officer himself, and the main burden of calls channelled off to Programme Enquiries, which can give a standardized, official reply. But if he can deal with an individual caller personally, the Duty Officer will. Sometimes he may privately agree with what the caller says, and will tell him so; but he cannot, of course, take any action himself. He merely passes it on to the proper quarters, and this is always done in genuine cases. So far as we are aware, no Duty Officer has yet written a book about the strange things he gets asked or told in the line of duty. A pity, for it would be a real collector's piece. Imagine, for instance, the sympathy required of the Duty Officer in charge on the night Grace Archer "died." Among the callers that evening was a man, who sounded quite young, who seemed beside himself with grief and who after midnight rang up again, this time quite maudlin with drink, moaning into the telephone that his life had been ruined, and finally bursting into tears. But this contrived death in *The Archers* was, as we know, one of the most blatant demises in radio history.

Duty Officers also have many other matters on their plate. They are required to receive VIPs, as well as speakers whom producers wish to put at their ease before a programme. Accommodation problems, the ordering of cars—all sorts of tasks come under their care, in addition to the loud protests of would-be Mrs Whitehouses and outraged Colonels. On one occasion a deputation of Pakistanis arrived unheralded at the big front doors of Broadcasting House. The Duty Officer of the day said "I will admit two, to hand in their written protest." And he added, as the commissionaire turned to go, "You can tell them they needn't take their shoes off." Diplomacy is part of his Duty. So is a sense of humour.

On night during the war, a mistake was broadcast in a late-night news bulletin. Raids were on, and almost everyone had bedded down. The phone rang in the Duty Room, and when the Officer answered, he heard a Very Well-known Voice on the line, saying "Get me the

Senior Official. I must speak to the Senior Official." The Duty Officer took his torch, and tiptoed round the Concert Hall, where members of the staff slept, but could find nobody who could be so described. Therefore, so as not to keep the illustrious caller waiting, he returned to the telephone to say that, as far as he could make out, he *was* the Senior Official. The Voice then carried on his complaint for several thunderous minutes, at the end of which Mr Winston Churchill said "And may I thank you, whoever you may be, for having the patience to listen to me."

PBX GIRLS

Equally important as Duty Officers, and often working alongside them, are the PBX girls at the BBC switchboards. They can, as we have seen, take a lot of the load from the long-suffering man's shoulders, and in their own right, they are probably the best collection of hello-girls in the country, and never more so than during the vintage years, long before the practice of inviting the public to telephone the BBC began. As adroit as any Bunny-girl in warding off the pestering people, they have been, in general, not only helpful but on many occasions much more intelligent than the average Admin. type at the BBC. The latter were often either craven or cross, men with double-barrelled names and single-track minds. But the PBX girls we knew in the years of radio's fame were characters in themselves.

On Christmas Eve, in the branch exchange at Rothwell House, a building opposite Broadcasting House which contained such dubious elements as the Features and Drama departments, the PBX girls would give a party for producers and other incorrigible types. These were sometimes allowed to take over the switchboard. Barsley has a keen memory of the mayhem, particularly the moment when he put a distinguished drama producer, trying to contact an even more distinguished drama producer, through to the boiler-house.

"One of the brightest gems among them was an Irish girl, Eileen O'Sullivan, and bless her heart, at the moment of writing, she is still there. Standards of presentation in the BBC are now so low that one morning, at 6.58, I heard a continuity voice, describing programmes for the day, begin by referring to Roy 'Plommley' (for thirty BBC years he had been pronounced 'Plumley') and continue by promising the voice of Chali*arp*in, an 'Adaygio' by Brahms, and a vintage recording of *Hear My Prayer*, with the celebrated boy chorister

Ernest 'Low' (Lough). Quick as a flash, Miss O'Sullivan, who knew all the answers, followed my instructions to see that whatever greenhorn had said all this it should not be repeated an hour later. And faith, we won the day!"

ADMIN. TYPES

"They fight by shuffling papers: they have bright dead
            alien eyes:
They look at our labour and laughter, as a tired man
            looks at flies,
And the load of their loveless pity is worse than the
            ancient wrongs:
Their doors are shut in the evening, and they know
            no songs."

Are these lines, from G. K. Chesterton's *The Secret People*, applicable to the BBC Admin. type? Probably not, but it is a great temptation to quote them, as Barsley did during the war, and Gilbert Harding after it. For years, members of BBC staff have been divided into two types: those who feared Admin. but fawned on it, and those who defied it and often thrived on their defiance. Every ordinary BBC man would *claim* to have a grudge against Admin., and pride himself that at times he outwitted "Them." But if the crunch and the confrontation came, many would climb down, and accept the inevitable, consoling themselves afterwards by breathing fire into their beer, and huffing and puffing to their sympathetic but impotent circle, or their secretaries. Between us, we invented the firm of Hackles and Umbrage Ltd. "Hackles raised. Umbrage taken. Distance no object." But at times the firm went into liquidation—in the local. As Ivor Brown once put it, "many a blow for freedom has proved a damned dull thud." The phrase "You can't win" was probably invented in the BBC, by those who had fought, and lost their case.

The obvious fact was, of course, that the Corporation, being run on Civil Service lines, was unable to accept anything unusual or dynamic, if not on paper. The Charter enjoined it to "inform, educate, and entertain"—in that order. The least important people were the producers of the entertainment. Presumably Admin. types listened to programmes like *ITMA*. If so they might have realized why Tommy Handley's first job was described as "Minister of Aggravation and

Mysteries." It was Laurence Gilliam, a life-member of Hackles and Umbrage, who once declared that if all broadcasting was to cease for six weeks, the only people who wouldn't notice would be in Admin. They would merely notice a slackening flow of material into their In-tray. The War, as Howard Thomas and others found, brought a welcome relief from Admin., whose cohorts disappeared into Ministries. This is how the great programmes were born. This is how John Watt enjoyed working sixteen hours a day away in Bristol, and Felix Felton, that restless, inventive character, found an outlet for his versatility there. The story is always ended the same: when the war was over, the Admin. cohorts came back again, to try ruling the roost. But their "bright dead alien eyes" were never quite the same. There were still the many infuriating moments which any producer could quote, shaking his fist at the man with the set face, the set of ideas, and the set of initials. "If DDT has really recommended, with NBG's approval, passed by SPQR with copy to LSD, that no action be taken, then——" and the extraordinary thing was that the loser would almost inevitably be the listener. He might be deprived of a good idea, a fresh treatment, a new technique, simply because the Admin. type wanted to win an internal battle. Programmes apart, there were other strange ways of treating BBC staff, and even more curious treatment for those on an outside contract. Barsley quotes one example from the days of his first assignment, the *War Report* series:

"I had been working since D Day on the regular shift basis, sometimes sleeping in BH, sometimes not. But at that time, in 1944, when Paris was about to fall, I was one of those who had to hang on day after day until the thing happened. When it was over, I went to see my Admin. man (we called him 'Pondweed') and asked if I could have a few days off.

" 'You mean,' he corrected me, in his neat office on the third floor which was unchanged since war began, 'that you wish to apply for compensatory leave?'

"I didn't know what compensatory leave was; I had merely worked for a fortnight on the trot, and, being then a freelance, the question of leave had never arisen. We were too busy to think about it. Pondweed sat back, his pale fingertips touching, and intoned: 'Compensatory leave may be granted in cases where a member of staff can be said to have worked hours exceeding those for which he was contracted.' But I wasn't a member of staff, and had no agreed hours. I was there when wanted. Paris had taken an unconscionable time being liberated. History had been made, and been broadcast. I had a book under contract, to finish within a fortnight. I—but what was the use? Strangely enough, I was granted my compensatory leave, and completed the 20,000 words, working in the country, within the ten days allotted. But, of course, it was the attitude of the Pondweeds of this world which had astonished me."

Another tiny but typical example concerns a piece of cake. Helen Mason, a producer's secretary, squeaked and skipped, on the pavement when she saw Fuller's van at the back entrance to BH (outside Scott's Hotel). "Oh, look, Fuller's cake for tea today!" Miss Redfern (General Office Supervisor) had seen the skip and telephoned the office and said Miss Mason must observe better decorum.

The Admin. attitude in those early days (and, given the chance, they would put back the clock today) was that entertainers were worth the same as "writer-fellows." One has only to trace the upbringing and education and background of the Admin. types to realize why they behaved as they did—and as, for instance, many publishers still do. To them, acting and writing is a form of vocation, like serving in the regular Armed Forces or seeking Holy Orders. That this labour of love should be paid as much as, say, an industrious Civil Servant was an insolent assumption, and those who went out to secure outstanding artists or writers on the cheap had often to use a lure more potent than a good lunch—namely, publicity.

Here, in an aside, Barsley is reminded of the day he persuaded Beatrice Lillie to take part in a radio tribute to Robert Benchley, who died in 1945. Lady Peel (her real title) was temporarily in England, but was proving most elusive. Dolly, her dresser and maid-of-all work, used invariably to say "Lady Peel is out" from the flat in 55 Park Lane, when her Ladyship could clearly be heard asking, in a loud whisper, who it was calling. Finally, the question of the fee was agreed: all that remained was to be sure that Bea would turn up at rehearsal time on the day. Barsley ordered a car to pick her up: but it was no ordinary car. Dolly admitted that when she saw the vintage Rolls-Royce, with its silver carriage-lamps, outside the door at 55 Park Lane, "Lady Peel gave a sort of a cry." She did more than that: she monopolized the Rolls at every available moment, to visit her mother, and to import an American GI friend to watch the show. Barsley duly sent in the hiring bill. This was eventually followed by a memo on the subject of transport for artistes, explaining to all producers that cars could be ordered only to convey artistes to and from the studio. The proof of the pudding was surely in the acting (Bea fluffed her way through the narrator's script inimitably: she had never been cast as a narrator before). But that to the Admin. man was merely output, merely a programme, merely a dainty dish to set before the listener. Far more important to him was the extravagance of the vintage Rolls. He had probably never heard of Miss Lillie. If she had been put down in the cast as Lady Peel, that might have made a difference: even more so if she had rung him up with her famous announcement on a Paris phone—"C'est Lady Parle qui peale."

No doubt almost every BBC producer or booking manager could gild this Lillie story.

How many members of the BBC have actually been advised by Management to leave the staff, in order to be paid adequately and separately? The list must run into hundreds, and once you're an "outside" man, the Management may haggle over fees and about your doing other kinds of writing, but they do pay something worth having. Otherwise, there's never been so much labour of love done anywhere as in Broadcasting House. The other trick, of course, well known in Fleet Street and advertising agencies, is for the staff man inside, given an idea from the outer-space of the freelance, to say "Yes, we'd thought of doing something on those lines ourselves," and the next thing is, they do it!

When Head of Drama, Val Gielgud once faced the formidable task of producing a most formidable man in an amateur production. The play, Edgar Wallace's *Sport of Kings*, contained a rather vulgar part, to be played by J. C. W. Reith. The Director-General's character is discussed elsewhere, but several of those who had a hand in this production agree on one aspect: once you had penetrated his shyness, you found a most accommodating response. Gingerly they switched the Cockney accent of the part to Clydeside, and Reith immediately responded. This hurdle over, Gielgud mounted an ambitious Ibsen-style production, but the only comment it evoked from one of the high-ups, Admiral Carpendale, was that it was "very long and very dull." No wonder Gielgud responded by describing the new Broadcasting House, the Admiral's pride and joy, as "an aesthetic disaster." On one occasion, he was showing René Clair round the building. They entered the august Council Chamber, with its solemn urns as part of the decoration. "Is this," asked the famous film producer, "where you keep the ashes of dead Directors-General?"

"HOW MANY PEOPLE LISTEN?"

Opinion has always been divided about Opinion Polls. It has been said, for instance, that Harold Wilson lost a General Election by trusting a last-minute one. There has been a similarly divided argument through the years about the importance of the BBC's Research Department's Listener Research, begun in 1936, with a former advertising man, R. J. E. Silvey, as Head, developing, with the return of television, into Audience Research, but continuing on the same lines.

The public is always asking this question about itself: "How do they *know* how many of us listen and how many of us watch, and whether we like it anyway?" This is no place to explain the sampling method or the Appreciation Index, details of which can be found in official BBC publications. The Department has its critics. One even went so far as to write "The real degradation of the BBC started with the invention of the hellish department which is called 'Listener Research.' That Abominable Statistic is supposed to show 'what listeners *like*'—and, of course, what they like is the red-nosed comedian and the Wurlitzer organ."[1]

Barsley, who has been a producer both in radio and television, can sum up for his colleagues, who are the main targets:

"For the programme producer in the BBC, the important item—and often the misleading one—is the Appreciation Index. True, the Corporation does more than ITV: it sends out part-time workers by the hundred to seek reactions. The findings are not electronic or computerized. But if a producer is unnaturally elated by a good result, chortling 'I've 18 per cent listening and an 80 per cent rating!' and imagines how well this is going down in the Higher Echelons, then that producer is made of puny stuff. True, in the eyes of the average High-up, the Appreciation Index is either a halo to wear or a stick with which to be beaten. The fallacy, of course, is that while the general percentage of listeners is involuntary and unselected, the Appreciation percentage is taken from people who have volunteered to belong to a panel, and these tend to be the more critical or disapproving types—the sort who would write to newspapers. A selection of their comments is quoted no matter how infinitesimal the number of replies. I once received a Research Report for a production on the old Third Programme which was solemnly divided into 57 per cent

[1] Lionel Fielden, *The Natural Bent*, 1960.

thinking this, 24 per cent thinking that, and 19 per cent not thinking at all. At the foot of the Report was given the number of letters received. There were nine in all. What's 57 per cent of nine people?"

BBC GIRLS

"You can see—it's stamped on their little bottoms that they're BBC girls."

This from a well-known, mildly lecherous author after a spell of scriptwriting within the Corporation. But if it can be said that there was a "BBC" type generally, as we have discussed, this didn't necessarily apply to BBC girls in general. Their training was uniformly good. The spoilt, slouching "temp," now offered such high wages by the economics of the day and by agency hysteria, would not be likely to get past a BBC personnel officer, at least not in the earlier years, when to work for the Corporation was something special. After training, a girl would probably start in some routine department, indistinguishable from any other branch of the Civil Service, and there, if she didn't appreciate the programme side of radio, and the chances to get into it herself, she might sit, rising slowly, grade by grade, until she had acquired the hauteur, perhaps, of an Admin. secretary, with an office of her own, a blue rinse and the MBE.

The girls who fought their way out, and became programme secretaries, could have the time of their lives as a very important ingredient in the production team, together with the girls with the delicate touch of a Junior Programme Engineer. Not for them the prospect of departure at 5.30 p.m. daily, a lunch-break of one hour, and a neat filing-system for a boss who was always punctual, usually sober, and sometimes willing to answer letters. Theirs was a dedicated job, which might entail loss of freedom, lack of food, loss of sleep, even loss of honour (though this was usually by mutual arrangement). The glittering prizes were the excitement of the programmes in which they were so irresistibly involved, the chance to meet celebrities, most of whom called them "darling" and so gave them a sense of *amour-propre* and the final opportunity to become producers themselves. Eventually, the lure of becoming a Television secretary became even greater: they could be regarded as almost enjoying the privileged position of a continuity girl in the world of the cinema.

The Girl Fridays on programmes were not glamour or good-time girls. Sometimes their responsibility could be very real: to a production secretary belong a dozen jobs, from knowing exactly how to use a stop-watch—timing being an immensely important factor, especially in news or a quick-moving feature—to cheering up a cast, coping with a maverick producer (including watching his liquor intake and keeping unwanted people at bay, especially Admin. types) and generally being the link between the private world of the studio and the world outside. They were anything but office-girls, and the producer whose desk was tidy and whose diary was up to date must be regarded as a rarity, particularly in the Features and Outside Broadcasts Departments. Many an anxious mother might have wondered where her wandering daughter could be, but BBC Girl Fridays didn't usually worry about mothers, if they could help it; again, the programme always came first. "And what greater glory could a man desire [we quote our author again] than to have a bright bundle of energy and eagerness at his elbow—to be captain of the big ship, towing a delicious little dinghy?"

This idealistic view is by no means always fulfilled. There is, we agree, the type of secretary who instinctively knows when to say, to the wrong type of caller, that you are Not In. (It is usually an importunate scriptwriter, a persistent actor, or an Admin. type querying expenses.) "I'm afraid he's not here," Girl Friday will say—in a kindly way, not in the po-voiced manner of the Admin. secretary, to whom everyone but a man with a set of initials is an intruder—when one is only five feet away. A tic-tac system works out whether (1) the caller shall be fobbed off finally or (2) left to wait for the contrived "Oh! here he is now," accompanied by the door opening and closing, or (3) asked "Can he ring you back?" This last remark, maddening to the freelance, probably standing in a noisy, stuffy telephone-box, should only be used with familiar, over-insistent callers.

But there can be the type of secretary who, partly through malice or sex-repression, will always put the Admin. type permissively through ("Yes, he's here, Mr Pondweed, I'll put him on the line"—as if one were a damp shirt hanging out to dry) but who will choke off an elusive girl-friend, who may never try to ring again. She also refuses to keep a file marked "Letters that will never be answered." A number of secretaries adored their bosses, thank heavens, but not to distraction. The programme came first. They all, without exception, tore their bosses to pieces over coffee: that is the way of all secretaries, and no more so than with production girls, who had plenty of stuff to tear in the shape of producers, notorious for their unkempt appearance and unruly ways, effectively hiding the lurking genius that each one fancied he possessed. To overhear something like "Old Randyballs doesn't realize it, but——" when you *are* Old Randyballs yourself, is tantalizing. If you can't smack them, join them, is my motto. Just ask one of them to go and get you a cup of coffee, there's a dear.

Barsley's tribute to BBC secretaries was included in a musical satire, when Marjorie Westbury played the part of Memoranda, and sang:

"I'm little Memoranda
I never miss a date:
Reliable and pliable
And never, never late.
"I tell you what you're going to do,
I hold your life together:
Don't you like my winter suit
Of red, limp leather?"

This was followed by the first performance of a Concerto for Typewriter and Orchestra, with one of the top BBC secretaries playing the solo part, including a dazzling cadenza. It was called, predictably, Typofsky's No. 1 concerto.

THE BBC "REP."

The Repertory Company of the BBC was formed in the autumn of 1938. As Norman Shelley, one of its early members, recalls, it was known as the "Munich Crisis" Rep. The remarkable thing about this company, unassuming, often misused, underpaid and taken for granted, has been its individual brilliance, its collective faithfulness to the BBC, and its durability. It is one of the few BBC institutions which has survived to the present day, as invaluable an asset to a producer as it ever was, though there are some who have always regarded the Rep. as a way of getting acting talent on the cheap, with disregard to the problem of unemployment in the theatrical profession. Bruce Belfrage, first manager of the Rep., under Val Gielgud, was firmly of the opinion that it should not have been continued after the war.[1]

[1] *One Man in His Time*, Hodder & Stoughton, 1951.

"You're overspending your budget: you'll have to use more people from the Rep." was what one often heard, as producer, from the departmental Programme Organizer. This has always seemed unfair to those Rep. members who were prepared to turn their hand to any part, for the sake of the security the BBC offered, and to give it their full attention. By 1941 the Rep. was thirty members strong.

Among those whom Shelley particularly remembers, in addition to Gladys Young and Barbara Spencer, is the late James McKechnie, whom he first saw in Scotland and immediately got in touch with Val Gielgud, saying "I think this man shows great promise, and he's not likely to be called up for military service." He recalls, too, the infectious giggles Jimmy had, and which he nearly burst himself trying to stop, and the devotion shown to Home Guard duties by Laidman Browne, "that dear Geordie man." He would give the all-round prize, however—and many would agree with him—to that quintessence of delightful radio, Marjorie Westbury.

That sense of humour and that sweet voice used to cause theatre managers to ring her up and demand her for a musical, and she'd say with a laugh "Have you ever seen me?" Marjorie has always, of course, been bouncing and buxom, and going about saying "The only chance I'll ever have in the theatre is one of the Ugly Sisters—and they can't find the other one!" But her versatility, quicksilver sense of humour and purity of voice have made her one of the most sought-after artistes in radio history. The quality of a long run like her Steve in *Paul Temple* has never been matched in any other medium. What a bubbling beldame for the vintage years!

The Forsyte Saga in its first production by Val Gielgud during the war was not only a landmark in radio drama but a great occasion for the Rep. company itself. Grizelda Hervey, who played Irene in both this and the later production by Hugh Stewart, has definite views about its effect. "We really became like a sort of family," she says, "completely wrapped up in the experience. For one thing, Muriel Levy, who adapted it, did a wonderful job, making full use of Galsworthy's own background in the person of Young Jolyon, played by Leo Genn, unforgettably. Malcolm Keen was Old Jolyon, and Ronald Simpson—dear Ronnie Simpson—*the* Soames to set the example for all people playing Soames thereafter. Elgar's Enigma Variations gave the perfect background. Yes, that was quite an event—and yet, incredibly, the BBC engineers destroyed the original recordings, by mistake! But not before this man Donald Wilson had heard it go out, for the first time."

Wilson is the man who fought the BBC for eleven years to get *Forsyte* on television. Endless objections were raised. It would be too costly. MGM had made a film of it in Hollywood (and as Grizelda Hervey pointed out to the American script-writers on the spot, a very bad film, not so much reflecting the English middle-class way of life as laughing at it). In one way and another, viewers were kept waiting. When the TV version was finally launched, of course, the BBC high-ups preened themselves on its beauty—and its box-office appeal. The experience is a typical one, though the BBC cannot really be accused of being much more reluctant than the average publisher or theatre manager. The trouble is, as the late Harold Nicolson pointed out, even in his capacity as a Governor, that "the BBC has an unerring instinct for the second-rate."

Grizelda Hervey, versatile as most members of the Rep., gave great insight to the part of Irene, as the woman who could not be wooed by wealth and property, but only by love. "The name Irene means peace, and in a sense that's what it was all about. Those were years in which many of the classics were brought to a much wider public by radio: not only Galsworthy, but Trollope and Jane Austen and Dickens and so on. It was a great period for the expansion of people's tastes. Apart from Irene, I think I liked playing in Somerset Maugham best: such a dramatic writer." Grizelda was also in nearly all of Martyn C. Webster's *Paul Temple* series.

As for Norman Shelley's own radio story, it dates back in all its wide range, to the 1930s. Shelley had known Savoy Hill in the 'twenties, singing "Fly be on the turmut" with Freddie Grisewood, and being greeted, with colleague Geoffrey Wincott, at a BBC party by Reith himself with the stirring words: "So, ye're both at it. Keep it up! Keep it up!"

Norman fought off the danger of type-casting. When Basil Dean, on the stage, accused him of being "infatuated with senility" Shelley pointed out that he had just been cast, by Dean, as a waiter aged about ninety-four. But when it came to playing General Booth on radio, his voices ranged from the age of sixteen to the age of eighty-four.

He is also proud of the Holmes–Watson partnership of twenty-five years' standing, with Carleton Hobbs, and claims it to be more successful than any portrayal on television or stage. Another memory, during the war, is becoming a sort of "one-man Churchill Rep." in reproducing the voice of Winston—that other "Winnie"—who would not give repeats of his speeches in Parliament.

"Of course, the old man insisted on listening to a trial run, for the European Service, and as he listened I'm told a slow slow smile spread over his face, as he said 'He's even got my teeth!' "

Here is Shelley's reply to those beginners who come to him saying "What sort of voice shall I use for this part?"

"Never think in those terms at all. What you must do is this: say to yourself, what sort of a man am I that I'm playing? If you can draw, so much the better, put him down on paper. Then think of the clothes he wears, the colour of his hair, the colour of his eyes: think of the food he eats, the things he likes to drink, the women he likes—or doesn't like—the books he reads, the house he lives in. Get all these clearly photographed in your mind, and the voice will come right—just as in the wartime scrambler telephone, this garbled thing went out, it will unscramble itself back into the listener's head, and the picture will come right. I've proved this to myself over and over again."

Perhaps the most convincing proof lies in the radio part he created in 1939 (his favourite role) Winnie the Pooh. "I can't tell you what a debt I owe," he admits, "to Ernest Shepherd for his drawings to A. A. Milne's story. When people say "But how did you get that voice?" I say, "It's Shepherd's fault. Then, of course, you've got to realize, he's tubby, his arms are stiff (they won't go sideways) his head's filled with sawdust—and his walk, oh, his walk!"

Shelley believes that if he'd never done anything else, his Pooh would have been sufficient memorial, surrounded as he was by the combined genius of such men as Geoffrey Wincott, Stephen Jack and Wilfred Babbage, in the original production by Josephine Plummer.

THE ENGINEERING SIDE

There's a sort of attitude in the BBC similar to that in the RAF when it comes to the engineering side. Intrepid aviators during the war would always sincerely pay tribute to the ground staff, "without whose tireless work the job would never have been done," etc. A hero-worshipping public, like a listening public, is apt to find this rather dull. There will always be people behind the scenes: of course the show couldn't go on without them, *but*—do we need to be told?

The great "but" in radio and television is that the public doesn't usually connect anyone directly with broadcasting unless his voice is heard and/or his face is seen. The near-miracles of engineering are taken for granted; so is the expertise of production and direction. We can quote an acquaintance saying "So you're a Producer. Do you have to be there when the programme goes out?" Even with broadcasting being initially such a matter of mechanics and with two of its most commanding D.G.s having had a technical background, the proof of the programme is bound to be still in the speaking or the seeing. The backroom boys have to be philosophical about it, relying on their own professional pride in the broadcast, and the part they played in it.

One BBC engineer's name, R. T. B. Wynn, calls for special mention, because he was a programme man: that is, he realized, even in the early days, that barriers existed between programme and engineering divisions, and that it was necessary to break them down. Far from being what some people called "greasers," R.T.B. is in fact the Hon. Roland Wynn, a Cambridge graduate who came from a distinguished family. He combined the ability of running his own staff with the knack of liaising with the programme side, and furthermore, had a flair for public relations which he had learned from working for Peter Eckersley, another pioneer from Savoy Hill days.

In the early days, engineers considered it their right to control every knob. They had the know-how, therefore they claimed the responsibility. It was after the "Fleet's Lit Up" fiasco that Wynn devised a method called Scheme A, the embryo of today's system of continuity. This meant that knob-control, in effect, could actually be in the hands of an announcer, a producer, or later his Programme Engineer in the studio. Thus the great days of the "P.E.s" began. Theirs has always been an important and exacting job, and one which can have finesse and artistry as well as accuracy. Every producer knows that his P.E. (or Vision Mixer in television) is worth his or her weight in gold. Their advice is very rarely ignored.

Scheme A was hotly resisted, by the diehards, but Wynn and Snagge both agreed that it was of vital importance, and Wynn fought his own division to bulldoze it through. As far as continuity announcers were concerned, it was also agreed that they should work within the area of the engineering control room, in case of a crisis. Many an announcer has been saved a blunder by the prompt action of his engineer. One way to seal the bond was to invite a representative of Presentation to sit on the selection board for prospective engineers, and vice versa. This started a new era in co-operation.

"Roly" Wynn was a Writtle man, in BBC parlance. That is, he

formed one of the Marconi team of pioneers who, with Eckersley, carried on experiments before 1922 in a small hut at the village of Writtle, near Chelmsford. He rose to be Chief Engineer of the Corporation under Sir Harold Bishop. As far as we can gather from Eckersley's enthusiastic writings, a rare old time was had by all at Writtle.[1] It is all in great contrast to John Logie Baird's first agonizing experiments with television. Baird, a sensitive and lonely man, had no cheerful team with him: his system was finally rejected: he came a cropper and died in frustration and poverty, long before he could see the successful results of his invention in other hands.

One of the most important aspects of BBC engineering lay in the increase use of recordings, and entire recorded programmes. Reith had always believed in the *mystique* of a broadcast being "live," and there are many actors, reporters and producers who prefer its excitement and its challenge. But as programme locations became more far-flung and planning more complex—not to mention the editing of items of unpredictable length—recording often became essential. The first Recorded Programmes Executive, Lynton Fletcher, was appointed in 1934, at the time of the celebrated Blattnerphone, which recorded on steel tape. The effect on personnel was striking. Sir Michael Redgrave, whose prodigious reputation on the stage and in films must not be allowed to overshadow his contribution to radio, recently recalled his first experience with the Blattnerphone for the present authors—and recorded it very casually on a very small tape-recorder:

"I remember the arrival of this sinister-sounding machine, and recording in a programme of poetry and music devised by Lionel Fielden and called *Mosaic*. With me were Fay Compton, Robert Lorraine and Freddie Grisewood. After a recorded rehearsal, we awaited the play-back. Well, Fay Compton's voice sounded just like Fay Compton: so did Freddie's—again, a fine voice. Then it was my turn. I began a poem with some line like, 'Oh, the lovely ships,' and when the words came out, they had very weak vowel sounds, and as I glanced embarrassed at the others, I saw Lorraine smile to himself, as if to say, 'Well, that'll teach the young man to speak more fully.' Then it came to Robert Lorraine's turn. He stood in front of the machine, arms akimbo, as if daring it to do anything to his voice. But what we heard, I'm afraid (because I admired Lorraine as an actor) was just what in radio one is supposed to avoid—the kind of theatrical projection at which he was expert in the theatre, but which didn't adapt

[1] See Asa Briggs, *Birth of Broadcasting*, page 71, and P. P. Eckersley, *BBC and All That*.

itself at all well to radio. At each succeeding word he seemed to shrink in front of the impact of this awful machine, and subsequently changed his style." Yes, the play-back can indeed be an uncomfortable moment of truth, and a great leveller.

The Blattnerphone was only one of a large number of different methods attempted in the search for the perfect recording device. It all goes back to Alexander Graham Bell and his phonograph, and the voices of Jenny Lind and Florence Nightingale and Tennyson reading "The Charge of the Light Brigade" on those wax cylinders. A magnetic recorder had been tried as early as 1898, but it was not until 1936 that the first tape-recorder called a Magnetophone made its appearance at the German Radio Fair. The first concert recorded by this method was a performance that year by Sir Thomas Beecham and the London Philharmonic Orchestra at Lugwigshafen (later the home of BASF, the big tape-recording company).[1] The maestro was nothing if not an innovator. Meanwhile the BBC stuck to disc recording, on records made of aluminium with a light acetate covering. Near-miracles could be achieved in editing with these, by dubbing from one disc to another. At other times a "jump" cut might be necessary, the young engineer making a yellow chalk-mark on the groove to follow, and dropping the tone-arm on to it while the disc was running. Done "live," this was a nerve-racking business and demanded exquisite sureness of touch.

But it cannot be contested that both the British and the Americans lagged far behind the Germans when it came to tape. The actual beginning of the present type of magnetic recording was in 1940, when H. J. von Braunmuhl and H. Weber took out German patent No. 743,411. It was a pity that there was a war on! Not until 1945 did one of the German machines fall into Allied hands. The Germans may have lost the war, but they had won the battle of the tape-recorder, and their former ally, Japan, has made a bid to continue the supremacy.

Until that time, the BBC contented itself with studio recording, and with the use of mobile recording gear for O.B's and Features. But the cars used to house the gear were the most unsuitable choice that could have been made. The Humber Pullman, a long, dull, black vehicle, was of the prestigious type, suitable for funerals of the slightly-less-than-Rolls-Royce standard, for delivering the Deputy-Chairman to his office or—most admirable use of all—for conveying

---

[1] See *Tape Recording*, by Michael Barsley (Michael Joseph, 1967).

a three-star general from the War House to his club for lunch. In fact, the BBC bought a second-hand lot which had been lightly used for just such purposes. These ungainly brontosauri, though roomy enough to contain the massive "E" Type recording gear, were not fitted for the job at all, and yet they were sent on long and sometimes urgent journeys. It was as if a hearse were to be asked to exceed the speed limit.

Let us take the example of one modest radio documentary programme in 1951, entitled *A Day in Naples*, for which Wynford Vaughan Thomas was the reporter, Barsley the producer, and John Vizard the engineer/driver. Instead of flying this small team to Rome and Naples with an equally small tape-recording machine (which had already proved its worth in the field for the previous three years—proved it, alas, only too well) it was decided to keep to the traditional method, by car. It took three days to reach Naples (instead of, say, a maximum of six hours by air). The car, straddling the Alpine passes, was well-nigh unmanageable because of its lack of manœuvrability. Then the necessary papers for admission to Italy were found to have been sent to a different frontier station. These were just three circumstances guaranteed to fray the nerves.

Only the imaginative genius of Wynford got the BBC into the country at all. At Molaretto, high in the Alps, we were halted. "There are no entry forms here," the Chief Customs Officer declared. Wynford, who had not been at Anzio for nothing, sized up his man by his accent. "But, signor," he began, in fluent Italian, "we don't want entry visas to Italy but transit visas, *through* Italy." "A transit visa? To where?" Wynford then spread his hands, beaming. "To the Kingdom of Naples!" he said. The effect was magical. The Customs Officer collapsed with laughter. "I must tell my assistant!" he cried. "He comes from the North!" and all the equipment was chalked and passed, followed by a *vin d'honneur*.

It turned out to be an enchanting programme of recordings, once John Vizard had recovered his composure after the drive. We recorded several songs by Roberto Murolo, a Neapolitan singer then unknown outside Italy, and by contrast, a story of a waiter in a restaurant who said he had once been given an audition for the San Carlo Opera, until there befell *"una piccola disgrazia"* which ruined his voice. "What disgrace?" asked Wynford gently. "I got VD," replied the waiter sadly. The recordings, including Pompeii, were done in three days. Then Wynford wisely flew back, and the long trek started home in the Humber Pullman. One tyre blew out on the Alps, and then the spare one went, somewhere near Arras. As we walked to get help it seemed like the end of the world. Nine days, when four would have done. Vast expenses, near-breakdowns of man and machine. It was, in fact, nearly the end of this way of recording a programme, but it's a valid example of the entrenched attitude of the BBC's recording department, and the word "Naples" is written on all our three hearts.

For all the excitement and experiment of the early days, there are those within the BBC who have sometimes found engineers unadventurous and highly suspicious of progress, rather like the late David Low's cartoon of the TUC as a large white cart-horse.

"It can't be done" is a phrase many an apparently madcap producer has heard. Ronnie Waldman told us of a case when he and his fellow producers required a quiz show to be held in four towns simultaneously. "The engineers thought we were crazy. How could we be sure of switching from one to the other, with howl-back and God knows what? Quite simple. We wouldn't switch: we'd just leave all four mikes open. But that would mean, they said, that each place would hear the laughter and 'business' of all the others. Exactly, we said: that's just what we want. The engineers washed their hands of all responsibility, but it all went like a bomb—and, of course, they were then as pleased as we were." Ronnie, of course, knew quite a bit about technicalities himself, which made a difference.

In general, there's great support by engineers for the perfectionist. The reputation of Dr Ludwig Koch as a recordist is as legendary as his voice and appearance. Creeping as silently as a deer-stalker towards his prey, Ludwig is part of the history of recording. He has been seen risking limb, if not life, lying flat on his face on a cricket field, near the batsman taking strike, with microphone in hand, to get the correct, the completely authentic sound of King Willow. At other times, in the winter, wearing mittens and a balaclava, he would look like a hunter: at others, his lean intent face might resemble one of the rare birds whose voice alone he hunted. One of Koch's recording engineers, Reg Pidsley, remembers some typical incidents:

"I went out many times with Dr Koch. It might be on a farm—and then there was the dawn chorus, that famous recording, with all the Doctor Huxleys and that, all up at Whipsnade. So we settled down for the night, and up with the dawn came all the little birds, and of course we hadn't got the tape-recorders they had now, it all had to be cut on the disc. Then after the dawn chorus was done, we had a walk round the bird sanctuary with the Warden, and suddenly Dr Koch stopped. 'Pidsley, Pidsley,' he says, 'not so fast.' He'd heard a bird song he wanted—the lesser tit-wit or something—anyway it had never been recorded before, the doctor said. So my colleague Bill Read scrambles up the tree and puts the big heavy mike up there (weighs about five or six pounds, enormous big thing) straps it up and comes down, and then we sit down to wait. Sure enough, the little bird came back, and sang, beautifully: but then Dr Koch puts his head out, and says 'Ah, Pidsley but what is that other noise?' 'Well, Dr Koch,' I said, 'it seems the little bird is perching on the mike.' And he'd been sort of making dough, you see, just like my cat does on my leg, but on the mike it sounded like an elephant with clogs on. So Dr Koch turns to my colleague and says 'But why did you put the microphone where the bird wanted to sit?'"

At the time of the Berlin Airlift, Pidsley was on duty throughout (he spent altogether two years in Berlin) and among celebrated recordings, made one of nightingales singing, as the planes went by carrying supplies. Proudly he played this to Dr Koch on his return to London, and the Doctor commented: "Very nice, Pidsley, very nice—but anyone could tell they were German nightingales!"

MUSIC AND THE MAGAZINE

"The greatest patron of music since Nero," a wag once remarked of the BBC, as the Music Department went on its untroubled way while the fires of rivalry smouldered and flared in other Departments. Certainly there can be no doubt of the continuing debt owed by the public to the men of music, be they directors or conductors or both. The Last Night of the Proms is now an annual event as exciting to many as the Cup Final, especially on television, when the bright, eager faces of those who prefer Beethoven and Brahms to a howling group of hippies are seen in dedicated close-up.

It wasn't all that easy to achieve such a triumph. Listeners today are probably unaware that it was the BBC which literally saved Henry Wood's Proms from extinction, just as the War saved *ITMA* from being taken off after six performances. Negotiations between Reith and Boosey, owner of the Queen's Hall, and a sworn enemy of broadcasting music, which he regarded as the death of the concert hall, are about as bizarre as a meeting between President Nixon and Chairman Mao. But the result was that the BBC took over the Proms without a break, and Henry Wood recalled the "elation" with which he conducted the first broadcast item, Elgar's "Cockaigne" Overture, now a Prime Minister's favourite.

The Musical Director of the BBC from 1923 to 1929 was Percy Pitt, and there is no secret about his disappointment at having to give way to the up-and-coming Adrian Boult from Birmingham. But in Boult's hands, greatness developed, grandeur bloomed until, in 1937, the legendary Toscanini conducted a series of concerts, with the BBC Symphony orchestra, which were about as difficult to get into as the Centre Court at Wimbledon on Finals Day. The renowned critic Ernest Newman declared "Wireless has placed the musical destinies of the country in the hands of the BBC." And there it has remained. We need only refer to the brilliant improvisations made on recent Prom seasons by Sir William Glock. This was news—especially with young people.

The BBC not only elevated the status of the orchestra, founding its regional examples in the early 1930s, persuading Sir Thomas Beecham to drop his prejudices and opening an old ice-rink in Maida Vale as a music studio. The Corporation began to interpret music to individuals, in the intimate way of the medium. Sir Walford Davies's immortal series *Music and the Ordinary Listener* made a tremendous impact on ears hitherto deaf to music's charms, as early as 1926, and the mantle has fallen, most worthily, on Antony Hopkins, who can breathe life—and humour—into a symphony or quartet which hitherto had only a number or a key. Pitt's *Foundations of Music* was taken up by that remarkable character Filson Young. George Thalben-Ball at the organ joined the immortals, and has persistently refused to leave them. At the Proms, the red carnation of Sir Henry Wood became the white carnation of Sir Malcolm Sargent. The excitement of those summer weeks remained.

Never have the vintages of classical music been so palatable as in those years; and for those who wished to learn more of the facts and structure behind the history of music, there was the evergreen weekly offering of a Grand Lady who retired just before the BBC's Golden Jubilee—Anna Instone's *Music Magazine*.

It was inevitable that the BBC should have a *Music Magazine* in its radio repertoire—to improve public taste and appreciation in music was part of the Reithian ideal—but it was not inevitable that the result should have been so outstandingly successful, varied, and apparently everlasting as the series begun during the war by Anna Instone and

Julian Herbage. A recent *Times* critic, Kirsten Cubitt, aptly summed it up as "the brainchild and creation of the man and woman whose arresting names are as much part of Sunday morning for thousands of listeners as peeling the potatoes or salting the joint for the oven."

Anna and Julian (BBC colleagues very rarely use their surnames) are also BBC "characters," which gives their series added flavour. Anna the wilful, Julian the careful: at one time the blend was rather tantalizing, and as we watched them walking down Great Portland Street at lunch-time, towards the now defunct Pagani's restaurant, we wondered what game of musical chairs was being played, and what they'd think up next for the programme. Alec Robertson had been the first presenter of the musical menu. Mark Lubbock, tall, white-haired, affable, would often be there, prattling about opera, and Constant Lambert, with his scarf and stick, might be on that slow walk to the pub, in deep conversation with Humphrey Searle and Stephen Williams as they all moved up to their favourite luncheon table, where choice wine flowed and the names dropped and another Music Magazine got under way. Yes, the group at Pagani's during the war was one of the last of the famous groups of BBC characters, taking their time, and not giving a damn what people thought about them. Toulouse-Lautrec could have drawn them: he'd have loved Anna's imperious, prima-donna profile and Julian's habit of stroking his minuscule beard as he gently disagreed with a voluble Alec. Gone are the groups. It is all now a matter of grabbing a sandwich, gulping a beer and throwing a nervous look over the shoulder, as if your name was already near the redundancy list. Anna, the old warrior, would have had none of that. Holding the title of Head of the Gramophone Department (a title as grotesque as Director of the Spoken Word) she wielded immense power, sending early disc-jockeys scuttling, terrified, to their places, to introduce *Housewives' Choice*, and frightening the lives out of the plug-money touts of Denmark Street. Anna has scarcely ever needed to raise her voice; her rebukes have been made more effective, as were the late Nye Bevan's, by her slight stammer. Gilbert Harding, David Jacobs, Bryan Michie, Stanley Holloway, Sam Costa—a whole gallery of famous men have been glad in their time of their week's Housewife chore for Anna. She herself obviously prefers the world of Music Magazine, but has been loth to relinquish her role as Dame of the Disc-Jockeys and the Queen of Needle Time. Julian, for his part, has been so long in the music side of the BBC, as Assistant Director, that his authority is unassailable. Take the two of them together, and you have the pattern on which all good magazine programmes are based.

CHILDREN'S HOUR

The disappearance of *Children's Hour* seemed, at the time, yet another example of the Corporation trying to be trendy—or was it realistic? What was the BBC up to—or rather, the all-powerful Board of Management? Children's Hour had always been recognized as part of the very life of broadcasting. What did Auntie mean by destroying her young? That children were no longer children? That they despised the Uncle-Image of Mac and David, that they watched the telly at tea-time instead, that they didn't have tea-time at all, but just lounged around in jeans, listening to pop and drinking coke, that they resented parents listening to the same programme as they did, that the time interfered with the schedule for the new Radio 4—or what?

"Yes," could be a general reply.

In 1933, when undergraduates of the Oxford Union voted that they would in no circumstances Fight for King and Country, the *Times* leader was derisively headed "The Children's Hour." Little did the leader-writer realize that he was in fact paying young Oxford a compliment, for in many ways the Department provided some of the most intelligent programmes in the whole BBC range, with an enthusiastic adult following as well. It never represented "kiddywinks," as it was sometimes called within Broadcasting House.

The secret of the *Children's Hour* quality lay with its creator, Derek McCulloch. A most unlikely choice indeed, a man who had every right to be embittered, a man whose First-War wounds never left him alone and who was to suffer further accidents, a man apparently withdrawn and not outgiving, almost a Wicked Uncle. You couldn't judge McCulloch by his published books, most of which are simple fairy stories traditionally illustrated. They were his side-line. The programmes, which were almost a religion with him, were indeed for young people, and covered a vast field of them, but they weren't of the sort to be told at mother's knee: they were often intended to help the children to appreciate the world about them, and to understand the issues their parents might be talking about, and the headlines they saw in the newspaper. They were, in a word, adult in their approach. It is a sad reflection that a publication called *The Children's Newspaper* also ceased to exist at about the same time, because it followed an equally adult format.

McCulloch's programme reputation was so high that he had only to ask for a top speaker to get him. If there was to be a talk about stars, the Astronomer Royal, no less, would be in the studio to give it. To explain politics, Stephen King-Hall might be the invited man. Vernon Bartlett would explain international affairs; Walford Davies or Adrian Boult would discourse on music. Johnnie Morris was the Zoo expert. They were glad to come, to put their subjects in a form which young people could understand, and this meant, in fact, in a form just as adult as that appreciated by the average grown-up, whose mental age in this case would probably be no higher than that of an intelligent youngster.

At the time our Vintage Era begins (1935) *Children's Hour* was put under the overall direction of the Drama Department, that is, under Val Gielgud. It regained its "independence" three years later. At the beginning of the War, a memorandum was issued from Head Office on the future policy for *Children's Hour*, along with other Departments. It has a rather pompous, *pas devant les enfants* air, cutting the programme by half, with orders to avoid subjects such as the War itself, and any mockery of Hitler or the other Axis leaders, but it took note of the fact that the programme had a sizeable adult audience. Gielgud had already increased the dramatic content, and such series as the historical playlets by L. du Garde Peach and Hulme Beaman's *Toytown* became radio classics. Characters like the Toytown Mayor of Felix Felton and Larry the Lamb assumed the fame almost of *ITMA* creations, and just as grown-ups read and re-read *Alice* and *The Wind in the Willows* and *Gulliver's Travels*, so they often listened in at five o'clock. The partial ban on recognizing that there was a war on was lifted as the tide of war began to lap our shores in 1940. Asa Briggs notes, too, that *Children's Hour* was chosen for the first broadcast by Princess Elizabeth in October, of that year, with Princess Margaret chiming in with her own "Goodnight" at the end. In a modern television parallel, Princess Anne, in 1970, participated in the *Blue Peter* series, an example of a series for young people inherited from radio's *Children's Hour*.

If the answer to our first multiple question is general, one real explanation seems to lie in the final reason, the re-fashioning of programmes into Radios 1, 2, 3, and 4, in which 4 was to represent mainly the spoken word, for adults. Therefore the 5 o'clock traditional space for children was a stumbling-block. It's also true to say that the BBC does from time to time appear to get almost jealous of the favourites it has created or any rapidly thriving section which seems to rebel against control. Perhaps it's also true that the grown-ups missed *Children's Hour* more than the young people, now glued to the telly or the record-player. But it would be a mistake to think of those who regret the dropping of established programmes as old squares. It depends what you replace the programmes with. It is perhaps ironical that the adventures of Larry the Lamb have been bought up by Commercial television.

The decision was, as Norman Shelley, one of *Children's Hour's* stalwarts put it, "nothing but assassination." One reason given by someone among the hatchet-men was that the programme "only had a listening figure of about two million." Two million youngsters, growing up. Norman Shelley thinks—and we agree with him—that this is a significant audience, if not an immensely sizeable one. But once the BBC Gods are on the side of the big battalions, they have dwindled to the stature of ITV Idols. They desecrate, but can find no substitute after the deed is done. Woe unto you, mandarins and managers of the BBC! Let us hope you do not stay long in command, for yours is a limited, opportunist outlook.

3

Corridors of Power

IN Broadcasting House, the seat of power, the Captain's Cabin in the great stone battleship, was the suite of rooms on the third floor, belonging to the Director-General and his aides. Until a few years ago, this was the only part fully carpeted, in royal blue. It was said that the staff lifts automatically stopped at the third floor out of reverence. The hinged doors opened inwards instead of outwards, and there was a small hall facing the offices of D.G. and his Controller, containing a bronze bust of Reith and a framed photograph of Foley House, which used to stand on the spot.[1]

There were staff jibes about "the passing of the Third Floor Buck," and John Watt, when Head of Variety, coined the phrase "Sno Use and the Seven Controllers." There was in fact only one Controller of Programmes in London: the others were in the Regions. On him fell the day-to-day working of broadcasting, and his orders and wishes, and sometimes whims, would be passed on the lower echelons, the Heads of Departments, with their Producers. There was usually an Assistant to the DG, and, as we shall see, once there was an Editor-in-Chief, with the name of Haley. Subsequently, Directors were set up, with a much higher status in sound than on television, where a director may simply be the man who puts out a programme.

Outside this hierarchy and concerned, supposedly, only with policy, not programmes, were the Chairman and the Board of Governors, who met in the semicircular Council Chamber—again, like a verandah in a ship—on the second floor. Of late, and well outside the vintage years, the responsibilities of the Chairman have been under dispute. There are those who have taken an extreme view of the present Chairman, Lord Hill. The retired Deputy-Chairman and one-time Acting Chairman, Sir Robert Lusty, declared in a letter to *The Times*, that Lord Hill ought to be impeached. More recently, Mr R. H. S. Crossman, MP, a prominent radio figure on Political Warfare, declared, in what was then his own paper, *The New Statesman*, that Mr Wilson, when in power, had appointed Lord Hill as Chair-

[1] Foley House was the home of James Watt, who invented the steam engine. Can it be accident that sound broadcasting came to be known as "steam" radio?

man of the BBC Board, following his term of office with the rival ITA Board, in order (*a*) to obtain the removal of the then DG, Sir Hugh Greene, within two years, and (*b*) to spread lack of self-confidence within the BBC. But these are matters for later consideration. Here are just a few of the personalities who strode the corridors of power during the Vintage Years, starting with "Mr BBC" himself.

LORD REITH

John Reith, the man who made the BBC, was a paradox: an extraordinary figure, full of contradictions. To the public, he was half-institution, half-legend. To his own staff, he was both an inspiration and a terrifying taskmaster. To his close friends he was a shy, unpredictable charmer, a man of great principles and boundless ambition who nevertheless often felt desperately insecure. Over and over again there were things he wanted to do, positions he wanted to hold—"Viceroy" was his one-word reply to Malcolm Muggeridge on that point—but he couldn't bring himself to attempt them without elaborate persuasion. He left a trail of glory behind him, a halo of respectability, a permanent reputation—and £76.

No one, in the many descriptions of him—he both invited and defied description—has ever managed to explain what really made him tick, and probably no one ever will, however patient and penetrating the analysis. His life is really made up of references to him: what he did, and what he didn't do. What he said, and what he left unsaid. What he created, and what he apparently deserted, the BBC.

Physically, he was formidable, a gift for the cartoonist, and he knew it. He played his height—about six foot six. He played his majestic appearance. He played his wound—an ugly scar gouged out of his left cheek by a First-World-War sniper's bullet. Sometimes he would deliberately present the scarred side of his face to intimidate people. (It also fascinated photographers.) He was autocratic, certainly, and he liked to be surrounded by yes-men, in the sense that he wanted people to do what he told them, and not to do things without his knowledge. Yet he would spoil for a fight with the highest in the land, and was the only commoner who invented a title for an ex-King, when he announced "His Royal Highness, the Prince Edward," one day in 1936.

Snagge adds: "He used his great height in another way, too. When he was Director-General, he always gave the impression of knowing a tremendous amount about the subject one was discussing with him. He seemed to have every detail at his finger-tips as he strode up and down, holding his coat lapels. What I never realized, until he told me about it long afterwards, was that on the top of a very tall book-case, where no one but he could see it, he would have a complete briefing typed out in advance by his secretary. Another example of his indecision, for a change. A long while after he had retired, he accepted an invitation to come to lunch at the BBC. Then he decided he could not face it, and he himself called in at Broadcasting House to leave a note saying he couldn't come. Hearing he was there, I rushed down and persuaded him to come after all."

Barsley remembers being sent round, as one of the producers of the Silver Jubilee programme on 14th November 1947, to invite him to take part. Reith was then Chairman of the Commonwealth Relations Board, with an office in Eaton Square. In the middle of the conversation, the telephone rang in the hall outside. He got up—and up, and up—and went out to answer, returning soon, to say "D'you know who that was? That was your Sir William Haley, wanting to know what I'd say." His answer was a courteous refusal: "I'm sorry to disappoint you."

Although exceedingly touchy, Reith had a strong sense of humour, and could enjoy jokes about himself, provided they were told in private. In his later years as Director-General he became irritated by the length of time it took to contact his Heads of Departments on the telephone, so he instituted a system whereby he would simply ask for "So-and-so—my ring." At once three sharp rings would sound in the man's office, demanding an answer by the man, not his secretary.

What Reith never realized was that these three rings were the quickest means known of emptying an office in Broadcasting House—and when Snagge told him about this after he'd retired, he threw back his head and laughed and laughed.

He never shed his strong Scots accent; indeed, it came on ever thicker in moments of stress, and on one notable occasion—the 1931 General Election—it caused chaos over the radio.

Announcers had all been carefully coached in the pronunciation of the names of constituencies and candidates. Suddenly, on the night, Reith decided to take part and announce some of the results himself. Instantly the telephones were jammed by people complaining—they couldn't understand what the man was saying. The announcer, Eric Dunstan, told him he thought he should stop but Reith insisted on having another go. The complaints redoubled, and in the end Dunstan walked out.

Snagge once took him to a Lord's Taverners lunch where they saw Ian Macleod, whom Reith had just defeated for the Rectorship of Glasgow University. Snagge said to Reith: "You know him," and he just said: "No." He refused even to meet the man, and when asked why, replied: "Because he never wrote to congratulate me."

His demand for exact, factual truth was unending, but at the same time he had an extraordinary capacity for self-deception. For instance, he always claimed, after he had left, that he never listened to the BBC at all. This was just rubbish: to some, he would often criticize particular programmes, and he once said to Snagge: "John, in my opinion the Be-attles [his pronunciation] are evil."

Conceited? Arrogant? Devious? He gave his enemies plenty of openings. Snagge was immensely fond of him, not least because he saw how exceptionally kind he could be to young people, and what trouble he took on their behalf. And yet, admirer though he was of his integrity and courage, he never completely understood him.

Reith was often the subject of exaggerated stories and cartoons, and like any Prime Minister he loved them. The "Spy" cartoon, an early one, shows the great height of the man, but portrays him as willowy: it misses the granite, monolithic image of later years, the eagle eyes, fierce brow, determined chin and the deep scar on his cheek.

He became the subject of parody, too, even for the sophisticated. In the late Herbert Farjeon's revue *Nine Sharp* 1937, the actor George Benson impersonated him in a Gilbertian take-off:

> "When I was a bairn, I lived up north
> In the land of the leal and the Firth of Forth.
> All through ma' youth in ma' ain countree
> I polished up ma' English verra carefullee.
> I polished up ma' English sae carefullee
> That I became the Ruler of the BBC!
>
> "That nae man's morals should be lax nor loose,
> I decided when I built Broadcasting Hoose,
> So I summoned up ma' staff and said, "Hoots
>   mon, hoot,
> If I hear of ye canoodling, ye gang right oot!
> I sat upon canoodling sae successfullee—
> There's never been a babby at the BBC!"

Reith held strongly to the view that, since radio was received directly into people's homes, there must be nothing to cause offence. There had never been a medium like radio before, and he was very conscious—many would say too conscious—of its possible bad effects as well as its good ones. In good faith, therefore, he drew up the rules, in consultation with his colleagues, and saw that they were carried out. He had the strength, the authority, and the determination to do it, and to see that his lieutenants enforced it. "What effect will this have on people listening at home?" was his oft-repeated criterion.

Today we have, in varying degrees, what is called a permissive society. There are milestones leading towards it, such as the court case over the publication of Lawrence's *Lady Chatterley's Lover*, with all the words which Murray had excluded from his Oxford Dictionary, and which Eric Partridge had partially concealed, with asterisks, in his *Dictionary of Slang and Colloquial Usage*, in order to keep within the law. This, and the other milestones marked S for Sex, are mainly visual, and are already becoming, in countries like Denmark, so permissive as to be ultimately boring. But this is only one classification. The radio Index included politics and religion (neither of which subjects, as Howard Thomas has pointed out, were allowed to be discussed in the highly erudite as well as entertaining *Brain's Trust*) all references to the Royal Family, to race and colour in a derogatory sense (Jack de Manio's fame once rested on the mispronunciation of a single word) to physical infirmity, homosexuality and so on.

Muir and Norden, that irrepressible pair, claim to have read all these prohibitions in the green books they were given as soon as they arrived in their office to write their first script as members of the BBC. These were supposed to be as closely followed in Variety as a certain little red book in China. After a while, Frank said to Denis "Have you finished yours yet?" Denis hadn't, so Frank waited until he had, and then remarked "You know, I think that when we *leave* the BBC we've just joined, we must write a script which begins 'My God!' cried the Queen, 'That one-legged nigger is a poof.' "

SIR WILLIAM HALEY

It may seem strange that the emergence of some of the most imaginative and vigorous programme material should have come at a time when there was no equivalent Director-General in overall command. The departure of Reith had been abrupt: the appointment of Ogilvie had been shockingly mismanaged, and the succession made little impact on the staff, still partially mesmerized under the Reith tradition. Who was F. W. Ogilvie, except Vice-Chancellor of Queen's University, Belfast? The men and women putting out the programmes never knew, and scarcely cared: certainly they knew nothing of the battle for mastery behind the scenes. What they appreciated was the new DG's apparent distaste for interdepartmental memos and red tape. Besides, there was about to be a war, and then it would be every programme for itself.

Ogilvie lasted until 1942, to be replaced by a double-headed DG consisting of Robert Foot ("Who's he?" asked the staff) and Cecil Graves ("Oh, him"). It made no difference either way. The BBC had, as someone put it, one foot in the graves. But this gave the Heads of Departments, all of whom had known Reith, not only a sense of service but a sense of freedom. With the programme dispersal to Bristol, to Woodnorton, to Manchester, to Bangor, the hold of Admin. weakened, or was swallowed up in Ministries. Then it was that the great programmes flourished, from *The Shadow of the Swastika* to *ITMA*, from *The Brains Trust* to *The Man Born to be King*, programmes made by inspiration rather than under supervision. As for keeping essential contact, Snagge quotes one example; "Though I was in London and he was in Bristol, I had closer contact with a man like Felix Felton than I had with a man in the next department in Broadcasting House."

By the time Haley became Director-General, in 1944, he had programmes to be proud of.

The main function of a Director-General should be to maintain the BBC's independence and keep away the pressures from outside. He has to carry the Board of Governors with him, and a strong DG always will. He is a person who will not only be the chief executive officer, but keep the Governors, in policy, away from the detail—that's his own job, and he has to establish his position when trouble arises, whereas the Board of Governors' job is to direct the overall policy. Frequently the Governors may say to the DG "We think you had better handle this with Downing Street, because you know the position better than we do. We think this is the right attitude to take." They may be ultimately responsible for policy, but it's the DG who does all the work.

No Director-General can expect to keep out of trouble when he's running an organization as big and as widespread as the BBC, covering entertainment, information and education. He's alone there at the top, and if he's a good man, he will never pass the buck.

Snagge gives a personal example of the Haley method:

"When I was in charge of Presentation on one occasion, one of the main newsreaders just wasn't there, and the bulletin had to be read by someone in the News department. I was out of the building, but was contacted, and shot back, but had to let him continue to the end, when Haley was at once on the phone asking what had happened, and why was the voice not that of one of the regular newsreaders? I told him I didn't know what had happened to the announcer, and Haley said 'I'm not interested in the announcer. You're Head of the Department and you are responsible for this and I want to know from *you* how it happened. I don't even want to know the name of the announcer, or to have it passed on. I want *your* explanation.' I was able to give it eventually, and admit that we had no shadow-announcer standing by. That was the end of it. When criticism followed, Haley told the critics, 'I've dealt with this. There's no more to be said!' He didn't bring it up again—in fact he stood up for me despite the mistake, instead of saying 'Snagge let the side down.' He'd got my explanation, and that was enough."

"An Editorial DG—the only one the BBC ever had," summed up Harmon Grisewood on William Haley.[1] "No one since Reith had sized up the job on a scale large enough for its true requirements. He understood the need for standards and had the guts to apply them."

This is true enough. Haley had been brought in as Editor-in-Chief, a newly-created post, which rather puzzled everybody, since he was very little known, apart from having been in Reuters and on *The Manchester Evening News*, a paper less erudite but more lucrative than its sister, *The Guardian*. (He wrote reviews under the pen-name of Joseph Sell.) But what was he doing in the BBC? We were alive to all sorts of conjecture, and since Haley appeared a very remote sort of person, this didn't give much clue, though there was a rumour that he was one of those in line for the next Director-General.

His eventual appointment shook a number of people, particularly the two members of the Board of Governors who voted against it— Lady Violet Bonham-Carter and Harold Nicolson. When the choice was being made, Nicolson was in favour of the first candidate, John Maude, Principal of Birkbeck College, "a man of great talent," he

[1] *One Thing at a Time.*

notes in his Diary. The Board agreed to interview the second candidate, of whom Nicolson had never heard, let alone met. "A clever man," he sums up, "but not at all suited to the cultural job which we had in mind." Then, to his "horror," Nicolson learned that the Chairman, having received the consent of Brendan Bracken, Minister of Information, had already gone ahead with the appointment. Nicolson and Lady Vi objected, and forced a vote, being defeated 5 to 2. Both were prepared to resign, Nicolson on both counts—that Haley was unsuitable and that the high-handed action of the Chairman was outrageous, Lady Violet on the second count only. She liked Haley and later described him as "far and away the best Director-General we had at the BBC during my spell as Governor." In the end neither resigned, but Nicolson noted "It is the absence of any corporate function which renders the BBC Board so contemptible a body." For the BBC itself he had a high regard, and was one of the principal speakers in our Silver Jubilee programme in 1947.

Haley gradually established himself as being a person who was putting the BBC back to the position of the Reith days—not in laying down the principles of broadcasting anew, but in rebuilding the prestige of the BBC and standing up for its independence, as Grisewood implies but Nicolson doubted. This happened during the war in a famous instance referred to in detail elsewhere in this book: the announcement of D Day in 1944.

As far as his effect on the staff was concerned, it was a reassuring one, once the discipline of war had passed and various re-jiggings were bound to be in the offing. Snagge, for instance, was told by Haley in 1948 that he was very prepared to let him continue in his position as Head of Presentation (having taken advice on this) but declared that at the end of one year he would, in the light of any further reorganization, decide whether Snagge should continue to do it. "It wasn't put in the form of 'probation' or anything like that, and I willingly accepted it, but realized this was a new sort of approach. The old idea was to appoint a man considered fit for a job, and let him continue in it, perhaps for ever. Haley wanted to reconsider the matter within a limited time. There certainly were to be changes, with the Light Programme replacing the Forces Programme, with the Regions restored to their original position of autonomy and with the Third in the offing—not to mention Television. Altogether it was a very interesting, indeed exciting moment in BBC history."

One particular and important experience Haley shared with Reith: his knowledge of engineering. He had been a radio operator, and therefore knew a great deal about the technical side of the BBC: he had the knowledge about what could be done in developing it. He could also talk almost on level terms with his engineers—a type of person who normally doesn't despise the ignorance of another man, and is indeed only too willing to enlighten, but who appreciates knowledge in another when he meets it, particularly if that man happens to be his boss. There must have been many a BBC engineer in Haley's time who said to himself "the old man knows his stuff."

An enchanting story about Haley, told by R. T. B. Wynn, Senior Superintendent-Engineer and one of the great figures of radio, reveals, on the other side, that the new DG could get up to tricks of his own, as Reith did. The scene was Haley's first news conference, in the august Council Chamber of Broadcasting House. The press was there in force, anxious to catch him out if they could, particularly on the technical side, since Haley hadn't come up through the ranks of the BBC, but had been a mere journalist like themselves. Haley had Sir Noel Ashbridge sitting beside him, the man he valued so highly that he had moved him from the post of Chief Engineer to that of his Deputy-DG. Ashbridge had a pipe in his mouth: he usually did.

When questions came, Haley adopted Reith's attitude of pondering before replying, as if weighing up the answer. On interrogation about technical matters, he invariably gave a lucid answer, so the pressmen went away, satisfied on that score. What in fact happened, according to Wynn, was that Ashbridge, sucking and blowing through an empty pipe, had been giving the answers briefly in morse code—puff, puff, puff-puff-puff, and so on. Haley, as we have said, had been a radio operator and knew the code backwards! So, if one wants a human side to Haley, there it is. His public image was very different.

One nickname given to him was "the man with two glass eyes." It was alleged to have been made up by J. B. Priestley, when meeting him after giving a talk. Actually, he did follow a policy of not appearing to make, as Director-General, any personal friends among the staff, which might be unfair to them, if word got round that someone was the DG's blue-eyed boy. But, if he kept this general aloofness, it was probably against his general character, and he would probably have preferred to be more friendly, as he was in private life. He could be a good and patient listener, and his ability to make a decision was never lacking.

Some members of the staff took a more irreverent view. One experiment in particular, the Haley lunches, was eventually looked on with dismay by those who attended. The idea—to mingle members of different departments round a luncheon table, to meet their DG informally and on common ground, may have been admirable. But this, according to one producer, is what happened:

"The lunches took place in a room on the third floor, and an invitation was the equivalent of a royal command, and planned on a rota principle. Participants were offered a minute glass of sherry when entering: the other refreshment was cider. In an atmosphere of almost desperate politeness, a Features man might try to strike up a conversation with a woman, or a *Children's Hour* organizer exchange banter with an announcer—and there, in the midst of them, would sit their host, almost in silence, like a man wrestling with a deep personal problem...." Many indeed were the excuses invented for not having to attend the DG's "get together" lunch.

Even more irreverent—blasphemous, even—was this hymn (we know the famous author, but will not disclose his name):

"Haley, Haley, Haley, Lord God Almighty,
  Buggering up the programmes, on Home and Light,
                                                  and "C"[1]
  Double-up on culture, Bach and Boult and Bartok—
  Hell on three wavelengths, blessed BBC!"

But even such critics respected him for the way he fought for the freedom of the BBC as an organization: if necessary, he would fight even Churchill, tooth and nail, over a question of principle, and his reputation abroad, after the war, was prestigious.

Haley has not so far written a book about his term of office, and probably never will, regarding the BBC simply as an organization of which he was in charge, and doesn't want to discuss any more. He would certainly hate to write of personalities or people, or disclose any information he had as Director-General, but would rather just get on with the next job, editing *The Times* or the *Encyclopaedia Britannica*, or whatever it was. No revelations here for Malcolm Muggeridge to unravel. This is not to say he forgot about the Corporation to which

[1] The original working description title of the Third Programme. A later—fortunately abandoned—idea was to call it "Minerva."

he had given so much undivided attention. He retained a personal interest in it, and A. P. Ryan, former Head of the War Reporting Unit, became his assistant editor on *The Times*. But his departure had none of the drama of Reith's departure, for Reith had stalked out of Broadcasting House without saying good-bye to anyone. His wife had paused to shake hands with the Chief Commissionaire: Reith strode by, but admits that his face was covered with tears. With Haley, nothing was here for tears: nothing was extenuated, nor aught set down in malice.

There is another story about Haley, which, though apocryphal, is in the style of his reputation. He is said, on his last day, to have gone round personally to say farewell to his senior colleagues, rather than to let them attend on him. One of these was not in his office at the time, and his new secretary, not recognizing the DG, asked if he would wait. Haley duly sat down in the outer office. Time passed, and his colleague still didn't turn up. So Haley rose, and turned for the door, whereat the girl said "Oh, are you leaving?" "Yes," the ex-Director-General is alleged to have replied, "I'm going to Fleet Street." "Well, that's quite easy," said the young thing. "You walk down to Oxford Circus and get a number 15 bus." Apocryphal it is, since *The Times* is published in Printing House Square. Significant it also is.

SIR HUGH GREENE

Hugh Carleton-Greene, appointed in 1961, turned out to be quite a different kind of chief from anything experienced by the BBC before. If Haley had been the first Editorial DG, Greene was the first Programme DG, although he had begun as a journalist (Berlin correspondent of *The Daily Telegraph* at a crucial time). His wartime job as Head of the BBC's German Section, with R. H. S. Crossman his right-hand man, was of the highest importance as a weapon in psychological warfare. The story of these days, and of the man once described by a member of his department as "a beast—but a just beast," belongs to a history of the BBC at war. Greene's outward character as Director-General gave a very different impression.

Here was a man who was completely friendly with everybody. To see him walk into the BBC Club, often with his coat-collar turned up, not on purpose but because he'd forgotten to turn it down, was to see a tall, slightly shaggy figure, grinning and full of quick, amusing answers, which might suddenly turn to equally quick and unanswerable decisions. Greene knew, from the moment of his very predictable appointment, that he had to keep his wits about him. When Snagge first congratulated him, saying "Good luck—I daresay we're going to see things happen," Greene replied, "Well, I don't know, but I think there's probably a bomb lying about under my chair somewhere, and somebody's already lit the fuse, so I'm just waiting for it to go off." It went off, but several years later.

A gay companionable character: the only DG, as one press critic put it, who would drink beer with his producers in a pub. He once bet Barsley, then Editor of *Panorama*, a pint that his brother, Graham Greene, would never appear before the cameras, and that pint held good for years. But he wouldn't discuss business unless specifically asked to, and unless the occasion was opportune. Otherwise matters of great pitch and moment were confined to the corridors of power, where Greene also excelled. Again, the story of this untidy, controversial figure as BBC boss doesn't belong to our span of radio, but the day when one bomb went off must be recounted, because it was a radio, not a television bomb.

The day the Nine o'clock News and the Silent Minute which preceded it were abolished was like the Day War Broke Out, since, in the writer Peter Fleming's words, "it became in most households an institution almost as sacrosanct as family prayers had once been."[1] Moreover, the wartime naming of announcers, made both as a security measure, and a means of recognition by secret listeners in occupied Europe, became equally popular with the home public. But nine o'clock was The Time, just as, to follow Peter Fleming's analogy, eleven o'clock was the acknowledged Hour of Mattins in church.

Nine had, in fact, been a comparatively recent arrival (1938). The six o'clock bulletin was the one which had caused such a row with the newspapers in the days of Reith and Carpendale. But the infant very soon acquired a halo. The Fellowship of the Silent Minute attracted many converts, but Greene, in his fragment of autobiography, remains unrepentant.

The decision, despite its shock, was realistic, in radio terms, apart from the drift to television. Nine o'clock became too late to allow a full-length concert or play afterwards, and besides the Third Programme, which recognized no fixed regular spots, was there as an alternative.

[1] Peter Fleming, *Invasion 1940*.

The name of Greene will always be associated with a change in the BBC's image. "At one time," he wrote, "the BBC seemed to be a pillar of the Establishment. The popular conception of a Corporation official—I do not know which word I dislike more, 'Corporation' or 'Official'—was of a bowler-hatted gentleman in striped trousers and black coat, entering the hushed precincts of Broadcasting House with tightly rolled umbrella at the Slope. I think the last of the breed went into gentlemanly retirement about a couple of years ago."[1]

SIR BASIL NICOLLS

Perhaps the word "Controller" was a misnomer for Sir Basil Nicolls (known within Broadcasting House as "Benjie" after his initials, B.E.N.); a Controller implies a tight rein: it has a discipline, a severity about it, a smack of the Ten Commandments. But outwardly, Nicolls gave no hint of this. He was a tall, commanding figure, true, and he was a man with a distinguished military record which included the heroic landings at Gallipoli. But the manner was more that of a patriarch than of a general, and the mannerisms were most deceptive. He had a habit, at his desk, of suddenly shutting one eye, and appearing to shoot an arrow from a bow through the window, at a building in Portland Place opposite, where Lady Cunard kept a nursing home. He would play with magnets on the desk, doing tricks with them, looking expressionless, apparently only half paying attention to what was being said to him, and people usually only went to see Benjie Nicolls about something important. But all the time he was taking everything in, and would have made up his mind by the time the speaker had finished.

He seldom demanded to see anybody in his office. If you wanted a decision, he might well guess this, and come to see you, and say "I'm here now, and I'd just like to talk to you about this." He strolled about the building, usually hands in pockets, giving this attitude of wandering, in time, and attitude, and actual movement. His room was often empty. He'd be out meeting people, finding out about things, but never interfering.

Unlike most men engaged in broadcasting at the top, he left no records of his achievements, though Professor Asa Briggs has been an assiduous and valuable collector of his most important minutes. Nor did he say much about his life at the BBC. Very few people, for

[1] *The Third Floor Front* (Bodley Head, 1969).

instance, know what happened to Nicolls on the night the bomb fell in Portland Place and set BH on fire. He was in fact on duty that night, in a little room on the lower ground-floor, which was severely damaged. His life was saved as if by a miracle, and he was found, by Laurence Gilliam, standing by the lift, his head wounded and his face streaming with blood, asking how things were, quite unconcernedly. It was Gilliam who got hold of an ambulance, and saw that he was dealt with quickly.

In other ways you couldn't frighten Nicolls. He'd be concerned with what you were doing or suggesting, and while he listened, apparently vaguely, he'd be sizing it up. He would really be keenly attentive, not only as to what was being said, but as to who was saying it. He was interested in the people engaged in broadcasting, not just in broadcasting itself. Towards the BBC he appeared to take a casual sort of attitude.

There were several examples in our own memories which reveal this. On one occasion, Nicolls was reproved because, of all things, he had hung his bathing-trunks out of the window to dry (Benjie was an athletic, sporting type). He was told it made the building look "untidy"—this, to the Controller of Programmes! He accepted the reproof, but confessed he couldn't see the reason for it, and his gentle smile disarmed all criticism. A more important example concerned Royalty. Nicolls, obviously, moved in the highest circles in his job: he was concerned, professionally rather than ceremonially, with Prime Ministers, Archbishops, Kings, Queens and Princes, and he could be relied on to do the job extremely well. But in 1947, on the occasion of the Royal Tour of South Africa, which was to have six weeks of elaborate radio coverage in a series narrated by Snagge and produced by Barsley, it was discovered by them that no alteration had apparently been made in the Corporation rule about the use of the royal voice. This rule stipulated that any speech or message by the monarch should be broadcast in full, preceded or followed by the national anthem. What had not been realized was that, with the distance involved, plus the quality of short-wave transmission, plus the impediment in the King's speech (his stammer, as his biographer Sir John Wheeler-Bennett confirms, was due to the fact that he was left-handed, but had been forced to "switch" hands by a ferocious governess) meant that his messages would have to be edited, for the first time in BBC history. The first scheduled speech was to last thirteen minutes, live from Cape Town.

We explained the dilemma to Nicolls, for his had to be the decision. Quite unperturbed, he admitted that he believed no alteration to the rule had in fact been made, and said "We'd better send a telegram." When it was pointed out to him that a telegram to the King's private secretary might very well not get there in time, and that a call could be put through to Frank Gillard, chief correspondent with the royal family, immediately, Nicolls said "All right. Go ahead." But as we left, he said, almost to himself, "But we'll *still* send that telegram." Gillard obtained royal permission within hours, and it is not known whether the telegram ever arrived. Yet the responsibility had been delegated to us, since we had to bring out the programmes.

The most celebrated wartime case was his reaction when Christopher Stone, who in closing a gramophone programme, sent birthday greetings to the King of Italy, adding, "We don't wish him any harm." Well, the storm broke. Italy was our enemy—Emmanuel's Garter banner had been removed from St George's Chapel, Windsor —and Nicolls had taken no disciplinary action. Thus spoke the Men from the Ministry. Nicolls took it all calmly. He didn't bang the table and say he was right, but regarded it somewhat as a storm in a teacup. This enraged the Ministry still more (Brendan Bracken was then in charge) and they more or less demanded that the BBC provide Nicolls's head on a charger. His staff rose in his defence. James Welch, Head of Religion, Gielgud, Gilliam, Uncle Mac and Snagge protested to the Board of Management and Governors, and threatened to resign if the Government and the Ministry were to be allowed to dictate what should or should not go on the air, and the dismissal of their Controller as the price of the mistake. The Board and the Governors backed them up, and the Ministry backed down.

Nicolls respected the mantle of Reith, with whom he had always been on the closest of terms, frequently lunching with him at the Athenaeum: he respected the Board of Management and the Governors. But in other ways he was an independent controller with a mind of his own. His memoranda were never unkind, in an organization noted for its asperity in this matter. Those who received them usually found something constructive and acceptable in them, but a Nicolls memo would rarely penetrate below the Head of a Department, and the Head would not necessarily interpret what the Controller had said, or how he'd put it, which was why, to the lower ranks, he was a mystery rather than a patriarch.

LINDSAY WELLINGTON

Lindsay Wellington, though he worked closely with Nicolls, seemed a very different type of man. In the first place, he was ambitious; ambition was a quality Nicolls never seemed to want to possess, or he might well have become a Director-General. Wellington possessed all the training and experience for a top job. He had been an assistant in the early days of 2LO at Savoy Hill, he'd gone through being Director of Presentation, he'd been in charge of programme planning, and during the war was seconded to the Ministry of Information (it would be interesting to know if he shared the Ministerial attitude over the message to the King of Italy). In peacetime he returned to the BBC as Head of Home Service under Nicolls, ending as Director of Broadcasting. Despite this impeccable and predictable career, he never had quite the understanding or, alternately, the brilliance which shone out of the gentle Controller.

Wellington made, in the Corporation's eyes, the well-nigh perfect executive. He shared one excellent quality with Nicolls, in that he rarely interfered with anyone engaged on an important job, but waited in the wings in case he was wanted. That he turned out to be a "play-safe" man became evident in time, also that, in any crisis great or small, he worked to the book—whatever that book was: it was certainly a sealed book to most members of the staff. He knew all about broadcasting, its planning, its requirements, its budget problems, and all the hundred and one items which might come up on a high level agenda. But he was not primarily a friendly man, and didn't properly understand the people under him, and what made them tick. He could be reactionary and conservative as well as remote, his yardstick being his interpretation of what Reith would have done, though by this time much of the Reithian laws and standards were in fact out of date.

It's probably true to say that Wellington made up for lack of wide and specialized knowledge by being sure of surrounding himself with experts: his expertise was in broadcasting as such, and as laid down in the book. He could turn to the experts if in any difficulty, or if in need of leadership. He didn't lead himself—though this certainly isn't to say that he bore any relation to the Duke of Plaza-Toro, who led his armies from behind. The main channels of post-war progress—the development of OBs, the continued, buccaneering success of Features, usually against all the rules, the experiments in mobile recordings, in short, the bold adventures—were not made in spite of him, but largely without any inspiration from him. Today, a reporting team of one man and his midget are accepted in all departments, but the opportunity was there more than twenty years ago, but received little blessing from on high, because the book stated that a reporter must be accompanied by a recording engineer, and no recognition had been made of the new approach.

Snagge recalls being "ploughed" as an announcer as long ago as 1931, when Wellington was Head of Presentation. On meeting him afterwards he was asked when he was leaving, since he had failed the test. Snagge replied that he had no intention of leaving after serving the BBC for six or seven years, just because of an examination. On a later occasion, he was sent for by Wellington. "He strode across the room, shook me by the hand, and said 'Congratulations.' 'Thank you,' I replied, 'but what on?' 'Oh,' he continued, 'It's been agreed that you should be offered the job of Controller Northern Ireland.' The job was held at that time by Andrew Stewart, a Scotsman. I then said 'Oh,' too, adding that I'd have to know more about it. 'That's all right, John,' came the reply, 'We'll send you over there and you can talk to Stewart yourself.' So I went, and came back convinced that the job was not for me—I wasn't suited to it, and told Ian Jacob, the Director-General, as much. I don't think Lindsay ever forgave me, because he'd arranged it, and, according to the book, I ought automatically to have accepted. Hence the handshake first, and the offer afterwards. I was only once offered another job, that of going back to my old field, and running Outside Broadcasts. This I'd have been delighted to do, but Wellington resisted my transfer for at least six months, and until he'd found a replacement. Otherwise he might in the meantime have lost one of the departmental experts he believed to be essential to him. Broadcasting, by the book, was everything to Wellington: he couldn't interest himself in other people, in their personalities, their private lives, their domestic problems, and so on. He'd lived for broadcasting and he'd got where he wanted, except perhaps the position of Director-General, which he might have liked —but then, Reith never got the job of Viceroy. Wellington was competent, capable, and knowledgeable, but some people may have felt he seemed to lack the human touch."

Sometimes in the corridors of power at the BBC, the cold draught could be felt.

4 The BBC Comes of Age

WHEN we come to consider radio programmes, rather than people, we find them equally departmentalized, into News, Outside Broadcasts, Talks, Drama, Features, Variety, Music, Religion and so on. This is not to say that the frontiers were all rigidly drawn. Some Talks were more like Features, the original difference being that in Talks actors were hardly ever used, but with the growing use of outside recordings Features began to use more and more real-life voices. Music had already been integrated into some programmes, composed specially for the purpose. The border between Drama and Variety was often crossed and, as we shall see, *The Brains Trust*, a discussion programme, started life under the banner of Variety, since it was meant to entertain.

There are obvious criticisms to be made of the Departmental system. It could provoke jealousy, intimidation, imitation, and above all, duplication. Those who crossed the borderline often came back with a winner, but sometimes a disaster. Among the "lower-deck" assistants in HMS Broadcasting House there was equal rivalry, but an equal determination, not always held in the upper echelons, to put the needs of the programme first.

1935 saw the BBC, no longer in childhood or adolescence, launch out into many major operations, particularly in the field of Outside Broadcasting.

We live in an age so apparently dominated by television that it must be difficult for a younger generation to believe that the events of those times—in Royalty the Jubilee, the Coronation, the Abdication, the Cup-Finals and Derbys and Boat Races in Sport, and indeed the Second World War itself—could be adequately covered by sound-radio, let alone be made vivid in the telling rather than the seeing. But this is as if to say that a photograph is *ipso facto* better than a painting because it is more life-like, or that invention always improves. In accepting the challenge of events great and small, the BBC added a new dimension to listening, and acquired a stature and importance in the world which it has never surpassed. Much of this was due to the handling of the material by Outside Broadcasting, BBC style, and this was not just a matter of mechanics, but of immense human drive and enthusiasm as well.

The early 1930s had seen a remarkable man in charge of OBs. Gerald Cock was a lively, energetic type as well as a good organizer, and though he did not remain at this post for very long, significantly moving on to the world of television, he had given the BBC itself a status it had long desired and deserved, by encouraging the entry into his Department men like Graham Walker, Freddie Grisewood, Howard Marshall, H. B. T. Wakelam, George Allison and R. C. Lyle, to name a selection in very varied spheres. In the entertainment world (for which he was equally responsible) Cock enlarged the reputation of the cinema organ by persuading Reginald Foort to play it, and of the music hall by getting impresario George Black to agree to outside broadcasts from the London Palladium.

When the time came to appoint a successor to Gerald Cock, the task was not an easy one. The Department needed someone who wouldn't just cash in on Cock's know-how and popularity, but would widen the OB potential still further and do justice to the great national occasion.

They got him: Seymour Joly de Lotbinière, formerly of the Talks Department.

His appointment was regarded with some apprehension. The only thing most OB people knew about Lotbinière was his height, alleged to be six foot eight inches, but some asserted it was officially six foot nine! This, of course, put him immediately in the Reith category. But although Reith was a mere six foot six, he had the beetling eyebrows and jutting jaw which "Lobby," as the new Head of OBs came to be called, didn't. Snagge's report on his one-time chief comments: "as it turned out, the four years before the outbreak of war saw a massive development in the OB programme, and Lobby revealed himself as one of the greatest Heads of Department of all time. He displayed exceptional drive, a wide breadth of vision, and proved to be an inspiring leader. He also became a personal friend to us all and was greatly respected."

How did Lobby fall on his feet? By assessment of the field: he agreed that the ground-work had been done, both in the commentary and in technical requirements. But, he told his staff, "the field must be extended, the range widened, the microphone must be taken to strange and interesting people, wherever they may be. In my view, the 'expert' on the subject is not necessarily the best man to broadcast on it. Technical experts are all very well, but more depth and projection are needed. You've got to be up to your necks in Outside Broadcasts." And up to their necks they were. The stage was set, not for the expert, but the expert broadcaster—and there's a world of difference between the two.

The man who really set the pattern was, in fact, the man who paid a random penalty later, Lieutenant-Commander Thomas Woodrooffe. The BBC engineers had produced the "lip-mike"—the miniature microphone which a reporter could hug to himself without extraneous noises interfering. Woodrooffe recognized its potential. With it he took all his commentaries, mainly sporting ones, in his magnificent stride. He established standards extremely difficult to surpass, even to this day. With a microphone which didn't pick up sound beyond a foot or so he could give an astonishingly fast and accurate race commentary. Alongside him, he had a race-reader giving him the order of horses, and *only* the order. Woodrooffe, with his great ability to talk and listen at the same time, would weave this very precise information into his highly stimulating account of the race.

It was impossible to better him on the great occasion. In 1937 he covered the Derby, the National and the Coronation of King George VI with a magnificent description of the scene from the top of Constitution Hill.

But to remember Tommy Woodrooffe is to remember two contrasting occasions. One—a happy moment—was in 1938, during the Cup Final between Huddersfield and Preston North End, he publicly announced his intention to eat his hat if Preston were beaten, and began to do so (this being radio, the listeners had to take it for granted) when the whistle blew.

The other occasion listeners were prepared to take for granted was the broadcast Tommy made, the previous year, at the end of an arduous week's reporting of Coronation week, which culminated in an eyewitness description of the Illumination of the Fleet, off Spithead, Portsmouth. All the top brass of the BBC were there, distributed among the wardrooms of various warships in the harbour. Tommy was assigned to his old ship, HMS *Nelson*. What precisely happened may never be known, but to the friend with whom he spent the previous night, he said "I'm so tired." Perhaps it's enough to say that he fell among thieves, who robbed him of his power of coherent speech, not out of malice but out of overwhelming friendliness and undergraduate tomfoolery. This has always been the hazard for the popular commentator, and Tommy's example has been held up for generations of would-be Woodrooffes who may receive the temptation of too-liberal entertainment before that inevitable moment of truth—the gleam of the green light which tells you you are on the air, and that thereafter anything you say, as the policeman tells you, will be taken down in evidence. The tragedy is that a producer was not assigned to help a man so overworked.

So much has been written about "The Fleet's Lit Up" broadcast, as it came to be known, and as the astute Jack Hylton named his revue which ran successfully for months, that it might seem unfair to recall the occasion, except that it is a classic example of mishandling, not only by the culprit, but also by his employers. Tommy, although penalized after the occasion itself, found it helped to boost the sale of his books about the Royal Navy, *Naval Odyssey* and *The River of Yellow Sands*, and he remained Editor of the Royal Navy magazine the *Ditty Box*. Public reaction over the years can be gauged when we come to deal with the BBC's Silver Jubilee programme in 1947. Then, after much trepidation, a repeat of some of the description was allowed to be broadcast—with Tommy's full permission.

The item was announced by that most loyal ex-army man, the late Lionel Marson, as follows: "This is the BBC Regional Service. The Illumination of the Fleet. We take you over now to HMS Nelson, for a commentary by Lieutenant-Commander Thomas Woodrooffe. . . ."

There followed a long pause, and a scuffling sound, after which a strangely unfamiliar voice seemed to heave itself out of the darkness, beginning "At the present moment the Fleet's lit up, and when I say the Fleet's lit up, it's lit up with little lamps. . . ."

One would have thought that these words alone would have brought those responsible for handling the broadcast swiftly to heel. But no. Tommy's reputation as a commentator was so well-known that his part in the event was taken for granted. Indeed, none of the Heads of the BBC in those other ships heard it go out at all, and had to judge it on the recording made at the time. But the main reason for the dereliction was that, owing to the control of broadcasts still being in the hands of a central room in London, there was no liaison between it and the OB men on location. Harmon Grisewood was the man on duty that night, but it is doubtful if he could have taken the responsibility at once. In his memoirs of radio, Grisewood does not even mention what part (if any) he played, though it served, as we know, a good purpose in drawing attention to the flaw in BBC organization, and strengthened the case for the continuity system of joint responsibility.

Those who have been able to study the recording may find, in one phrase, an interesting and probably instinctive flashback in Woodrooffe's mind to his previous Coronation broadcast, when the royal coach came down Constitution Hill after the service, in the gathering dusk, and was, in fact, lit up inside. At that time Tommy's words were, if memory serves us right—"here it comes, that glorious, scintillating, coruscating coach—and it's all lit up with little lamps!" Typical good Woodrooffe stuff, but could it not be that, as he gazed at the lights of the Fleet anchored at Spithead, he saw the "little lamps" of the Coronation Coach? The phrase is repeated about four times in the broadcast, which ended when the lights of the Fleet were extinguished and Tommy cried "They've gone! No magician could have waved his magic wand with greater acumen—and now they've gone, and there's nothing between us and heaven!"

It is on the word "heaven" that Harman Grisewood, who was brought up in Vatican City, is said to have ordered the broadcast to be faded out, with the usual apologies about technical difficulties and poor transmission. The listening public, however, was entranced. Telephone lines to Broadcasting House were jammed. One ecstatic listener from Sweden cried "I didn't know the BBC had such a sense of humour!"

The immediate sequel to the event—which didn't cost Tommy Woodrooffe his job, only a six-week suspension, after which he was back in his usual tremendous form as a sports commentator—has, we understand, never been told before. All the main BBC hierarchy were present at Spithead that night on various ships, but apparently none of them listened to Tommy's historic commentary. Therefore, there was no BBC post-mortem that night, apart from the complaint which Harmon Grisewood no doubt filed. To the many calls from the press, a BBC spokesman shirked the issue by repeating that the broadcast was merely "unsuitable," so the newspapers went into action.

Came the dawn the day after the Spithead Coronation Review. A special compartment had been reserved on a non-stop train from Portsmouth to London. In it sat Sir John Reith and his colleagues. They had not yet seen the morning papers, but at the last moment a panting minion thrust them into the carriage, and they were blaring with such headlines as "The Fleet's Lit Up." One wonders what conversation took place on that non-stop journey to London? This event, when the BBC honestly looks back on it, must have been one of the Outside Broadcast Department's funniest if not finest hours.

The burning of the Crystal Palace, in 1936, gave Seymour Joly de Lotbinière, whose name somehow suggests a Crusader *en route* for Acre or Jerusalem, the chance to shine, not as Head of Department but as commentator. He was with a recording van returning to London when Paxton's immense building, reconstructed from the Great Exhibition of 1851, and built entirely of iron and glass, with two towers nearly 300 feet high, was seen to be ablaze. "Lobby" stopped to watch, and record, off the cuff, what he is said to regard as the model commentary for all time—and he had no scruples in telling his commentators as much. Here he had a tremendous spectacle on his hands, and like a good commanding officer, he went straight in, and carried on for about half-an-hour.

1936 was a particularly testing time for the OB Department. Coverage of a wide range of sporting events was keeping commentators busy, but also during the year there was the death of King George V—and the Olympic Games in Hitler's Berlin, which achieved film immortality from his friend, Leni Riefenstahl, but which did not show on film the refusal of Hitler to present an Olympic Gold Medal to Jesse Owens, the American negro, who, surprisingly for the Aryan Nazis, won the coveted 100 metres race, and three other Gold Medals, on the same day.

There was also the glamorous maiden voyage of the *Queen Mary*, in the same year. Every effort was made to give full BBC coverage— and this was primarily the Outside Broadcast Department's job—to the first trip of this wonder-vessel, whose progress had been halted for two years by industrial strikes, ever since Queen Mary, in the only known utterance recorded by the BBC, said briefly about Cunarder No. 534, in a low, deep, almost guttural voice: "I name this ship Queen Mary. May God keep her and all who sail in her." The traditional message, behind a glass screen spattered with rain, ended in a successful launching. The story behind the naming of the ship has several variations, including the theory that the Cunard-White Star Steamship Company wanted the vessel called "Queen Victoria," but when Sir Percy Bates, Chairman of the Company, approached the Monarch, King George V, with permission to christen the liner "with the name of the greatest Queen who has ever lived," His Majesty replied "I'm sure my wife will be very pleased."

There had been one near-disaster when the ship came from the

The BBC Comes of Age 71

fitting-out basin in Glasgow to the open sea. This proved to be one of the most exciting voyages that BBC members on board can ever recall. Under tugs, and with her engines going, she came out of the basin without incident. But after going downstream, this vast mass of ship, this wonder of the world, was hit by very strong winds. Her bows grounded on one bank of the river. The stern then swung round and there she was, across the tide with her bows and stern embedded on both banks. The tide was beginning to fall, and there was near-panic when it was realized that, within minutes, this greatest ship of all time would be exposed to the definite possibility of breaking her back.

This apparently desperate situation could well have been reported today, by live TV coverage from a helicopter. All the BBC commentators of the day could do was to fix a microphone on the bridge, though the engineers were warned off during the handling of the immediate emergency, and retired to a small control-room, hearing orders being given, which could not be recorded. Perhaps the final one was, in those days, best left recalled and not recorded. A very Scottish voice on the bridge suddenly shouted "She's moving!" and then after a pause "Thank Christ!"

The BBC certainly made a great effort to give the Maiden Voyage the full treatment. In 1931, at the height of the dockyard crisis, King George V had said in his Christmas broadcast "What misery a silent dockyard may spread among the people." Cunard had by then spent two million pounds: the final bill was to be more than twice that. Their statement on 10th December 1931 said "the directors have reluctantly decided that it is necessary to suspend the construction of No. 534 pending some change in prospects." For two and a half years she remained idle in the yards. Then the word was given to resume work. Four thousand men were immediately taken back.

By the time the day of departure from Southampton came, the public was swamped by statistics of the voyage, enlivened by a section-by-section preview of the interior, with its décor by the Zinkeisen sisters, Dame Laura Knight, Tom Webster, and the famous A. R. Thompson mural of swinging London in the Observation Bar, and edified by the Poet Laureate's tribute to:

> " . . . this rampart of a ship,
> Long as a street and lofty as a tower."

The passenger list makes fascinating reading today; so many of the 2000 "souls" aboard were accompanied by maid or valet. One collector's item read "Miss Frances Day and Chauffeur." In the Errata list of corrections there appeared, among the "Not sailing" category—Miss Frances Day's chauffeur. But what was of interest to the wireless public was the BBC's inclusion—Mr Henry Hall, BBC Dance Band Leader, Mr John Snagge, BBC Commentator, Mr John Watt and Mr Eckersley, BBC Producers, and Mr Jack Buchanan, entertainer for the BBC, supported by Mr Larry Adler.

There were months of preparation for the OB staff, for this was to be the first ship-to-shore series of broadcasts ever to be attempted on public radio. The BBC shipping expert, George Blake, worked with the engineers on the chief problem—how to get good quality sound from a short-wave floating transmitter. Henry Hall had even composed a special tune for the occasion, "Somewhere at sea," and there was an atmosphere of euphoria among the lucky ones to embark on such a glittering voyage. It had all of John Watt's favourite word—*panache*.

The departure from Southampton was comparatively quiet and sober. Perhaps the general public had heard enough about the wonder-ship. But not so, as John Snagge reported, the Americans crowding into Manhattan.

"The day was gloriously sunny and our reception stupendous. Every small boat that was afloat came out to greet us. River fire-floats were there, squirting their jets of water high into the air, creating great rainbow cascades. Steamers kept up a constant hooting. Girls dressed in Scottish kilts were playing bagpipes.

"John Watt, my producer, and I were leaning over the side watching this great scene, as we were not due to do another broadcast until we actually docked at Manhattan. Suddenly we both noticed two typically English gentlemen in bowler-hats who were sitting in deck-chairs on the promenade deck. They were not paying the slightest attention to all the fuss and excitement and, as they continued to read their New York newspapers, one turned and exclaimed: 'What's the good of these papers—they don't even give the cricket scores!' "

The BBC must have sent out at least fifty broadcasts from *Queen Mary* on the Maiden Voyage and after, and had twenty-five points wired for microphones on board. One American commentator on the voyage was to become a veteran voice on big events: Red Muller of Blue Network, a colleague in World War II and on the Astronauts' flights.

The BBC Comes of Age 73

It was "Lobby" who gave the ordinary outside broadcast its impulse and impetus, and who built up the image of the single commentator who was completely in charge of events, but charged, himself, with building up a word-picture sequence which was not only intelligible to the listener, but exciting as well. In the old days, a second voice used to say "Square 4" during a football match, so that listeners, scrabbling for their copy of the *Radio Times*, would know where they were. Radio commentating is, obviously, a blind medium, but blind people don't always want to be helped across the road: they acquire an extra-sensory perception. This is what radio speakers always ought to seek to give listeners: an image in the mind. Obviously it was easier for the fantasy performers like Tommy Handley, but commentators too, reporting on live events as they were happening, could capture the imagination of the listener without relying on "Square 4."

When, after 1937, BBC Television entered the field of sporting commentaries, the first of many and continuing arguments began over the payments of fees. BBC Television made separate contracts from those of Sound Radio. Radio had not normally paid any fees for public or sporting events, any more than a journalist from the press would expect to pay for his seat on the ground. But the trouble began when big sports occasions were booked by promoters for showing in cinemas, not on television screens (this continued for many years, involving many top men from Cassius Clay to Dr Billy Graham). BBC radio still, quite rightly, refused to pay.

The OB department went on from strength to strength, nevertheless, with Charles Max-Muller in charge, and a loyal team to feed him with the best they could give. One forerunner and pacemaker whose name dropped out of the lists is Michael Standing, who was to become Director of Outside Broadcasts, and later of Variety, and a Naval Correspondent in *War Report* (1944-45). Michael was renowned for what is known in radio and television as *vox-pop*—the voice of the people given *ad lib* and *pro tem*—to give our description a completely Latin title. The whole business is so commonplace now —it is used, particularly, in that degenerate form of telecommunication, the Commercial—that its origins are largely forgotten. Independent Television News was the first to catch on to its visual possibilities, but by that time the invention of the portable tape-recorder had made it easy for any radio reporter to collect snatches of conversation, to be edited later in Broadcasting House.

Michael Standing's unique, pioneer-project was called "Standing on the Corner." It took place on Saturday nights, when Michael would stand unobserved, with a microphone and a trailing wire, on a street corner, and chat, live, with people he would question on what had been happening that week. Probably very little of his conversations survive, even in the massive archives of the BBC, that never-failing source of material for fill-up programmes. But it was a bold venture—and it was so unlike a man like Michael Standing to do it. But it led to endless repetitions of the same sort of interview which are so boring today, when men with much less perception and knowledge than Michael Standing pester the private citizen for his or her views on anything from lunch-time abortions to the price of tapioca.

"Lobby" took charge of Outside Broadcasts at a difficult time. All the opportunities were there: the horizon was widening week by week, and television was in no position to make a challenge. But Reith, that enigma of the BBC, its creator but not its conservator, had departed, and there was no heir of his calibre. In his Autobiography, *Into the Wind*, there is characteristically no mention of either Gerald Cock or Lotbinière. The index is full of politicians and pundits, who were Reith's main preoccupation. The BBC staff was the staff, and that was it. Let them get on with their jobs. Yet Cock and Lotbinière between them set the seal on the most expert Outside Broadcast team in the history of radio.

We could, of course, learn from speakers of other countries. No one could do a cricket commentary better, at that time, than Howard Marshall. No doubt John Arlott and Brian Johnston would agree. But when a Canadian called Bob Bowman appeared, from the ranks of the BBC News Department, to make commentaries on boxing and, above all, ice-hockey, we knew we had not only a different voice but a different technique.

Stewart Macpherson, another genial Canadian who had the same style, and was to prove it in the field of battle as well as in sport, helped to revolutionize the style of OB commentating. It's doubtful if anyone could talk quicker than Max Robertson at Wimbledon in a men's doubles. This is expertise: but it's also the realization that in radio you have to make the event sound exciting even if it isn't. You have to extract the last ounce of interest there is, or you're wasting the listener's time. There have been marathon cases when a commentator has been left with a major "fill-in" because something has gone wrong. Classic examples are Wynford Vaughan-Thomas in

Capetown in 1947, at the end of the Royal Tour, when Frank Gillard's closing commentary from HMS *Vanguard* was cut by the breaking of a cable and Wynford was left to describe the scene of departure for more than half-an-hour. He could be forgiven for such phrases as "here, under the clear blue African sun" and "the Guard of Honour are standing on their horses." Richard Dimbleby had the same experience, filling-in for forty-five minutes this time, on television, when the Royal Party arrived late on the River Thames.

THE BOAT RACE

The Oxford and Cambridge Boat Race is a phenomenon among sporting events, and has for nearly forty years been an "exclusive" for BBC radio and television. It could be described as the most popular amateur sporting event in the world—so amateur, in fact, that there's no money in it at all, except for the golden sovereign of 1829, year of the first race, which Snagge eventually found in a coin-shop, and which has since that day been used for the toss—an important moment of choice for the man who wins. So amateur that it is, in essence, a private challenge from the President of the losing University Boat Club of the previous year to his opposite number. If the challenge is not made within a certain date, then the race is declared void. This has never happened and probably never will, but according to the rules it could, more than 130 years later.[1] The only financial reward comes from the television fee paid by the BBC, seats in official University launches, and the sale of programmes. It will be interesting to see if this Simon-Pure amateur status can continue to be maintained. A sponsorship offer was refused in 1971, and it certainly seems that the race will go on for as long as the Port of London Authority keeps the Thames clear between Putney and Mortlake during the period covering the race.

The Boat Race is not, and never has been, a contest between the two champion rowing-crews of Britain. It probably does not even represent the best crews the two Universities could provide. Young men do not go up to their colleges primarily to row, and many a first-class oarsman has been unable to take his place in the eight because of examinations, which must take precedence. Yet to have rowed in a "blue boat" is triumph enough for any oarsman. It matters not if you

---

[1] The closest shave was in 1950, when Christopher Davidge, of Oxford, failed to send his challenge by the customary letter. He sent a telegram saying "one gauntlet," and the race was on.

"won or lost, but how you played the game." This was originally written of cricket, but it applies equally to rowing.

It may seem strangely antique, in this world of commercialized sport, when fancy footballers with flowing hair have a quarter-of-a-million pound tag on them, when boxers stick out for a million pounds, win or lose, and when lawn-tennis players, once supremely amateur, have incomes in the big-money, that the Oxford and Cambridge Boat Race has held its magic unchanged for so many years. One secret may be the simplicity of it all: every year the same Universities, the same two colours, dark blue and light blue, the same course—though it was once rowed in the opposite direction.

From a broadcast point of view, it is admirable both for radio and television. The cameras get closer and can catch the sense of struggle on the crews' faces, but the radio description, as Snagge knows after making a world-record unbroken number of thirty-seven consecutive commentaries in forty-two years (the war intervening) is heard by people all over the world who have never been near either Oxford or Cambridge, but for whom the race is a hallowed tradition.

"To get a rowing blue is a great honour," says Snagge. "I never got one, though I rowed for my college eight (Pembroke, Oxford). The training is rigorous—first on the Isis or the Cam, then on the Thames tideway itself, and often in poor weather conditions. It is always a gruelling course, but things can get so bad, with a cold wind whipping the water, and snow on the ground, that, as happened in 1859 and 1951, a boat may sink. On the latter occasion, Cambridge won the re-row by the biggest margin for fifty years—twelve lengths. They were a world-class crew, and went on to beat both Harvard and Yale.

"As well as sinkings, I've seen some incredibly close finishes, sometimes by the few feet known as a 'canvas.' I've also been caught out: once when there was an engine-failure in the BBC launch. The commentary had to be taken over by the TV launch, and I was left, saying—God forgive me—'I don't know who's ahead. Either Oxford or Cambridge is leading!'—words which have clung to me, over the years, like a tin can tied to a dog's tail. But they didn't stop me doing the commentary the following year, and I was very touched when, in 1970, after I had made my thirty-fifth commentary, they gave me a silver salver to commemorate the fact. I suppose I've become a sort of fixture, but it's one event I won't ever miss if I can help it. In 1971 I'd been ill, but managed to get out of the nursing-home two days before the race. Thanks to my running-mate Tom Sutton, I'd been kept fully informed about everything, and all went well. I went back to the nursing home soon after. That's what the Boat Race can mean to you!"

A commentator has to know, and describe each year, something of the history of the race. It was first rowed in 1829, largely owing to the initiative of Charles Wordsworth, of Christ Church, Oxford (nephew of the poet William Wordsworth). Then, the Oxford crew appeared in dark blue and white striped jerseys, canvas trousers and black straw hats with a blue ribbon. Cambridge wore white with a scarlet sash. Light blue only became their colour when a certain Mr Phillips, in 1836, realizing that this was the colour both of Eton, the college which had been the mainstay of Cambridge rowing prowess, and of Caius College, Cambridge, dashed into a haberdasher's shop just before the start of the race, bought a length of light blue ribbon and had it fastened to the prow of the boat.

The first race was held at Henley, but after much argument the course was moved to London, and this is probably when the reputation of the race began to rise. The crews rowed at first from Westminster to Putney, but after 1845 from Putney to Mortlake. By 1971, Cambridge led with 64 wins to Oxford's 51: in 1877 there was the celebrated dead-heat, when John Phelps, who had rushed out of the bar of a Mortlake hostelry, was heard to cry "Dead-heat for Oxford by ten feet!" It is not true to say, as some declare on recent form this century, "Cambridge are bound to win." Statistics show that Oxford won two long sequences, 1861-1869 and 1890-1898, while Cambridge's longest spell of victories was 1924-1936.

"From the BBC point of view," says Snagge, who has had many distinguished visitors in his launch, including Prince Charles, "the Boat Race has always been regarded as one of the key fixtures of the year. Perhaps that's partly because so many BBC men have been to one or other of the two Universities. It ranked, from the first, with the Derby, the Cup Final and the England-v.-Scotland match at Twickenham, in the BBC list of events they wanted to broadcast. In the early years, of course, there was no communication between the launch and the shore, and you had to check your timing visually, depending at one moment, for instance, on a man on the top of Harrod's, waving a white handkerchief."

One famous broadcaster has cause to remember the Boat Race. In March 1949 a young Canadian actor and reporter called Bernard

Braden came over to Britain, and approached the BBC. After only a few days here, he met Laurence Gilliam, and asked if he could try reporting the English scene. The Boat Race was due and Gilliam asked Barsley, who edited and produced the topical magazine programme *Mirror of the Month*, if he had room for a Canadian who had never seen the event. Braden was given a place in the launch. So began Braden's first broadcast in Britain, which was recorded and reflected in the radio *Mirror* that evening.

He said he felt a bit overwhelmed at first by the importance attached to the occasion. "We do have little affairs we call boat races in Canada. I even got a little satisfaction out of thinking the sixteen oars being dipped into the Thames this morning were fashioned from Canadian spruce. How sensitive can you get?" One of a group of small boys asked "Oo yer stickin' up fer?" Braden had to be asked three times before he understood. "The Cambridge crew arrived in a bus, the Oxford crew in two Daimlers—if that means anything.... Well, I could go on like this for some time, but the important thing, of course, is the race itself. The fact of the matter is, I didn't see it. I had a seat in the BBC launch behind the commentator John Snagge, and shortly after the race began we fell behind, and the other launches obscured our view and threw spray at us. Fortunately for me, Mr Snagge absorbed most of this. My wife heard the whole thing on radio, and she told me Cambridge won...."

British listeners were to hear many more examples of the caustic Braden humour, but this was a characteristic beginning of a spectacular radio and television career on BBC.

SPORTS REPORTS

In 1927, when the "C" of the BBC was altered from Company to Corporation, one of the biggest immediate changes was in running commentaries on sport. "For five years," says Snagge, "we hadn't been allowed to do it, owing to pressure on the Post Office from the press, claiming the right to publish reports on sporting events, reports which must not be "scooped" by immediate, on-the-spot radio reports. As a Corporation, the BBC now had the right to broadcast them. The question arose—what was the best way to do it? The public was staggered at the thought of being able to sit at home, and actually hear a goal being scored, or a horse passing the winning-post at the time it happened.

"We had a great challenge, and to start with, made a howling mess of it. There were BBC staff members who knew how to play various games, but were probably not used to talking into a microphone. In January 1927, I gave my first football commentary, and to help me out, the London announcer, Rex Palmer, was sent up to Stoke to watch them play Hull City. Neither knew much about the game, or the players in it. A goal was a goal, a foul was a foul, and that was it."

Not until experts arrived on the scene—experts who could handle a microphone—were there any commentaries worth listening to. One of the first was a rugger match between England and Wales at Twickenham, and it produced a commentator worthy of the occasion, Captain H. B. T. Wakelam. He survived right through to the later years. But in the early days, the BBC was deluged with advice from the public as to how a running commentary should be done. One glorious example was the listener who wrote in, suggesting that the right man to do the commentary was the man who saw most of the game—the referee. A microphone should be strapped to his chest. But how could contact be maintained with the amplifiers and the transmitter? Perfectly simple: an elastic lead could be attached to one of the goal-posts. It was a long time before the BBC, after the war, devised its own comprehensive sports programme.

Sports Report has been running for twenty-four years, which is about the average age of the young team now engaged on it. Angus Mackay was the father-figure, who retired in 1972, and he built up the fastest, slickest programme which radio can provide—and they can provide a much wider variety of immediately topical material than television. The series, through the years, has become prestigious enough in its field to be worth anyone's while to appear on it.

"We never let anyone down," he told us, "or make a Charley of anybody. We take the programme seriously when seriousness is needed. J. B. Priestley made no bones about talking for us, or the Duke of Norfolk, the Archdeacon of Westminster, Stanley Baker, David Frost, people from many different spheres. Then on the lighter side, Bob Hope, Bing Crosby, Tommy Steele, Peter Cook—you name them, they've been here. There are obvious experts like Sir Stanley Rous. Then there are the characters—great sportsmen like the late Learie Constantine. He was delightful. When you asked him to do something, he'd grin that big grin of his and off he'd go, so well that you'd have difficulty in wrapping it up within the time. Learie was with us till nearly the end. I remember that on his last broadcast he had to sit down: he was too ill to stand for more than a few moments."

What a career that was, indeed. Social historians will recall how, before the war, when Captain of the West Indies, he was turned out of his hotel, the famous old Imperial in Russell Square (now alas knocked down for a modern lump of a building) because of a colour bar there. (The Anglo-Dutch family, which still owns it, had a lot of explaining-away to do.) Learie became professional for Nelson in Lancashire, and ended up, not only in the House of Lords, but a Governor of the BBC. To Angus Mackay, he was one of the "old mates" of *Sports Report*. "Success didn't alter him one little bit."

Eamonn Andrews's rise to fame is very closely connected with *Sports Report*, for which he worked even when he had become well-known on television. It was a devotion of a rare quality. The Eamonn trail began, as he himself admits, very modestly. He was known to us first as a junior boxing champion from Eire, introduced by a fellow-Irishman, the late Brian George, Head of Recorded Programmes, in the Cock Tavern, Great Portland Street. Everyone knew Brian, and liked him. He shared with Louis MacNeice not only a pub, but a passion for rugger. He was the sort of man who remained on equal terms with everyone, never ignoring subordinates, but pulling them in to join in the round he'd be ordering. He had a prodigious memory, and if you asked him about some long-forgotten disc, he'd tap his teeth with his pipe and close his eyes as if asleep, and when he opened them, he'd have remembered it. He forced this big, cheerful bruiser of an Irishman on nobody. But a man like Angus Mackay saw in him a quality he liked, even though it was based merely on hearing one radio appearance in *Ignorance is Bliss*, when Eamonn had deputized for Stewart Macpherson. Mackay asked Brian George for an introduction, and this was the beginning of an association which lasted from 1950 until 1963.

"Eamonn had nothing when he began: merely his return ticket to Dublin. We gave him a try-out, and he was good. The difficulty was to get him for the all-important Saturday show, but we fixed that, and though he had many tempting outside offers for Saturday work, he refused them, and stuck to *Sports Report* throughout. One of Eamonn's greatest assets was his liking for people, and this communicated itself. Some speakers would come into the studio and almost die of fright on you. But they didn't with Eamonn. This explains why he got on so well with the *What's My Line* visitors. He put them

Eric Maschwitz, ex-Head of Variety and just back from Hollywood, appears on *In Town Tonight* with his successor John Watt

Radio Times Hulton Picture Library

One of the "BBC girls" in harassed mood.
Where would the Corporation be without them?

BBC Copyright Photograph

"D'you think they'll get it, Gordie?"
Ronnie Waldman with Gordon Crier, bright boys of *Band Waggon*—and beyond
Radio Times Hulton Picture Library

"Lobby"
Seymour Joly de Lotbinière who, as Head of Outside Broadcasting, first brought all Britain to the listener (1953)
Radio Times Hulton Picture Library

"Around the World in Sixty Minutes"
Laurence Gilliam, Head of Features, discusses one of his famous Christmas Day programmes with Producer Alan Burgess (1953)

BBC Copyright Photograph

The Brain behind the *Brains Trust*

Howard Thomas, now boss of Thames Television, faces questions to the Joad–Huxley–Campbell team in 1941

Radio Times Hulton Picture Library

Drama—and "How"

Val Gielgud, BBC Head of Drama, and Stephen Potter, Gamesman and producer of the "How" programmes. A peaceful wartime session (1940)

Radio Times Hulton Picture Library

He wrote the greatest play in radio

Dylan Thomas, author of *Under Milk Wood*, photographed in 1946. The play was first produced in January 1954

Radio Times Hulton Picture Library

Poets' Corner

Louis MacNeice at the graveside of Dylan Thomas, Laugharne, Carmarthenshire, November 1953

Radio Times Hulton Picture Library

"Children's Hour"
Uncle Mac (Derek McCulloch) supervises a broadcast by John Rorke and Jack Train

BBC Copyright Photograph

ITMA: a rehearsal at Bangor, one of the BBC's wartime centres, in 1942. Left to right: Tommy Handley, Jack Train (Colonel Chinstrap) and Ted Kavanagh

Radio Times Hulton Picture Library

"We've both done twenty-five years' service, dear boy."
Stuart Hibberd and John Snagge in 1949

BBC Copyright Photograph

would be that he's too nice to be a commentator: that he'd almost rather not hear about controversy or unpleasantness in sport, because it was so unsportsmanlike."

Angus Mackay warns "beware the specialist" only in so far as the expert may tend to know too much about his own subject, and be too wrapped up in it. The alternative pitfall is to expect a commentator to be able to handle anything. In the 1930s, for instance, the versatile Raymond Glendenning, his moustache as magnificent as his voice, would be on racing one day, on football the next, on boxing the one after that and no man could be expected to master all three in so short a time. Moreover, though in those days we wouldn't suggest there was any cheating, lack of recording facilities meant that no check-up could be made on any commentary. In football, a commentator could be some way behind the play, and provided he was on the ball, as it were, when it went into the net, the rest of the time his job was to make the game sound exciting and entertaining. This is one of the arts of commentary: to go on saying an event is just plain dull is to beg the question "Then why broadcast it?" But at the other end of the scale, to whip up enthusiasm when it doesn't deserve it is in itself a form of deception. A good commentator knows how to strike the balance: and a good commentator, according to Mackay, must above all be a good communicator. He mustn't think about what he's going to tell, but rather about what the listener wants to know.

Perhaps this attitude is something of a dig at Stewart Macpherson. We had known him chiefly as a lively war-reporter who never pretended to be a hero (indeed, he sent a message from the battlefield at Arnhem, inquiring about "coming home for dental repairs, which are getting urgent"). As a quiz-master he was often brilliant and incisive, with occasional ludicrous lapses in general knowledge, as in one *Twenty Questions*. The object was "a cow." "Is it animal?" asked a Questioner. "Yes," replied Stewie. "Is it a mammal?" was the next question and the reply was "No." He later admitted he didn't know exactly what a mammal was!

But what Angus Mackay found, on reading an article by Macpherson in a Sunday paper about his broadcasting methods, was that he commentated with a pageful of phrases beside him, which he could "plant" as required. They were not spontaneous. "And that," says Mackay, "destroyed a big illusion I had held."

Royal Broadcasts

IF the public image of the monarchy has changed, this is partly due to the influence of radio and television, and the use the "royals," as BBC men call them, have made of them. The growing-up of the Prince of Wales and Princess Anne, in a television age, has brought them much closer to ordinary people, and they respond in an up-to-date way. The "divinity that doth hedge a King" remained for years a silent divinity except for those privileged to be near the monarch when a speech was made.

Reith, who realized the power of the medium under his command, saw the emotional value inherent in the royal voice, linking the peoples of the Empire. The first occasion was the opening of the British Empire Exhibition at Wembley in 1924. In a sentimental radio programme "Let's Remember," broadcast in 1951, C. Gordon Glover set the scene, to the accompaniment of Tolchard Evans and his Tuneful Twenties Dance Orchestra playing *It Ain't Gonna Rain No More*:

Narrator: Over three inches of rain fell in those last weeks before curtain-up, but on April 23rd, upon the Day of Shakespeare and St George, our wonderful Wembley opened ... opened by His Majesty King George the Fifth, before the representatives of Empire and a vast concourse of the people ... and the voice of the King was heard not only at Wembley, but, for the first time in history——

Voice: —simultaneously from 2LO and all stations of the British Broadcasting Company....

Awe-struck Woman: But it won't somehow seem possible—to hear the King's voice....

Man: The King on the old crystal....

Newspaper Voice: A Newspaper Competition. This newspaper offers a prize of an up-to-date four-valve wireless receiving set for the best account, in not more than two hundred words, of "How and where I heard the King's speech...."

Woman 1: The bother is, I shall be out shopping—oh it is a botheration!

Woman 2: That doesn't matter, dear—they're going to have

loud-speakers in all the big shops—look, here's a list of them in the paper....

Newspaper Voice: It's the biggest thing that has yet been planned. It will be history, wonderful and magnificent if it succeeds, and abysmal disappointment if it be marred. One can hear little children in the far-distant villages saying—

Child's Voice: I heard the King....

It did succeed, and the King's declaration and prayer was broadcast. An echo of this last thought was in King George's Silver Jubilee broadcast, on 6th May 1935, in which he sent a special message to the children:

"Let me say this to each of them whom my words may reach: the King is speaking to *you*."

King George's first Christmas Day message from Sandringham in 1932 was, however, the radio scoop for which Reith had waited five long years, since it again refers to the wonder of radio and was spoken specially for it. Preceding it was the special Christmas Day Commonwealth link-up, described later in this chapter. Thereafter the Christmas Day broadcast became a famous "live" event on radio, and Queen Elizabeth II was later televised, being filmed earlier. One year (1969) the royal message was not broadcast or televised, and this became a controversial point. Did the initiative come from the Queen (as presumably it did) or was she advised against it? In a letter to *The Times* Snagge and Barsley jointly suggested that the message should have been carried on radio alone.

The most memorable Christmas quotation of all came from George VI in 1939:

"I said to the man who stood at the Gate of the Year: 'Give me a light, that I may tread safely into the unknown:' And he replied 'Go out into the darkness and put your hand into the Hand of God. That shall be to you better than light, and safer than a known way.'"

For many the magic faded when the BBC altered the time of 3 p.m. and put out a recording in the morning. To some, it was as bad as scrapping the nine o'clock news, or admitting that the Commonwealth didn't exist. A compensatory treat for viewers in 1970 was the informal television portrait of the Royal Family's year, done in the intimate, close-up way known with the Dutch and Scandinavian royal families, and presenting much the same image.

But in the heydays the 3 o'clock broadcast was part of the nation's life, and followed a certain protocol. The Head of Outside

Broadcasting, first Gerald Cock, succeeded by Lotbinière, had to be there to supervise the arrangements. Both have received the coveted Victorian Order. The first time "Lobby" attended, in 1935, was the last message given by King George V. After the broadcast, he came back seemingly very pleased, and confided to his close friends that he had, later, been presented to the entire Royal Family, at their Christmas Party. We were deeply impressed by the story. Only a long time after did Lotbinière hear from an aide that the King, having completed his talk, hurried back to his family and asked them to wait, so that he could show them "the longest man I have ever met."

"Lobby" doesn't mind the re-telling of this story.

Also present on many Christmas Days was the same engineer, R. H. Wood, a man who was always in demand by royalty: something about his calm way put them at their ease. Wood was equally celebrated, in the Corporation, for his malapropisms, such as: "As he's buttered his bread, so he must lie on it" and "It's the last straw in the gearbox."

There have been many royal occasions other than at Christmas Day. King George VI, whose speech impediment was such a trial to him that his message, in the last year of his life, had to be recorded and edited on tape, was at his finest when opening the Festival of Britain, live, from the steps of the Royal Exchange—a magnificent speech.

Snagge was assistant to Gerald Cock for the 1935 Jubilee broadcast. King George V was due to speak at 8 o'clock from Buckingham Palace, after what had been a gruelling day for him.

"I was awaiting, in formal morning coat for Cock's arrival, at about 7 p.m., in a small room adjoining the Regency Room, decorated in green and white, and overlooking the Palace gardens. The faithful R. H. Wood was with me. I was suddenly informed that His Majesty was tired, and anxious to have his microphone balance test at once, as he had been sitting in the garden, and could then have a further rest before the broadcast took place. I realized I would have to carry out these orders myself. I therefore stood by, and the King came into the room, asked my name, and then said: 'I understand I am to speak for a few moments.' He sat at the table. R.H. gave the O.K., and he read three sentences. He then looked up at me and said 'You know, if you talk you get tired, and if you get tired your voice gets tired.' He then added 'What time do you wish me to be back here?' I told him the broadcast was at 8 o'clock. The King repeated 'What time do you wish me to be back here?' I said 'If possible at five to eight, Sir.' He replied 'Very well. I will listen to the Prime Minister before I speak.' With a courteous word of thanks, he then left the room."

This left Snagge with a problem. He could listen to the preceding programme until Ramsay Macdonald spoke, but it seemed impossible that the King could both listen to the Prime Minister's introduction and be at the table to broadcast at eight.

"Panic stations set in. I got hold of a member of the Palace staff, who told me that I should speak to the King's page. 'The King's page?' I echoed, imagining a diminutive youth. He was sent for, and the man who appeared was about six foot four inches in height, immaculately turned out, with all his decorations. I put my problem to him. His reply was 'If His Majesty has said he would be here at five to eight, he will be here at five to eight.' I pointed out the impossibility, with the PM's broadcast and the Page intoned again 'If His Majesty said he will be here at five to eight, he will be here at five to eight.' It seems they all repeat themselves at the Palace, but the King *was* there, and so was Gerald Cock!"

THE ABDICATION BROADCAST

The most famous royal broadcast was made by ex-King Edward VIII after his Abdication in December 1936. He had previously made several appearances at the microphone, and Snagge remembers him visiting Savoy Hill in 1928, to make an appeal, as President of the British Legion. "The studio was a very tiny room on the first floor, and His Royal Highness was received by Admiral Carpendale. It's always been a matter of interest to me as to whether speakers prefer to be left alone, or to have someone with them, either out of sight or sitting opposite them, as a sort of audience to whom they can talk. No two people, in my experience, react the same. HRH was most insistent that I sit opposite him. Meanwhile, the large figure of Carpendale loomed near the door, and the Prince asked me, obviously not knowing who he was, 'What's he doing here? Please ask him to leave—he's putting me off.' You can imagine how I felt, having to shoo my boss out of the studio, knowing he'd have to meet HRH after transmission. It isn't true, by the way, that a special microphone is made for royal braodcasts. Special cases are sometimes made to house the latest types, or to screen the red light. One of those stood on Snagge's desk for years, built in wood shaped like a foreshortened Cenotaph, and on it the inscription:

'Used by His Majesty King Edward VIII Broadcasting House, 1st March 1936, Windsor Castle, 11th December 1936.'

What a span of royal history is covered in those few short months. Those in the know—and this applied to anyone who received *Time* magazine or other US papers on subscription—could read about Mrs Simpson and there were special instructions for the BBC monitoring service at Caversham to log any American broadcasts on the subject.

When the crisis came, it came with devastating swiftness, sparked off in a sermon by the Bishop of Bradford, appropriately named Dr Blunt, who made only an oblique reference to royal behaviour. The *Daily Mirror* was the first newspaper to break the year-long agreed truce among the press, and appeared with the banner headline

KING WANTS TO MARRY MRS SIMPSON: CABINET SAYS NO.

This was the first time most people had heard of the lady. Opinion soon divided itself into pro and anti the monarch and his behaviour, a division largely into generations. One of the embarrassing adherents turned out to be Oswald Mosley and the Blackshirts, with their slogan "STAND BY THE KING." It is difficult to assess King Edward's political outlook. Certainly he set a standard of informality which shocked court circles and the Establishment, which were otherwise very pleased with the popularity of his royal tours to the Empire countries. "He carries the flag and he carries the bag," as one politician summed up. He also had his following among the unemployed, who remembered how he broke away from the official party at a shipyard to talk to workers, and said afterwards "Something must be done." But, in the view of Baldwin and Dr Cosmo Gordon Lang, the ship of state would founder if the King were left on the bridge. They endured their unpopularity stoically. A satirical poet (Christopher Hollis) wrote a quatrain on the Archbishop which is remembered to this day:

" My Lord Archbishop, what a scold you are,
And when your man is down, how bold you are.
Of Christian charity, how scant you are—
You old Lang swine, how full of cant you are!"

One can imagine, in this more tolerant television age, what use would have been made of the situation, if there were a *That Was The Week That Was* on the screen.

Relations between the BBC and Edward, both as Prince of Wales and as King, were good and informal. From time to time he rang up on a point of information, or to make a comment. At one time, the telephone rang in the Children's Hour studios. A voice said "I'd like to speak to Mr McCulloch, please." One of the assistants asked who was calling. "The Prince of Wales." "Oh, come off it," said the assistant, "then I'm the...." "This is the Prince of Wales," the voice went on. "Will you kindly ask Mr McCulloch to speak to me?"

Reith's greatest challenge came over the proposed Abdication broadcast in December, described fully in his autobiography.[1] The King had foreseen the potential use of the wireless as the best means of communicating directly with his people, and he must have guessed that he could count upon the support of an independent BBC. He was certainly not mistaken in this. Reith, as history shows, took history into his hands. But what baffled him as he drove to Windsor to introduce the monarch personally, was what title to give him: he couldn't be "the abdicating King" or "ex-King Edward VIII," obviously. But he was still a Prince of the blood royal, and that is how Reith described him in that supreme moment, as the country listened with bated breath, for a short speech, in the writing of which, it was said, Winston Churchill had a hand, though this was later denied.

"This is Windsor Castle. His Royal Highness, the Prince Edward," said Reith.

In his broadcast, Edward spoke these memorable words:

"You must believe me when I tell you that I have found it impossible to carry the burden of responsibility and to discharge my duties as King as I would wish to do without the help and support of the woman I love."

As he spoke, we remember that at this stage his voice rose and yet deepened in intensity. It was a sudden, stabbing moment of truth, spoken not as King to people but as one person to another. To many it may have been, as Emile Zola described the Dreyfus affair, "a moment in the conscience of mankind."

It was one of the most dramatic, and to many listeners, heart-rending broadcasts ever made, but at the end of it, despite the

[1] *Into the Wind* (Hodder & Stoughton, 1949).

tremendous strain of the occasion, a simple but significant touch followed, as Snagge was to recall.

"The broadcast over, the ex-King, instead of immediately entering the car which was to take him to the south coast and the waiting destroyer, moved across to where the BBC Outside Broadcast van stood, and, to their surprise and immense pleasure, thanked the engineers for their part in sending out the broadcast. This despite the immense pressures and cares on him: it was typical of the man."

OTHER ROYAL BROADCASTS

The mechanics of broadcasting always seem to have interested royal users. King George V, a diehard traditionalist, had nevertheless been deeply moved at the thought that his words were going to unseen millions of his people, and his message, "This is the King speaking to *you*," had an inspired touch. At the launching of the *Queen Elizabeth*, with the clouds of crisis darkening, the Queen Mother spoke of "Courage and brave hearts." The words may be written for them, and they may not have any professional delivery, but the sincerity comes out, and it was sincerity which Haley described as the chief asset of Tommy Handley, the friend of royalty.

A Snagge memory of the Fleet Review at Spithead in 1937 adds a personal sidelight:

"My task was to be with Commander 'Rocky' Knight, RN, at Farewell Jetty, as the Royal Yacht steamed out of Portsmouth towards the ships at anchor. Our equipment was a recording-van, with an improvised green hut on top. By worming one's way into this, one could look out over the harbour. We were standing watching the scene, some two hours before the yacht was due to sail, when a dockyard policeman came up and asked us to keep out of sight. We clambered back into the van, and there soon appeared, at the foot of the steps, Princess Elizabeth—she would have been nearly eleven then—beckoning to her sister to look inside the van, at our embarrassed figures. She then called to her parents, and the King and Queen strolled across towards us. His Majesty asked 'Can we come in and have a look?'

"The steps were steep, and our driver, Saunders, will never forget his proudest moment. 'These very hands,' he would often recount to me, waving them, 'picked up their Royal Highnesses, and lifted them to the top.' The party talked with the engineers for some ten or fifteen minutes. Then the King left the van and asked Knight and myself if he could see the commentator's position on top. We managed to get there and he asked many questions about the technique of commentary work, and gave us several details on the procedure of the ceremony to come, which we found very useful. What a temptation it was to throw in a line, later on, such as 'His Majesty was telling me just an hour or two ago to look out for such-and-such,' an aside which would presumably be permissible today. Dimbleby broke this royal barrier when he said at one point in a commentary 'The Queen Mother has just explained to me that....' On that day, we got a special wave from the family as the yacht steamed out, and that was enough."

In 1947 the Royal Family left on a prolonged tour of what was then the Union of South Africa. This was the first royal tour to have full BBC radio coverage, on a scale never attempted before, with top commentators like Wynford Vaughan Thomas, Audrey Russell, Frank Gillard and Godfrey Talbot reporting, Snagge introducing and Barsley producing. It was also the first time the royal voice had been edited[1] for the quality of transmission was unreliable, and there were so many different speeches of welcome in the six weeks of the series. The editing was done on disc, for tape-recording was still, in Britain, in its infancy, and sometimes there would have to be "jump-cuts" on transmission, in which the ice-cool fingers of the "jeep" (a nice young thing called Joan Coates was one of the experts) would lift a needle from one groove and re-place it exactly on another, with only a fractional pause—a harrowing moment worthy of the highest citation for bravery!

During this tour, Princess Elizabeth came of age on her twenty-first birthday, and made a very popular broadcast, sitting on a lawn, with the roar of the Victoria Falls in the background. In this she dedicated herself to her people and she has certainly lived up to her dedication. The Duke of Edinburgh, too, with his outspoken and challenging utterances—unpopular in some quarters—had made great use of the microphone and the television cameras, but his off-the-cuff remarks at such gatherings as the Lord's Taverners (of which he is the official "Twelfth Man") are not broadcastable! Princess Margaret and her husband, however, are two who have made only formal use of the BBC. Lord Snowdon, as one would expect, excels at the making of television documentary films.

[1] See page 61 for the reference to Sir Basil Nicolls.

CHRISTMAS DAY ROUND-UP

On Christmas Day 1932, in his opening sentence, King George V paid a significant tribute to the wireless:

"Through one of the marvels of modern science I am enabled this Christmas Day to speak to all my peoples throughout the Empire."

It was the first time that many millions of listeners, including those on the new Empire Service, had been addressed directly as "my people," and the effect was incalculable. "I take it as a good omen," His Majesty continued, in his gruff but kindly voice, "that wireless should have reached its present perfection at a time when the Empire has been linked in closer union. For it offers us immense possibilities to make that union closer still."

These words may well have been inspired by the idea which Laurance Gilliam conceived, in combining broadcasts from the Commonwealth into a radio link-up, preceding the monarch's Christmas message. This series continued for a quarter of a century. Another passage of King George's talk reinforced the idea:

"I speak now from my home and my heart to you all. To men and women so cut off by the snows, the deserts, or the sea, that only voices from the air can reach them."

"Voices from the air." The phrase became a challenge, not only to the BBC men putting out the programmes under Laurence's dynamic direction, but to reporters and BBC representatives all over the world. To them fell the task of selecting the speakers and the items representing their corner of the earth as it was at that moment, in peace or in war, in poverty or abundance. It was an honour in the great days of radio to be associated in any capacity with its greatest annual programme.

The long list of narrators was impressive—Robert Donat, Laurence Olivier, Ralph Richardson, John Snagge, Howard Marshall, Chester Wilmot—and one Christmas, the voice of the first lady of radio, Gladys Young. Music specially composed came from Benjamin Britten, William Walton, William Alwyn and other famous names.

But the element which gave the programme its unique quality was the sequence of contributions from overseas, linked by the narration into a single theme, and crowned by a single title, such as *The Gifts of Christmas*. It was Gilliam who welded all these facets into a whole, getting his far-flung team to work for him as no man in the BBC had ever done before. Alan Burgess helped in many a Christmas Day round-up, and said this of Gilliam in a programme commemorating the vanished series, broadcast in 1969:

"I worked for Laurence Gilliam for eighteen happy and eventful years, and if there was a man better fitted to be Head of a BBC Department than Laurence, then I've never met him or heard of him. He was enormous in size, in zest, in spirit, immensely generous, immensely committed, involved in every aspect (of every aspect) of sound radio. And, of course, a programme of the scope and size and complexity of a live, round-the-world hook-up, with large orchestra, speakers waiting in Sydney and Southampton, Tooting and Timbuctoo, and every second counting, because we had to be 'out' for 3 p.m. exactly, for the royal message, was tailor-made for Laurence.

"I remember when I first joined Features in 1946, he took one look at me and said 'Oh, yes, you'd better lend a hand with the Christmas Day programme,' which meant that I put Edward Ward on the Bishop Rock lighthouse, where he was marooned for a month, and spent Christmas Day with Wynford Vaughan Thomas at the bottom of a coal-mine. Eighteen years later, I was still lending a hand. When you think of this broadcast on Christmas Day you think of Gilliam. His job was to set the scene for the royal speech. It had to be a colourful setting, a moving setting, with speakers reflecting the time, the emotion of their part of the world in that particular year. To do this, he was prepared to spare no expense, or mileage or time: if twenty-four hours wasn't enough to get the job done, he was prepared to invent an extra two or three. Even today, more than ten years after Gilliam's last royal programme, broadcasters everywhere smile a little wryly and regretfully at the memory of all the trouble and all the fun Laurence put them to. I don't think there's much doubt that if he were alive today, and the Christmas programme still going on, Laurence would have a man on the moon to greet Her Majesty."

Howard Marshall, himself both a narrator and a reporter, on different occasions, added this:

"It was a very important broadcast, but it was performing one of its major purposes, which was bringing people together round the world, and it was a very formidable responsibility, and always a great thrill when it was leading to the voice of the monarch, when everyone was talking perfectly naturally and then it came to the King—it was beautiful stuff. It became for one thing a traditional way of life. On Christmas Day, everybody automatically switched on. But it was a memorable experience, and in those days, when you waited for your man to take over from your cue round the world, it was a great relief to find him doing it so sweetly and so smoothly. There were no faults, no mistakes, and this was due to the remarkable amount of rehearsing Laurence made us do. We were all pioneering. It was very exciting. I don't think you get the same feeling even in television today, which is so much more complex in all its apparatus."

The apparatus was elaborate enough then, by radio standards. It is invidious to single out individuals from a team like that, but the name of Charles Ladbrook, the programme engineer who was at the controls so many times, and who worked with Gilliam more closely and more instinctively than anyone else, stands out, unfailing and unflappable.

The technical difficulties involved in the project, as it grew more ambitious each year, were immense, and though there were stand-by recordings for each item in case the circuit faded or broke, sometimes the running order had to be changed, not only on rehearsal but on transmission. Muir Matheson, acknowledged expert in conducting music for films, found this programme a real challenge, and explains why.

"The orchestra's job was to add linking passages, and set the scene for the Commonwealth countries as they came in. Well, a snowstorm in Canada is a vastly different thing from sunbathing in Australia, so we were always terrified they might be switched." The links might have to be varied in length, perhaps stretched to have the right fanfare as an introduction, for if it came too soon, Muir said, "you'd get a rocket from the producer. You see, with earphones on, Laurence could give me a piece of his mind, and I could never answer back! But the orchestra—it was usually the London Symphony—were good at cutting and expanding. Also you had to be prepared for hitches, and have something ready as alternative. I don't remember any hitches, but you had to be on your toes. I used a system of hand-signals—say, to hold up four fingers, meaning cut four bars. Nobody seemed put out at anything unusual."

The producer of this tribute programme, John Lane, had served on the Christmas round-up for ten years, on recordings. When we asked about costs, he couldn't really attempt a detailed answer. "Laurence was a great spender: the cost didn't matter to him provided the assignment was worth it, sending reporters in search of material to Africa and Asia and Canada and the West Indies. He knew he had the ear of a vast public—in those days radio was everything—

and he knew that no one would throw it in his teeth if he spent several times the programme budget. He had a staff of about twenty around him for two months, and needed all of them. Then there were the reporters he sent out, and the BBC reps all over the world. A small army, in fact, but Laurence was a broad, big-canvas man."

Getting the Commonwealth material in, meant, in Laurence's firm and unalterable view, sending out his own men to set up and introduce the items, or perhaps setting up several and being actually present at one. This was not caused by mistrust of the BBC man permanently on the spot: Laurence was well-travelled enough to know many of them anyhow. But he also knew that, being perhaps the sole representative in their own neck of the woods, they might be subject to sudden pressures, news requirements, or administrative problems. By briefing his own Features staff, he could rely on them sticking to the pattern of the programme, and through daily experience of Laurence, they would know what to expect of him, and what he would expect of them, wherever they might be.

In these days of live colour pictures from the moon, the problem of a live radio hook-up cued into a programme seems a simple one: but it may be said that each invention makes something of a laughing-stock of the one before it, and no one can claim that it took less derring-do for the Wright Brothers to get a machine off the ground than for NASA to put men into space or *Concorde* to take a hundred passengers through the sound barrier. The effect, too, on the listener on Christmas Day, hearing "voices from the air" afar off was just as exciting, and as exciting for those taking part, and those arranging their item, too, as anything before or since. Some Christmases brought greater poignancy than others, some greater happiness or triumph: some were just traditional. The most eloquent moment, apart from the royal message, was the final item, in which the monarch was introduced by whichever of the Commonwealth speakers appeared the most suitable, in voice or situation.

For Barsley, Christmas 1950 became the most remarkable experience of his life, culminating in the most distant live outside broadcast in BBC history up to that date, with the microphone in a hospital ward in South Japan. It marked, too, the first lone excursion of a long-distance reporter taking with him a portable tape-recorder.

"The whole assignment was offered to me in a flash. This was typical of Laurence. As if giving me the itinerary of a journey to Slough, Reading, Oxford and all stations to Birmingham, he told me he was sending me, at a fortnight's notice, to India, Pakistan, Ceylon, Singapore, Hong Kong, Tokyo, and a hospital at Kure, near Hiroshima. In each of the first five places, I was to choose likely Commonwealth speakers for an item, record them, and have the tapes flown back before hedge-hopping on. At Kure I was to assemble some of the wounded, flown back from Korea, and if possible introduce them live.

"I listened open-mouthed. I had never been out of Europe before.

" 'You'd better get all your jabs done now,' Laurence went on. 'There's about five of them.' Then he gave that heaving chuckle of his which I can hear still. 'You're a lucky devil, but it's going to be a tough job.'

"That night, having been duly punctured and scratched at the BOAC surgery at Victoria, I wondered why on earth I'd been chosen. Perhaps it was partly because I knew about the all-important tape-recorder, and had been one of the first people to try it out, on the first leg of the Monte Carlo rally.[1] But then, I thought, I'm so unmechanical I can't mend a puncture in a bicycle tyre. Laurence was taking a risk; but he always did. And what on earth was the Far-East going to be *like*?

"To cut a long journey short (the whole story is told in another book[2]) I boarded a BOAC Argonaut at London Airport North one bleak November morning, glimpsing my family from the window, the two little girls with the green and white ribbons of Wimbledon High School, and wondering if I'd ever see them again—and I reached south Japan six weeks later, flying this time with a parachute attached, in an American transport plane, under the rank of Sergeant Barsley. The wonder of the scenery was to be matched by the miraculous performance of the tape-recorder, which I had nicknamed 'Buster,' and which caused astonishment wherever I went. For my part, I found myself able to record plenty of feature material everywhere I went, enough it turned out, for six half-hour programmes produced after my return, two of them recorded in countries which weren't even in the schedule, French Indo-China and Thailand.

"This was an early reminder of what a roving reporter can be faced with *en route* when apparently talking to himself with a sort of devil-box slung over his shoulder. I was arrested in Karachi for talking into 'Buster' in the market ('You are broadcasting secrets

---

[1] It was an American machine made by Stancil-Hoffman in Hollywood, one of six delivered to BBC Features under Marshall Aid.
[2] *Behind the Screen* (André Deutsch, 1957).

about Pakistan'), played an irate customs official's voice back at him in Delhi (I have never seen an Indian turn so white), met Ralph Richardson, Trevor Howard and Carol Reed filming in Ceylon, flew straight into the riots of Singapore, over the mixed marriage of Dutch girl Bertha Hertogh to a Malayan, and there, in the ladies' loo at the Stork Club (chosen for its acoustics) had recorded, incongruously, messages of goodwill from commandos, under curfew (of one of them, Sergeant Bulpit, I sent a message to Laurence saying RECOMMEND SERGT. BULPIT CAREFUL PRONUNCIATION TO INTRODUCE KING), made a forced landing in Saigon under French rule, where I recorded enough night-life for a whole programme, ate mice in Hong Kong, and was given a bath after dinner by four hissing girls in a restaurant in Tokyo, ending with a visit to the half-restored ruins of Hiroshima on Christmas Eve, the day before the programme.

"Christmas Day dawned fine and clear. The hospital matron, stalwart Miss Shebbeare, had given every support to the task of getting the item out on time, which meant at about six minutes to three, London time, but alas! six minutes to midnight, Japanese time. I was very pleased at the news that my Sergeant Bulpit was to follow us in presenting the King: I didn't know they'd found his family, too, in London. I add 'alas!' because it seemed likely that some members of the hospital might be a little over-merry, at that hour, and I was entirely on my own as far as the BBC was concerned. The Allied radio engineers were Australian, and had begun celebrating Christmas with bottles of Foster's powerful ale before ten in the morning. As the day wore on, I began to get more and more anxious. The prayers I'd offered up to Auntie BBC at morning service in the hospital chapel had to be answered. The speakers, under solemn promise to keep the alcoholic intake down to the minimum, had to be men of their word, and with one exception they were. Our recorded rehearsal with London, trying out the vast circuit for the first time late on Christmas Eve, seemed to me hopeless. The difficulty was to get the right cue, which was to be given to me from Tokyo by Bernard Forbes, our representative there, with whom I had spent a very pleasant time. He was to say 'Over to Michael Barsley in Kure, K - U - R - E,' spelling it out because the previous item, by Rene Cutforth, came from Korea, a confusing similarity of names.

"By evening, it became obvious that the Australian crew were getting a bit out of touch: theirs was an almost impossible task anyhow, with only out-of-date, military gear. So I took a chance, and called in Japanese engineers, from the local radio station. The hospital ward and control were suddenly full of about seventeen little men, pattering around like figures in a pantomime. 'Here they are, with love and hisses,' I said to myself, and the Christmas spirit made them acceptable to the Ozzies for once. I realized London was frantically trying to get in touch with us, but we couldn't do anything, but just get ready to chance it. The hospital chaplain had assembled a choir in the corridor, to sing a carol. One of my speakers was a fellow Scouse, from Norris Green in Liverpool. Then my Canadian speaker slowly slid under the table. I remember shouting 'Get me another Canadian!' and a desperate search taking place in the wards. Just in time, one was wheeled in. I got his name, and said, 'Look, you read this message. Use this chap's words. Got it?' He'd got it. The seconds ticked by. Only the Japanese were impassive.

"The only way I could follow the programme, as it was coming faintly from London, on the Overseas Far Eastern Service, was by pressing a tiny Japanese radio set to my ear. Reception was very bad, but at last I could hear Cutforth's voice which I knew so well. We were due on next. 'Stand by everybody—starting the carol when I point, padre.' Then Bernard Forbes, a tiny voice from Tokyo. 'Over to Michael Barsley in Kure, K - U - R - E!'

"I pointed. 'O Come all ye faithful. . . .' Scarcely believing, I began, 'Hullo, BBC . . .' and it came, right through, live, and my daughters recognized my voice. It came, landline to Hiroshima, then Tokyo; short-wave to San Francisco, California, over the Pacific; land-line to New York, short-wave to Broadcasting House. The longest radio jump in BBC history. Two hours later, I was shovelled aboard a train for the long seventeen-hour journey back to Tokyo, and awaiting me was Bernard, with a telegram which meant more to me than anything else in my BBC Life. MAGNIFICENT JOB CONGRATULATIONS GILLIAM."

DEATH OF KING GEORGE VI

The King is dead. Long live the Queen!

Inside the BBC, orders went forth. Ordinary people suddenly became key people, moving swiftly and with a purpose. No one unconnected with their part in Operation Demise, as it might be called, stopped them, even to say "Good morning." Usually the BBC reacts superbly to the great moments of history: sometimes it falls flat on its face. While Sir William Haley supervised arrangements for Winston

Churchill's tribute, to be broadcast the following evening, activity within Gilliam's orbit was immense and multifarious, with every Department co-operating, both home and overseas. Lines were booked for recording tributes from Australia, Canada, New Zealand, India, Ceylon—it was the Christmas Day round-up formula all over again, with the added sharpness that the King's death, though ultimately expected, had happened so suddenly, with the new Queen and Prince Philip far away in Kenya.

Finally, on 14th February, Leo Genn narrated *The Commonwealth Mourns its King*, a worldwide operation mounted within a week. Churchill's tribute was quoted, followed immediately by a taxi-driver, Ted Gould of Stoke Newington, who had picked up a fare near Buckingham Palace that day, just after half past ten, and was almost the first to spread the news:

"I called up our control-room, which keeps in radio touch with all our taxis, and told them: 'This is the saddest news you'll ever broadcast. The King is dead.' I could hear the announcement every few minutes, because the drivers were shocked, and couldn't believe it, and kept requesting confirmation. My next fare heard the news coming through, and broke down, and asked me to take her to St Martin-in-the-Fields to pray...."

Then the reporters: Rene Cutforth saw the salute of guns in Hyde Park the following day ("There's a cold breeze, but it's a soft day, with blue shadows. They're burning the dead leaves at the Bayswater end of the Park, and the yellow smoke mingles with the clean white discharge of the guns"). Richard Dimbleby's memorable description of the lying-in-state at Westminster Hall, with "that ruby [how suddenly he emphasized the word] which King Henry wore at Agincourt." Wynford Vaughan Thomas, the evening before the funeral, speaking in St George's Chapel, Windsor ("Here lie Tudor and Stuart sovereigns ... under the soaring tracery of the fan vaulting, the banners of the Knights of the Garter hang their heavy splendours of velvet and gold....")

In between, many ordinary, non-professional voices from many countries. One of those, a woman from Blackheath, at the lying-in-state, said:

"The moment was gone, almost before I realized. I just thought: oh dear, I haven't got time to say goodbye. As I went by, I made the sign of the cross. The men can raise their hats: women can't. Lots of good men die, and we don't hear about it...."

The microphone caught the unprepared, confused reactions and the heartfelt phrases with great impact, and, with an immediacy which television could not achieve, garnered messages from the ends of the earth. At home, it was an inspiration to call in Johnny Carey, then Captain of Manchester United, to talk of the King's love of sport, and the "special dignity" he gave it (a dignity much needed today in many a top game). A bagpipe lament followed from Scotland, and then Albert Thompson, postmaster at Crathie: "My memories of the King and his brothers date back to their childhood. I used to watch them on Sundays, the four boys in Highland dress going to church with their tutor, walking over the bridge from Balmoral, and up the steep park into the kirk...."

A choir from Wales; a countryman from Wiltshire; a Channel Island fisherman speaking of the Duke of Normandy, the Islanders' own Duke, giving his first words in French: a factory-worker, a miner, an Ulsterman (one of "The King's Men") all were woven into the tapestry of words in the familiar but very apposite Christmas pattern. Then the Commonwealth messages came in, wider still and wider. Lieutenant-General Berryman, an Australian who had twice made arrangements for royal tours—the second of which never took place—told of his astonishment at the knowledge King George possessed about things Australian. Mr Holland, New Zealand's Prime Minister, had only recently been talking to His Majesty at length about the projected tour. Then a Maori choir sang a farewell hymn.

From Canada, Leonard Brockington, a seasoned broadcaster known to many of us in Broadcasting House, recalled the royal visit thirteen years previously when, as he vividly put it, "the pictures on the postage stamps and the images on the coins suddenly came to life ... our children welcomed him with songs, when he set forth upon our Canadian earth. They will follow him on his last journey to his own dear English earth ... for they know that he was a good man, who did good things."

From Kimberley, South Africa, where he was farming, Group Captain "Sailor" Malan, DSO and Bar, DFC and Bar, victor over thirty-two Luftwaffe planes, remembered that, for the investiture of himself and his friends, the King waived the command to visit Buckingham Palace, and came to the airfield himself for the awards, and to lunch in the mess afterwards.

An Indian Minister, the widow of Pakistan's late Prime Minister, the Begum Liaquat Ali Khan; Vernon Abisaykera from Ceylon; a Gold Coast Paramount Chief, Mene Azzu Mate Kole, the Koner of Manya Krobo, and the drums of the Bemba tribe in Northern Rhodesia, followed the story in their own fashion. Captain Anthony Kimmins, RN, continued—a memory of the King's visit to Malta, with only a small escort, during the war, across Bomb Alley: Private Speakman, the VC of Korea, and an RAF Squadron Leader from Cyprus, spoke for the other services, the last one recalling that "the King was a fully-fledged RAF pilot, and we knew that his wings had been earned the hard way, and we had heard how proud he was of that flying badge." For France and the Allies, Jean Marin, one of "Les Trois Amis" in wartime London, spoke feelingly, and in New York, Mrs Eleanor Roosevelt broke off a press conference at the United Nations to pay a spontaneous tribute.

It all seems a long time ago. People have gone, names have changed, radio's measure has shrunk, and television has taken the main credit in the big occasions. But for the thinking man and woman, who doesn't merely remark "Doesn't Prince Philip look cross?" and Who's that bearded man in that funny hat?" (probably a King-at-Arms) the varied pattern of voices and places was enough, and no television could better the magic of the words from Bunyan's *Pilgrim's Progress*, the King's favourite book, as spoken in the brogue by Duncan McIntyre:

"After this, it was noised abroad that Mr Valiant-for-Truth was taken with a summons. . . . When he understood it, he called for his friends and told them of it. Then said he 'I am going to my fathers, and though with great difficulty I am got hither, yet now I do not repent me at all the trouble I have been at to arrive where I am. My sword I give to him that shall succeed me in my pilgrimage, and my courage and skill to him that can get it. . . .'

"When the day that he must go hence was come, many accompanied him to the riverside, into which, as he went, he said, 'Death, where is thy sting?' and as he went down deeper, he said 'Grave, where is thy victory?' So he passed over, and all the trumpets sounded for him on the other side. . . ."

Music up and fade . . . Programme Engineer "Laddie" Ladbrook says into his mike, "OK, Control room. Out at 2215 GMT. Recording number 17465. Your report, please. . . . Stand by studio. Message from Laurence; OK. Leo, Duncan—he'd like a word with you. Right. Now, chaps, who'll buy me a drink?"

We had one at "The George," without realizing how appropriate the name of the BBC local had become.

QUEEN MARY

As far as the BBC was concerned, Queen Mary remained the silent Queen and, as we have said, the only existing record of her voice came at the launching of the ship named after her. On television, her familiar toque and parasol were the royal trademark. Her shyness and her unfailing dignity endeared her to the people in a very special way: so did the very human stories of her foibles. During the war, as Queen Mother, she was very bored at being sent out of London to the Duke of Beaufort's estate at Badminton. One day she read a report that a large mine had been washed up on the shore at nearby Clevedon. She asked her Secretary to find out when it was due to be detonated. The officer commanding the local Sapper squad was astonished: he'd probably not considered it, but blurted out "tomorrow at eleven," or some such time. The reply came "Her Majesty will be there." The bomb-disposal squad surrounded the mine with additional explosives, in case this Royal Command performance didn't go off with a bang. Promptly at the hour, the familiar maroon Daimler, in those days the pattern of royal cars, appeared on the cliff top. Her Majesty alighted. The officer, after, presumably, a quick prayer, gave the order, and the mine went off to schedule. "Thank you," said the Queen, and drove away.

The BBC's Bristol headquarters contained, among other Departments, the Children's Hour, and Queen Mary desired to pay the studios a visit. The usual BBC "bull" of whitewashing and tidying up took place, and to restrain the programme staff, a large notice of NO SMOKING went up in the production room. Queen Mary entered, sat down in an ordinary chair, laid aside her parasol, took out a packet of cigarettes and offered them round. The particular brand of cigarettes will be revealed, to everyone's astonishment, on the next page.

When Queen Mary died in 1953 with, as one BBC man remarked professionally, "perfect timing—in between the Boat Race and the Grand National," there was a tremendous surge of sympathy and admiration in the country for this remarkable royal figure. The feeling was so intense that it was realized by those responsible for the radio obituary that this must be no formal one. Douglas Cleverdon and Barsley had been compiling material and recording speakers over a period of three years, under the top secret heading "Demise of the Crown," but they were willing to throw all of this overboard in order to catch the mood of the nation. Gilliam, in overall charge, was in enthusiastic agreement, and every rule and protocol went by the board, in order to mount a regional link-up within about forty-eight hours. Sir Compton Mackenzie, who well knew the story of "Princess May" of Teck, was alerted in Edinburgh, and flew to London, scribbling notes on scraps of paper as he came, to present the tribute.

The Regions had freedom of choice, and each responded in a characteristic way. Everyone expected there to be a piper at Balmoral, but the item was made perfect by the addition of a ghillie's memories of the ball for the royal servants. "I danced with the Queen, and so lightly she danced." From Wales, the Royal Treorchy Choir sang their hearts out, but it was the West of England contribution which caught the personal image of the Queen best of all. The speakers were woodcutters on the Badminton estate, describing how Queen Mary would come and talk with them during their break. "She'd hand cigarettes round, too," said one on rehearsal, "Woodbines they were...." This revelation—for Queen Mary did indeed smoke Woodbines—had to be partially concealed, the trade name being replaced by "the cigarettes in the little green packet," the nearest they ever came to being By Royal Appointment to Queen Mary.

CORONATION DAY

"A-bunting we will go, a-bunting we will go,
 Long-livey, long-livey, long-livey—
 A-bunting we will go!"

This was one studio clarion-call invented for *Coronation Day Across the World*, a reminder that, in a Features programme of whatever magnitude, cheerfulness always broke in. This, indeed, was to be a Gilliam hook-up bigger than any Christmas Day epic, with an intake of nearly forty items from overseas alone, and with the OB Department at full stretch, in the kind of co-operation which always worked so well. Moreover, though we in sound radio knew that the TV Coronation would sweep the board, we had arranged to broadcast the progress of the TV film as it was rushed out to Canada and the US in a hair-raising race between the BBC's Canberra jet, with the RAF, and an American-hired Canberra. We caught our man, the late Tom Sloan, at Goose Bay in Labrador for the hand-over of film, then Leonard Miall in Washington, proclaiming that we had a world scoop.

The muster of locations in this ninety-minute broadcast read like a mixture of Baedeker and Bradshaw, and stretched from Buckingham Palace to Fiji. As for the European items, we handled five countries in twelve minutes. The most amusing moment was when John Snagge said "Over to the House of Lords!" which was followed by the raucous singing of *Daisy Daisy*. The explanation was simple: the "House of Lords" is the name of a famous hostelry in the Hague, near the Parliament buildings, and the voices were those of Dutch revellers. This was not the last fling of Features: the Christmas Day programmes continued for a year or two more, but the end of the Big Show in radio was near. Leo Genn spoke the final words of the script:

"Thus Coronation Day is coming to an end. Here in London the huge, cheering, warm-hearted crowd salutes the young Queen as she stands on the balcony of her floodlit Palace, while the fireworks make exciting arabesques of multi-colour coloured light in the sky. It is the end of a day, and the beginning of an Age...."

Snagge had close experience of two Coronations, and comments on the difference between them, from a BBC point of view:

"So far as the ritual was concerned, they were identical in form and order—the service was the same, the route was the same, the royal coach was the same: the only distinction was that one had been for a King, and the other was for a Queen. But in 1937 it was the first time such an event had come the way of broadcasting, and there was no precedent. All Lotbinière and his OB team could do was to consult the Abbey authorities, the Earl Marshal, the representatives of the Services taking part, and to read the published accounts of the King George V Coronation in 1910. We were faced with a continuous programme from 10 in the morning till about 5.30 in the evening, without once going back to the studios. Over 100 OB microphones were in operation, all controlled by R. H. Wood, that engineer-friend of royalty, from a headquarters in the crypt below Westminster Abbey. My own role was a fairly simple one, which was in two parts. I had the prologue to do, watching as the coach left the Palace down the Mall; then at the end, I took over from Tommy Woodrooffe and that 'glorious, scintillating, coruscating coach' as the procession came down Constitution Hill, and went round through the Palace gates, followed by a description of the great crowds as they chanted 'We want the King!' All the commentators had been as nervous as kittens, because there was no rehearsal, but we came away with a feeling the broadcast had been pretty well done, under the circumstances.

"In 1953, the procedure was much the same—indeed, R. H. Wood was still there at central control room—but by that year, the public had become more aware and more critical of broadcasting generally, and we knew, of course, that we were very much in competition with BBC Television. For my own part, things were quite different. I was stationed at the very heart of things within the Abbey, the counterpart of Dimbleby, and, as Norman Shelley told me about his Winnie the Pooh, I wouldn't have minded if this had been my only broadcast, so privileged did I feel. But it meant, not just a one-shot commentary at the time, but rehearsal after rehearsal, and long talks with the Duke of Norfolk and with Dr McKie, in charge of the music, and many others. There was an opportunity to time all the pauses, and to alter one's script up till the last minute. Everything could be in order—*but*—and this is something a commentator always has to face, and on this occasion Richard Dimbleby and I had many a talk about it beforehand—what was one going to do, what was one going to say, being all on one's own, if anything untoward happened during that long service? You couldn't ignore it if anyone fell down, or if Her Majesty felt faint in her heavy robes and had to retire, because all the papers would have it afterwards. No matter what preparations you made, there was always this fear of the unknown quantity.

"The other problem, which I hadn't reckoned on, and which took me completely by surprise, was the realization of the effect your own emotions might have, when, after all the rehearsals and all the time and trouble you had taken, it came to the real thing, the true, live ceremony, with the golden carpet, the blue brocade—when you saw the royals come in, when you saw the peers in their full robes, and Sir Winston Churchill in his Garter robes, and the crowned Heads of State, when you saw the whole ceremony, mounting in traditional rite and splendour to its incredible climax of colour and sound—when you saw all this from the supreme vantage-point, in all its detail—*that* was the test, to do a professional job under the strain of your own deep personal emotion. Whether the emotion you felt was conveyed to the listener, I wouldn't know. It must have had some effect, even though there were times when you experienced difficulty in speaking at all. You're on your own, it's up to you—and the best of luck, chum!"

6 Drama and Variety

THE Drama Department has always been one of the mainstays of BBC radio, and consistently one of its best branches. In the earliest days the wonder of the wireless was its ability to communicate at all, by giving news, information and events. Music and Drama followed, as embellishments of the original spoken word, and became, with Variety, the regular output on which the reputation of the BBC rested.

Radio, as we shall see, revolutionized the performance of plays as soon as a dictum was realized, and enforced—that the performance should be rehearsed and directed within the studio, not merely relayed from an existing production in a theatre. This may seem a very obvious necessity now, but in those years, when the BBC was alternately despised and feared by managements—and this included newspaper proprietors and sporting organizations as well as theatres—it is surprising how long it took for the lesson to be learned, and for the advantages of broadcasting to be seized rather than opposed.

"THE POLISH CORRIDOR"

The Drama story of our period is dominated, during the early years, by the personalities of two men who came to be known as "The Polish Corridor"—Val Gielgud and Eric Maschwitz.

Val Gielgud was a man with interests so wide, talents so diverse and influence so deep, that it is not surprising that he exercised great influence in the BBC, though it was a discreet and patient exercise, not exulting in victory nor being humbled in defeat. It is sometimes difficult to believe that he retired from the BBC as long ago as 1963—on his sixty-third birthday. Val created radio drama as we know it, created it by a mixture of good sense, good taste, and an indefinable flair, giving it a flavour as superior as that of an Abdulla Turkish cigarette over any King Size Filter-tip. He wrote a number of books, all but two of them as a sort of therapy in thrillers. The exceptions are his history of BBC Drama and his autobiography *Years in a Mirror*, in which he sums up his attitude to the BBC as follows:

"The organization I knew was led to years of discretion by the hand

of Lord Reith, and experienced at the hands of Sir William Haley. In Sir Hugh Carleton-Greene's stable stamps a horse of a different colour."[1]
He would not be led to further prophecy.

Yet, as Eric Maschwitz recalls, Val was the "Cinderella" of the Gielgud house in Gledhow Gardens, South Kensington, where Mabel Constanduros also had a flat. Ellen Terry had been his aunt; brother John was a successful actor; brother Lewis a diplomat in Paris. But, says Maschwitz, he was at first "an awkward young man, rather too conscious of being the odd man out. He blotted his copybook after coming down from Oxford by eloping with the daughter of a Russian countess, since when he had been first a typewriter salesman, later a provider of jokes for a humorous magazine, then a stage-manager, with intervals as an unsuccessful actor."[1]

Val used to return to Oxford for occasional parties, still wearing his scarlet-lined cloak and flourishing his sword-stick. Maschwitz himself was a Cambridge man, a contemporary of Lance Sieveking, who originally lured him into the BBC; a contemporary, too, of the late King George VI, who played tennis with him at Trinity, and seventeen years later, when decorating him with the OBE remarked "It seems a long time since we played tennis together at Cambridge!" Eric kept the original citation framed on his wall as a piece of history, for though the presentation was from King George the citation had been given by King Edward VIII during his brief reign.

Within the Corporation there was a touch of comic espionage about these two, in the way they plotted together to upset the weekly routine meetings of the Programme Board. Like Tweedledum and Tweedledee, they would agree to have a battle, but only during the meeting, and only in order to pull the Chairman's leg or brighten things up. Eric brought original ideas, not only into the *Radio Times*, which he edited for five years, but into everything he did subsequently. Like Val, he was an individualist, who defied Administration and cared little for authority.

Val Gielgud has always been a quiet man, liking good company and good humour. Wilfred Pickles tells the story of his visit, when in Manchester, to Pickles' local club for a lecture on BBC Drama. The local publican, drawing him a half-pint beforehand, said "You're a Portuguese, aren't you?" Val replied that he was English. "Then what have you got that black beard for?" demanded the publican.

[1] *No Chip on My Shoulder* (Herbert Jenkins, 1957).

Instead of being offended, Val was highly amused, and used the story as the beginning of his talk.

Thirty-five years is a long time to spend with any organization, but it may seem less long if it engages different sides of a man's output. Val Gielgud was given a surprising amount of freedom, and was acceptable as a pioneer and a leader both in Variety and Drama, not to mention Features, which he commanded until the war years, and was reluctant to relinquish, much as he admired the man who took over. He started working for the BBC on the *Radio Times* in 1928, assisting Eric Maschwitz, his office "looking down upon the graveyard of the Savoy, with its shrill autumn chorus of starlings." His opinion on the Savoy Hill organization agrees with that of Jack Payne: Gielgud found it a "rather slap-happy family party." For instance, he considered the Grand Goodnight of J. C. Stobart, invoking the moon and stars and all the field now open to astronauts, to be "embarrassing." But he was willing to take on the very formidable task of being responsible for Variety and Drama simultaneously.

Maschwitz and Gielgud were also called, by the popular press, "the Variety Twins." Neither of them, in reputation or experience, seems to bear any resemblance to later impresarios and tycoons in showbiz—the Lew Grades and Littlers and Delfonts, for whom at that time the music-hall meant everything and the radio nothing. This was perhaps because they had no ambition in the field of earning big money: they were concerned with putting on as good a show as they could for this new, vast, listening public, rather than competing in tycoon stakes. In this way they were, no doubt, conforming to the BBC's non-commercial image, but their professional enthusiasm meant that the play was the thing, not the profit. (On behalf of variety managers, it is fair to note an exception in George Black, who, after long opposition, began to sense the potential of the wireless when choosing a performer.) True, Christopher Stone, the first disc-jockey, failed on the stage, but Wilfred Pickles won fame. To his astonishment, he was offered star billing at the London Palladium, and this was only partly due to his acting ability. Black shrewdly realized what publicity Pickles's name had received during his brief—and not entirely successful—stint as a BBC news-reader. Another of Black's wireless discoveries was Henry Hall, with the BBC Dance Band. The Mills Brothers, too, got to know the value of radio coverage for Bertram Mills' Circus. Promoters like these—and at first they were rare—not only "allowed" acts to be performed on the wireless: they went out of their way to give full co-operation, and it paid off. Maschwitz called Black "one of the very greatest figures that ever graced the lighter side of the theatre."

Although not a writer, Gielgud shared Maschwitz's flair for putting his finger on a mistake, but equally instead of criticizing he would suggest something in its place. Maschwitz went further. He might say about some sketch "I think there's something wrong here," and would sit down there and then and rewrite it, and it would be out on the air an hour or two later. He had been known to go to a full rehearsal of a show, object to things in it, go away, work till four in the morning and return with the entire score rewritten. Like Sir Arthur Sullivan, he could manage with little sleep.

The World War saw Features and Drama drafted to a place near Evesham called Woodnorton. Gielgud commented: "It is the appropriate setting for a nightmare. Once the home of an exiled Duc d'Orléans, it sprouts fleurs-de-lis on everything from weather-vanes to bath-plugs, and has a bear-pit in the garden.... To my horror one may not smoke in it. I have had to take to my bicycle again—after fifteen years. My billet is vile. Its owners seem to regard one as if one were a mediaeval *condottiere*, likely to steal the silver and ravish the daughter as opposed to hoping for bed and breakfast!"

He shared an office with Laurence Gilliam, Howard Rose and that engaging Scotsman Moray McLaren. How sad to behold four such inveterate travellers and gourmets so constricted in place and diet. *Où sont les fromages d'antan?* Stephen Potter found himself at a farm with the biggest collection of caged birds in the country, "and wallabies running loose." Gielgud's sketchy diary of the time, contained within his autobiography, is full of exasperation. He gets a memo from Head Office saying that half an hour is long enough for a play, and that they should preferably be "of Children's Hour type." When he puts up a Christmas idea suggested by Ed Murrow, that President Roosevelt should be asked to introduce the King, the BBC Establishment receives it coldly, sheltering behind the Ministry of Information's attitude, that it seemed to be too much of a publicity stunt. "I wonder," observes Gielgud tartly, "what Goebbels would have done in similar circumstances."

There are compensations. During visits to London, Gielgud stays in Bloomsbury, and in 1941 plans a series of plays called *The Saviours*, with Clemence Dane. Noel Coward looks in, talking excitedly about, of all authors, E. Nesbit, whose books he knows by heart, particularly

The Railway Children. A good muster of players assemble for a Shakespeare series, including Fay Compton, Marius Goring, Leslie Banks, Sarah Churchill and Robert Helpmann. The Drama Department's move to Manchester is one step nearer civilization, but the Nazi bombing follows the BBC. By 1943 they are back in London. Constance Cummings stars in *The White Cliffs of Dover*; Eric Linklater has written a play called *Cornerstones*; John Dickson Carr, a favourite author of Val's, has produced an idea called *Appointment with Fear*; the Controller of Programmes has suggested a series of Saturday Night Theatre performances, suitable for the average listener. It is something like old times again, and when Gielgud sends out a questionnaire asking listeners to choose their favourite plays, he is astonished to get some 12,000 replies.

Maschwitz's work on the *Radio Times* was to prove valuable in his later BBC years. Its topicality helped him in forming the weekly *In Town Tonight*, for which he chose that memorable signature tune, Eric Coates's "Knightsbridge" March. The paper not only gave him the *entrée* for meeting anyone in showbusiness, but the opportunity of choosing writers like James Agate, J. D. Beresford, D. B. Wyndham-Lewis ("Timothy Shy"), Lowes Dickinson, Sacheverell Sitwell, L. A. G. Strong, R. H. Wilenski, Filson Young (his literary adviser)—and Compton Mackenzie, with whom he planned a great adventure at the microphone.

His adaptation of the latter's *Carnival* was the most ambitious drama production to date. Gielgud shared the infectious Maschwitz enthusiasm for it. Peter Creswell was chosen as producer. But first—catch your author, that's the golden rule. Laurence Gilliam caught Dylan Thomas in a pub, and out of it came *Under Milk Wood*. Maschwitz tempted Mackenzie, whom he had never met before, with oysters, at Wheeler's in Soho. The enthusiasm caught on (as it usually does with Monty, once you challenge him with something, and invite his full co-operation) and the two became lifelong friends. It's strange that Mackenzie, his senior, should have outlived Eric, but he never burned himself up in the Maschwitz manner.

As a production, it apparently used so many studios that, as Eric put it, "we practically tied Savoy Hill into knots," with two orchestras and a double-banked sound-effects staff. Hermione Gingold played in it, so did Harmon Grisewood. The part of Jenny Pearl, the Edwardian chorus girl, was taken by Lillian Harrison. It comes as no surprise to us to learn that Maschwitz never received a penny for adapting it, nor for writing dozens of other scripts, long or short. The BBC has always rightly withheld payment for charity work, but has also, through the years, gladly accepted the offer by any members of staff willing to display an additional side of their talent for the one basic salary.

Snagge recalls an example of Maschwitz's almost compulsive sense of the ridiculous. This was at the Television Centre, where he held the job of Head of Light Entertainment. Her Majesty the Queen was due to arrive on a visit to the studios, and every BBC man of note was gathering in a room after lunch, the Director-General, the Chairman of the Board of Governors, several Governors and Heads of Departments, the lot. Eric Maschwitz was seen to appear gaily from the bar, and announce to the Chairman and all present "By the way, if a parcel arrives at Reception in the shape of a sword, I've arranged for it to be sent to my office, and I've laid on the dubbing theatre!" Only Maschwitz could have thus heralded the knighthood of George Barnes.

On an earlier Royal visit, to Broadcasting House, Val Gielgud had laid on a demonstration of a BBC Control Panel, which conjured up the sounds attending a Royal procession. These apparently delighted the King above all else, and he lingered so long there that Queen Mary "had to give voice to the unanswerable words, 'Come along, George!'" This occasion followed a previous honour, the Royal attendance at the London Palladium, in which the BBC played a part by broadcasting it. Radio "Variety," far from being in the "I say—I say—I say," custard-pie category, became respectable and sought-after, and a dazzling era opened. Maschwitz's account is studded with names—not only the stalwarts of BBC programmes (Tommy Handley, Harry Hemsley, Clapham and Dwyer, Leonard Henry, Olive Groves, George Baker, Mabel Constanduros and all) but outside favourites like Burns and Allen, Jean Sablon, Chevalier, Eddie Cantor, Greta Keller, Hildegarde, Noel Coward, Gertrude Lawrence, Bebe and Ben Lyon, Larry Adler—the list was everyone's dream command-performance.

But as usual, Eric Maschwitz was able to compete with other facets of his genius. For outside work, he had chosen the odd name of Holt Marvell. Snagge, for whom Maschwitz made one or two OB commentaries (including the Boat Race and the return of Amy Johnson at Hendon) believes it may be some sort of anagram. His occasional incursions into commentary were limited to his own field, but laced with individual phraseology, such as describing the Mayor of Croydon and party awaiting the fabulous Amy as "wearing full canonicals."

But Holt Marvell's greatest achievement was to write, for composer Jack Strachey and American singer Joan Carr, a "little number" called *These Foolish Things*. At first it was a flop. Even Keith Prowse, the ticket agency to whom Maschwitz was contracted, released him of all responsibility. Patrick Waddington sang it in a Maschwitz West End revue. Still no luck. After all, it had been hastily written, on vodka and coffee, as Eric sat, unshaven, and in his pyjamas, at the piano one Sunday morning, after six eighteen-hour days in the radio studios. Long after, as sometimes happens in real life, a famous singer and personality found it lying on top of the same piano, and Leslie Hutchinson ("Hutch") the West Indian singer, began to try it out.

> "Gardenia perfume lingering on a pillow,
> Wild strawberries only seven francs a kilo,
> And still my heart has wings—
> These Foolish Things remind me of you. . . .
> A tinkling piano in the next apartment,
> Those stumbling words that told you what my heart meant,
> A fairground's painted swings—
> These Foolish Things remind me of you. . . ."[1]

A generation has sung it: nearly two generations. The BBC, of course, paid Holt Marvell nothing for it, but from royalties it gave Marvell and Strachey a regular thousand a year. His other hit, *A Nightingale Sang in Berkeley Square*, evokes the same sugary nostalgic orchids-and-white-satin atmosphere, and was composed, with Manning Sherwin, in the appropriate South of France setting of Le Lavandou, near Cagnes, where the *Small Hotel* song was born.

Eric Maschwitz left the BBC, reluctantly, in 1937 (to return, years later, to BBC television, and finally radio again). He had become too deeply involved in the stage, and the cinema, with such landmarks as *Balalaika*. The Corporation could not hold on for long to a man like that. It had used him. He had used Them. BBC life had been a great joke from the time he commented on the Variety Departments initials (VD) as representing a disease. But it was a successful invasion of two worlds. When he returned from Buckingham Palace with his OBE, for services to radio, he found an MGM contract awaiting him, offering a sum of six figures for the film rights of *Balalaika*.

[1] Words by Eric Maschwitz, reprinted by permission of Boosey & Hawkes Music Publishers Ltd.

MABEL CONSTANDUROS

Among the versatile "ladies of the air" whose work was to affect the Drama Department, no one could overlook Mabel Constanduros. Her grandfather, Thomas Tilling, was the pioneer of transport in London, and a name always connected with trams and buses. But she herself possessed driving force and, strangely enough, it emerged from a quiet, ordinary, happy family life and an equally inconspicuous marriage. Mabel might just have settled down in the London suburb of Sutton, with her sister living nearby (they married the two Constanduros brothers). Not a suggestion that she would one day top the bill at the London Coliseum, and become a household word for creating the cockney family she called Buggins.[1]

As a child she was proud of her grandfather (in rhyming slang of the time a "Tom Tilling" meant a shilling) and very fond of her parents. Her father, she decided, judged people the way he judged horses—and that was meant as a compliment. After education at the Mary Datchelor School in Camberwell, she became interested in theatricals, and joined the local drama club. Other members included Leslie Howard and Mabel's life-long friend Gladys Young, for whom she was writing in 1925, three years before the Buggins Family sketches were attempted. A training under the imperious Elsie Fogerty, that tiny, Queen Victoria of a figure with piercing blue eyes, helped Mabel, as she helped so many, in her career. Later they would greet each other uproariously, like old school girls swapping memories of their mentors.

The Buggins series became a success from the start, both on the wireless and the stage, and in books. Mabel unashamedly enjoyed her "applause by post," as she called her fan-mail. In character and conversation, Grandma and Mrs Buggins are very reminiscent of an earlier favourite Constanduros character, *Mrs Green*, written by Elsie Evelyn Rynd, and published at the beginning of the century. Eventually, the old cottage Mabel bought at Bury in Sussex became a meeting-place for many writers and radio performers. She teamed up with Nancy Price, and appeared in her production of *Lady Precious Stream* with Leon M. Lion. She played in A. P. Herbert's musical *Derby Day*, and turned Stella Gibbons's satire *Cold Comfort Farm* into a play, taking the part of Mrs Agony Beetle, in company with Felix Aylmer and Roger Livesey.

[1] Her life story is told in *Shreds and Patches* (Lawson & Dunn, 1946). Many of her sketches were also published. She died in 1957.

Mabel was never more enthusiastic than when in collaboration. With Howard Agg, a young man who wrote to her by chance, she made several popular adaptations from the classics. With Denis, her nephew, she wrote a suburban triumph in *Acacia Avenue*, with the sort of family situation repeated today so often in television plays. Denis, who later, in the West Region where he lives, invented an unending and highly successful local family called the Luscombes, joined forces with his aunt in providing a typical "English Family Robinson" in 1937.

Mabel was adaptable to any style, from satire to soap-opera. Barsley found her the mainstay of his first BBC script, the wartime satire *Is Your Genie Really Necessary?* on Christmas Day 1943. She encouraged him to go on writing humour, saying "You can be as good as *ITMA*." This encouragement she offered to many people, while maintaining a prodigious output herself. She may, however, have guessed that her own family style of programme would eventually be taken up by others and that the name of Dale was likely to become a source of grievance to the man she so much admired, Val Gielgud.

As Head of the Drama Department, he could not escape being responsible for the Dale family and its cosy, predictable doings. Mabel had been all in favour of domesticity, but of *Mrs Dale's Diary* Gielgud could only lament, blushing and with bowed head, that the series was "aesthetically contemptible and sociologically corrupting. The persisting drip-drip-drip of such programmes destroyed all possibility of criticism. The audience was gradually drugged into belief in the reality of a dream world ruled by bogus values, and entirely occupied by trivialities. . . . In the long run, I had to ask myself the question: was it worth while to make the continuation of the Dales a resignation matter?" His was "a confession of ignominious failure." But the end of the Diary came quietly, despite an injection of the familiar voice and laugh of Jessie Matthews into its final episodes, replacing the part played with such assurance over the years by the late Ellis ("Luggy") Powell, a fabulous, bibulous character who in no way represented the suburban gentility of the Mrs Dale.[1]

THE ARCHERS

About *The Archers*, a product of BBC Midland Region, Gielgud felt less pained, realizing that in Godfrey Baseley's account of a farming

---

[1] The demise, under Lord Hill, was noted in a very short Barsley letter to *The Times*, which ran: "Up, Hill: down, Dale!"

family and its problems, there was a large degree of horse-sense, plus pig-sense, plus cattle-sense—in all, farm-sense. "Acceptable hokum," he said, and left it at that. Here Gielgud seriously misjudged the Archers' public, which was genuinely interested in the issues of the countryside. These have always been carefully and topically woven in by the scriptwriters. Archer-worship rose even higher on occasions. By some diabolical coincidence (or was it carefully contrived?) producer Tony Shryane killed Grace Archer on the night Independent Television was born—and stole the headlines. "It was almost as if," one listener wrote, "there'd been a death in our family." Against it all the fanfares, all the speeches, and all the waving of Sir John Barbirolli's baton at the opening ITV ceremony beat in vain.

The Archers continued in triumph, but in 1972 it suffered a casualty which, in our opinion, reflects a type of BBC attitude which springs from a desire for innovation, at any cost. Godfrey Baseley, creator of the series, was sacked from his own creation. The country wine of the future can no longer be classed as vintage.

HOWARD ROSE

Gielgud was fortunate in having Howard Rose as his right-hand man in production, as long ago as 1929. Howard, well-known for his meticulous, perfectionist approach to his cast—a trait which some actors, like Bruce Belfrage, found unbearable—argued from the first that the cast should come to the studio where, Mahomet-like, he could then take them through their parts line by line.

The best account we have of the Rose method is a look-back by actor David Kossoff, who joined the BBC Repertory Company in 1945 and made his first named appearance in a Barsley production, a documentary on Barrow-boys. His first drama part of any consequence was in Saturday Night Theatre, produced by "that dragon of a man," as Kossoff calls Rose. "Mr Rose's way was to tell everyone, raw recruit or elder of the theatre, exactly which word should be stressed. He acted everybody's parts, and after showing you how, would say, time after time, 'I can do it, why can't *you*?' So terrified did I become that despite the comfort and sympathy shown me by the fellow members of the cast, by the time I went on the air, I had completely lost my voice through sheer nerves. I made my début hoarse!

"There is a sweet end to this story, and I admit only to a very little malice in remembering it, for Howard Rose was a deeply kind man and behaved so to me on many occasions. But it had to happen and one day it did, in another big production by Howard, with, in the leading role, the newest young West End heart-throb—a very handsome well-trained actor who had done all the things, in rep. and in small parts, to make him deserve his fine reputation. He had not broadcast very much and as he approached the microphone for his first speech of the play, the late, and by me deeply lamented, Laidman Browne whispered to me 'You will see, he will open his mouth and Howard's voice will come out.'

"And it was so. The young man was hardly able to say three words at a time before he was being told over a thunderous loudspeaker how to do it. He kept his temper far longer than I thought he would, and then closed his script. He waited for the very long and detailed suggestion over the loudspeaker to end, and it ended, of course, with the words, '*I* can do it, why can't *you*?' Then he replied with great dignity, 'Well Mr Rose, *you* do it.' And walked out."

Val agreed with Howard's view about production in the studio, a point which seems obvious now, but which wasn't so obvious when the wireless carried no guns, in that it offered no real money. Bruce Belfrage's first job, as Drama Bookings Manager, gave him a real taste of the Admin. attitude towards "entertainers." For example, when, in an inspired moment, he approached the American actor Ernest Truex to take part in a BBC play, for fifty guineas (Truex's normal US radio fee would have been in the 500 dollar bracket) after dining and wining him, he sent in his acceptance gleefully. But he received a memo from the Man at the Admin., one Mr Cruttwell, curtly declaring that the sum was outrageous and that "a fee of five guineas was perfectly adequate." It was then that Val Gielgud switched on the charm and exerted the influence, and the day was finally won.

TYRONE GUTHRIE

The mid-Thirties brought the Drama Department, with its attendant Features, into maturity, and into recognition as a medium which Filson Young, that remarkable "programme consultant" from 1926 to 1938, described as having intimacy. "Plays," he said, "should be heard in darkness." This was perhaps an extreme view, but L. du Garde Peach, one of the regular and most highly-regarded radio playwrights of that era, capped this by declaring "When there is nothing to look at, there must be something to think about." It would be dangerous to carry this dictum into the television age, in which, all too often, there is the assumption that "When there is something to look at, there need not be so *much* to think about." Val Gielgud, while encouraging experiment (the Columbia Workshop Programme of America was introduced in the form of an Experimental Hour in 1937) criticized producers who "concentrated more on knobs and switches than on actors and acting." Again, there's a modern parallel here with television, and even more with the cinema, where the work of the director and the editor may bring, for all its brilliant adroitness, disaster to a good story or theme. Pity the author, pity the actor, when the camera is king.

The most remarkable BBC play of the late 'twenties, Tyrone Guthrie's *The Squirrel's Cage*, comes before our Vintage Years, but no one could deny that its vintage (1929) had a freshness and bouquet which lasted for a decade. This, and its follower, *The Flowers Are Not For You to Pick*, are far ahead of their time, even though Guthrie, in a sweeping phrase typical of him, dismissed them as "straws in the wind."

"It is hoped," he added in his preface, "that in some not too far distant future, the human spirit may find sincere and effective expression in terms of mechanized drama. By then the technique of these plays will be as dead as Queen Mary, as dated as the dodo."

Guthrie was wrong, of course. His plays and their technique had a considerable influence on later writers such as MacNeice and D. G. Bridson, and there is a haunting quality about his use of the repetitive phrase. *The Squirrel* is about childhood fear and adult monotony: the suburbanites get no further than the animal rotating on its wheel. *The Flowers* is also about fear and human prohibition, as its title implies. The important thing to emerge from them is the role of the listener. Guthrie explains:

"The impression, though limited, is highly concentrated in quality.... It is partly created by the listener himself, as he collects the author's clues. The microphone play is more intimate, more subtle, because it is received by each listener privately at home. It demands a great deal of creative energy and technical ingenuity of the artists; a great deal of imaginative concentration of the listener...."

Guthrie used all the techniques available: *The Squirrel*, with Mabel Constanduros and Michael Hogan, was produced in four different studios. In *The Flowers*, he devised a way for listeners to recognize his hero amid a babel of different voices. He gave the actor Harold Scott a slight stammer—a distinctive banner in the verbal field of battle. "Canned drama," he called it, just as John Watt was to sum up television drama as "amateur theatricals in an iron lung." But strangely enough, Sir Tyrone Guthrie, that gallant crusader, made his last offering on radio, recording, just before his untimely death, the favourite quotations he had treasured in his rich and rewarding life.

The inventiveness of Guthrie and Lance Sieveking led to further radio experiments which were not just gimmicks. Edward Sackville-West produced *The Rescue*, and Geoffrey Bridson, a poet as well as Assistant Head of Features, made a notable contribution in his *March of the '45*, which wrings high tragedy out of an historical situation, again with repetitive phrases, like a bell tolling. The way was now open for writers like Dylan Thomas and Louis MacNeice.

LOUIS MACNEICE

Louis MacNeice ought strictly to have remained, once Drama and Features were made separate departments, with the former. But his association with Gilliam was much closer than with Gielgud—not that the transfer of allegiance caused any bad feeling. Being already a well-known poet of the Auden, Spender, Day Lewis school gave him a distinction apart from radio, and this might have set him somewhat apart from his fellow roughs in the BBC, who mainly jested, quaffed and swore. But Louis himself did all these things, and in their company. After all, there were other poets in Features, including, as we have said, Geoffrey Bridson, and Terence Tiller, and W. R. Rodgers. Not one of them remained aloof.

This is why the award of the CBE to Louis in 1958 gave us private amusement as well as admiration, for the BBC's policy towards the Honours List had always been a very correct one, and successive governments accepted its recommendations as if they came from a branch of the Civil Service. The normal routine was that Heads of Departments more or less automatically qualified for the OBE, Controllers for the CBE, and ultimately (but not always) Directors for a K. Once Barsley made a note of this procedure—quite altruistically, since he once declared "I never wanted to be Head of anything: I might have ended up the shrunken head of a shrunken department—or even the head of John the Baptist." He discovered that one

Controller in the Regions hadn't got his CBE. On pointing this out at a BBC staff party, he was assured by a Director (who hadn't by then got his K) that "this would be put right at the next Honours," and so it proved. The real one-upmanship, of course, was to get the MVO or CVO, which is in the personal gift of the Sovereign: this Lotbinière received, being closely associated with royal broadcasts. Senior women producers or top secretaries usually qualified for the MBE, to go with a magnificent self-assurance.

But MacNeice, in the catalogue of men on the BBC staff, was a mere Producer (Features) Grade A1 minus, or whatever it was, and to be awarded a CBE might seem most inappropriate. "I went around for days feeling I'd almost done something wrong," he remarked. The award was, of course, for services to poetry, and besides the printed poems, most of his radio plays are in verse form. His manner and appearance, however, belied the traditional myth of a poet wild-eyed, tangle-haired, bearded and withdrawn. Louis was one of the quietest and best-mannered of a rowdy bunch of writers and producers, and since he was Irish this seemed indeed a remarkable thing. He would as soon have beer as wine or spirits, and was often to be found at lunchtime in "The George," perhaps with Hedli Anderson his wife, and with Gilliam, Dillon, Terence Tiller, Dylan Thomas, R. D. Smith, Alan Rawsthorne the composer, David Thomson—indeed any of the congenial Features types, including the engineers. His voice was slow and rather nasal, and he had a way of curling his lip in argument as if slightly contemptuous, which was quite unlike him, unless the contempt were deserved. His passionate hobby was, of all things, following and watching Rugby football.

In the introduction to one of his two great radio plays, *The Dark Tower*,[1] he had some illuminating things to say about the medium in which he worked. At first, like many of his literary friends, he was against the BBC, and broadcasting in general. Then radio began to impress him. "Sound alone," he summed up in 1943, "is for most people more potent, more pregnant, more subtle, than pictures alone and for that reason—regardless of the material pros and cons of television—I hope that sound broadcasting will survive, dispensing with people's faces."

"When you have written for the page," he goes on, "you do not see your readers reading you . . . but in broadcasting you can, given the

---

[1] Published by Faber & Faber in 1947. *Christopher Columbus* appeared in the same year, and with the same publisher.

right speakers, force your listeners to hear the words as they should be heard. . . . Every transmission of a play or feature, however unimportant the programme, should have—and usually has—the feeling of a First Night: it is something *being made* by a team of people."

This is what made Louis one of the major figures in Features. His productions were brilliant exercises in the medium, and he could count on the intent interest of his technical staff and the full co-operation of composers like Benjamin Britten and William Walton, for whom a radio feature "in the round" was an adventure. Louis wrote of it "this pleasure in a thing-being-performed-and-shared. . . . Radio writers and producers can talk shop because their shop is not, as with poets, a complex of spiritual intimacies but a matter of craftsmanship. The popular assumption that all radio professionals resemble civil servants is flatly untrue."

Any Admin. type could vouch for this! But MacNeice adds this consoling thought: "with ingenuity and a little luck a creative person can persuade (or fool) some of the Administrators some of the time." Not many Commanders of the British Empire talk like that. Louis usually wrote his own scripts and produced them as well, as did a number of his colleagues in Features. It gave a new dimension to the job. One of the pioneers was that complete professional D. G. Bridson. But it had its attendant dangers since, as Louis admitted, Writer A might not agree with the way Producer A was dealing with his script, or alternatively, he might agree all too readily and uncritically, and it might be better if Producer B were called in. Radio writers, anyhow, should know something about production: "the script is only half the battle, and the writer who merely sends in a script and does not go near the studios is working largely in the dark."

The MacNeice programme which made the greatest initial impact was *Christopher Columbus*, with music by William Alwyn, produced by Dallas Bower in 1942 to celebrate the 450th Anniversary of the discovery of America. Since the United States was our war-time ally, no doubt the choice of subject was doubly important, but MacNeice made no concessions to topicality. It was, he said, "an untypical radio play because it involved so much music, and particularly vocal music," and he was set to concentrate on "the emotional truth of the legend rather than to let it dissolve in a maelstrom of historical details." A stunning cast was led by Laurence Olivier as Columbus, and included Robert Speaight, Marius Goring, Cecil Trouncer, Gladys Young, Margaret Rawlings, and Hedli Anderson.

In a foreword to the School Edition,[1] MacNeice almost apologizes for his idealistic attitude to radio plays twenty years before. "I feel I am returning to an innocent but quaint and archaic period. The nickname 'steam' radio is properly nostalgic: rarely has such an up-to-date medium matured, and indeed aged, so rapidly." He regards his faith in the potency of sound as now being out of date, though he still clings to a belief in its subtlety. "Television is addiction-forming to a far greater degree than sound ever was. And most people, after all, are lazy. Listening to radio is far harder work than just watching a baby screen: without any visual aids you have not only to follow carefully but also to use your imagination." He goes on to claim that radio can make things larger than life, and create fantasy, where television cannot.

MacNeice's fellow poet, W. H. Auden, in a foreword to the last collection of his radio plays,[2] while recognizing that such plays "permit almost instantaneous changes in place and time" and "are perhaps the ideal medium for 'psychological' drama, that is to say, the portrayal of the inner life," agrees that, since the advent of television "radio drama is probably a dying art."

There are some who would disagree. A minor art, maybe, but are not the minor arts still attractive, and is not steam radio, like a steam locomotive, something to be prized and promoted here on earth, even if television wants the moon to play with?

THE MAN BORN TO BE KING

Of all the departments in the BBC during these years, the department of religious broadcasting seemed to us to be one of the least adventurous—still, perhaps, in awe of the Reith tradition. For instance, we know that questions on religion or politics were forbidden to *The Brains Trust* even in 1941. One can imagine the inward frustration of a Joad or a Huxley. How different in these more adventurous days, with a Muggeridge musing in a boat on the waters of Galilee, and Jesus as a Superstar.

Reith was not himself narrow-minded about religious broadcasters. He gave every encouragement to such outspoken and uncompromising speakers as "Dick" Sheppard from St Martin-in-the-Fields. Professor Briggs quotes Reith as saying, of Sheppard's preaching, "It

---

[1] Introduction by MacNeice, 1963. Published 1964.
[2] *Persons from Porlock and Other Plays for Radio* (BBC, 1969).

was the work of a man who understood profoundly the needs and sorrows and fears of humanity. The subtle mingling of humour and sharp visual imagery and sincerity had an aptness and reality which more complex sermons would have lacked entirely."[1]

There were other famous, sometimes fruity, voices which earned a large following: the sonorous tones of Canon W. H. Elliott from St Michael's, Chester Square; the radical approach of Dr Cyril Garbett, that great Archbishop of York who refused the senior see of Canterbury; the vigour of Canon Cockin from the University Church at Oxford; the graceful style of Father Agnellus Andrew; the breadth and wisdom of Father Bernard Walke from Cornwall; the dry pessimism of the "gloomy Dean," W. R. Inge; the forthright Scots voice of the Reverend George Macleod; the complete list is a creditable one. These men were personalities, not just parsons. They were not the type described in a Barsley poem written in that very year 1941:[2]

> "Back from their pews in time for the News,
> The faithful flock has hastened,
> For the polished word of an Oxford Third
> Has left them cheerfully chastened.
> Respectable Mattins in suits and satins
> Is not for the wretched sinner
> But for those who nod to a friendly God
> And go to a well-cooked dinner."

The Daily Service started in 1928 had already achieved a permanent place in broadcasting. The massive and sometimes misled Central Religious Advisory Committee already consisted of fourteen members in 1931, including Father Martindale, SJ, and Sheppard himself. It was not until 1939, when the Rev. F. A. Iremonger left the BBC to become Dean of Lichfield, that the new Director, the Rev. James Welch, formerly Head of St John's Training College, York, recalled the name of Dorothy L. Sayers, creator of the famous Lord Peter Wimsey detective stories, but also, in 1938, author of a Nativity play written specially for radio, *He That Should Come*.

The play cycle that was to follow is an acknowledged landmark in BBC general history, not merely religious history. Though the Peter Wimsey thrillers gave little hint of the writer's interest in

---

[1] *Dick Sheppard by his Friends*, edited by Howard Marshall (1938).
[2] *Horizon*, edited Cyril Connolly, June 1941.

religion, *Gaudy Night*, her long novel about life in a woman's college at Oxford (Miss Sayers was at Somerville) suddenly becomes serious and theological halfway through, just as Evelyn Waugh's *Brideshead Revisited* starts with a brilliant satire on Oxford undergraduate types, and ends in doubt and death, Roman Catholic style.

Dorothy Sayers was a real character, apart from being a highly successful novelist (most of that breed being personally rather disappointing and business-like).

She started her literary career as a copywriter in a London advertising agency, situated above Donald Soper's Methodist headquarters, Kingsway Hall. Pamela Frankau had also been employed there, and her book *I Find Four People*, was concerned with the place. So, too, was Miss Sayers's *Murder Must Advertise*, which contains some satirical but not altogether unkindly references to the staff. At the Agency she was always referred to as "Miss Sayers." To Val Gielgud, Head of BBC Drama and, as we shall see, producer and godfather of the *Man Born to be King*, she was always Dorothy L. Sayers. The L was as compulsory as in a driving-test.

Miss Sayers's last three novels were, it can now be admitted, typed in the offices of the agency, which was proud of her association with it. Indeed, the murder in the book was committed at the foot of an iron spiral staircase within the old building. Years later, the agency dedicated the staircase to her with a special plaque and a notable party, the sole liquor provided being that from one of their clients, who made a famous gin-sling.

Miss Sayers was also responsible for writing parodies on behalf of another client. To call it "a world-famous Dublin stout" would be the equivalent of calling Harrods "a well-known store in Knightsbridge." Barsley, who worked in the same agency a few years after Miss Sayers's departure, recalls that her most famous wartime parody (hitherto unpublished), began:

> "I will arise, and go now, and get my Guinness free,
> And a small cabin build there, of clay and bottles made. . . .
> Nine beanos will we have there,
> And live alone in the b—— loud raid."

It is (as they say in obituaries) a far cry from the Miss Sayers of a firm of Incorporated Practitioners in Advertising to the Dorothy L. Sayers who was invited to write a cycle of plays for Holy Week and Easter, on her own terms, by the BBC.

Before we come to the book of the play itself, and the production, the first words should be those of Val Gielgud, whose role of producer was insisted upon, as one of the terms, unless the contract was to be cancelled. In his own autobiography,[1] Gielgud described his first meeting with her in 1938 (he had been annoyed because she criticized his novel *Death at Broadcasting House*, and he had proved that technically she was in the wrong). "As a sworn admirer of her detective novels, I had expected to meet a feminine version of Lord Peter Wimsey; something of an intellectual and academic snob, with an exotic taste in wine and cigarettes. I confess to having felt a mingled sense of shock and disappointment when I came face to face with a square-shouldered, tweed-clad, evidently practical woman in pince-nez with something of the air of an amiable bull-terrier. On her side, as she told me later, she had anticipated the worst by the beard that I then wore, and my gossip-paragraph reputation. Fortunately we lost no time in finding tastes in common which developed into a mutually appreciative affection. We both loved Oxford. We were both extremely positive in the expression of our opinions. We both hated humbug, waste of time, and bad cooking...." He forgot to add the one piece of expertise which was entirely Wimsey. Sayers was married to a wine-merchant.

After the first Sayers condition came the second. Robert Speaight was to play Jesus. She had accepted Welch's dictum that the actor concerned ought to be "a believing Christian and a member of the Church," and Speaight filled the requirements. But by now the BBC was, if not alarmed, at least apprehensive at unleashing such an innovation in, of all programmes, *The Children's Hour*—for of such, maybe, might be the Kingdom of Heaven, but into their shell-pink ears would be poured the poison of a modern Jesus who had, in the phrase of the now defunct newspaper the *Daily Sketch*, made Admiral Carpendale's Broadcasting House into "a Temple of Blasphemy."

Gingerly feeling their way, the Corporation allowed Miss Sayers to hold a Press Conference (a rare occurrence in those days) on 10th December 1941, only a few days before the first performance was due to be transmitted, live, on the Sunday before Christmas. Though the journalists present were generally in agreement, a storm broke. Words like "irreverent," "blasphemous" and "vulgar" were used. Miss Sayers had all along insisted that the speech should be modern,

---

[1] *Years in a Mirror* (Bodley Head, 1965).

and that the plays were "to present the story not in the form of a devotional exercise, but primarily as a piece of real life, enacted by human beings against the stormy social and political background of first-century Palestine.... I am anxious," she added, "to avoid genteel piety in the stained-glass manner...." I want to make Our Lord really real."

She read extracts from the first script, and by some journalists these were used in evidence against her. Letters poured into the BBC, after the familiar pattern of complaining before the event, and a question was asked in the House of Commons. The BBC obviously had to take note of this: members of the Central Advisory Committee were sent copies of the script by post, and asked to answer by post, telegram, or telephone. Only one reply was doubtful. Members of many denominations sent their blessings and good wishes.

Transmission of the second play in the series was postponed for a fortnight, so that the Advisory Committee could go through it again— the average age of the Committee being about sixty! The Archbishop of York asked permission to read each play before it was broadcast (no doubt he looked forward to doing so) and the BBC reaffirmed its decision to continue with the series. "If blame there is," wrote Welch in his preface to the book of the plays, "let it be left at other doors than those of the craftsmen." Welch was also anxious to stress that the opposition was not from the laity or members of congregations, but from church leaders themselves. He received hundreds of listeners' letters: "I learned something I hadn't learned before, and I was very grateful," wrote a factory forewoman. "It's changing the atmosphere in our house. Where before there's been resentment and criticism, you can feel it dying away in the presence of Christ." Another: "I've always been brought up a God-fearing man, but I would truthfully state that I learned more about my religion in half an hour today than I ever did in the years of Sunday School." A schoolboy wrote "I don't go to church now, but it might have been different if we'd had these plays some years ago."

The plays, being on radio and not on stage, did not need to have the licence of the Lord Chamberlain—though the BBC, characteristically, thought it necessary to consult him—and the veteran Minister Dr Scott Lidgett, in considering the impersonation of Our Lord, saw no difference between Robert Speaight speaking as Christ and a clergyman reading his direct words from the Gospels, in a church. The Archbishop of Canterbury, the Minister of Information, the Director-General of the Corporation, the Prime Minister himself, were all targets from private individuals or bodies like Mr H. H. Martin's ever-watchful Lord's Day Observance Society. However, not only was Miss Sayers grateful to Mr Martin for the publicity, but the Editor of the *Church of England Newspaper* added "I feel that this is all to the good because it attracts attention to the broadcasts."

The remarkable thing about the series is that so many years elapsed before it was published in book form. The radio series ran from December 1941 to October 1942—one of the darkest periods in our nation's history. But the text was not available (the BBC do not lend out scripts except under special circumstances) until it was published in 1966 by Victor Gollancz Ltd. By that time, Miss Sayers was dead. What can explain the incredible gap between performance and publication? During the year 1966 alone it was reprinted twenty-three times. Mr Gielgud was particularly proud of the Dedication:

"These plays are for Val Gielgud
who has made them his already."

Dorothy Sayers wrote a long introduction to the play-cycle, which was evidently intended for publication. She rightly states that there was no standard of comparison for such a venture—except possibly the Passion Play at Oberammergau, which is a rarity performed every ten years, and performed only for those tourists who have the money to attend personally: radio and television companies have tried for years, unsuccessfully, to obtain the rights of this closed (carpenter's) shop.

Something of the contemporary attitude of the playwright can be detected in her description of the primary characters. Herod the Great was "no monstrous enemy of God, he was a soldier of fortune and a political genius, a savage but capable autocrat." Matthew the Publican was "a contemptible little Quisling official" (again the contemporary phrase) fleecing his own countrymen in the name of the occupying power and enriching himself in the process till something came to change his heart, and not presumably his social status or his pronunciation." Pontius Pilate was "a provincial Governor faced with what is generally called Whitehall. . . . Caiaphas was the ecclesiastical politician appointed like one of Hitler's bishops by a heathen government. . . . The Elders of the Synagogue are there to be found in every parish council, always highly respectable, often quarrelsome, and sometimes in a crucifying mood. . . ."

As far as the language was concerned, Miss Sayers wrote that "no attempt has been made at a niggling antiquarian accuracy in trifles. The aim has rather been that of a Renaissance painting whose figures in their modern habits mingle familiarly with others."
She cites the example of the Wedding at Cana, which reveals some knowledge of Jewish marriages: the Last Supper with Eastern table-manners and the Passover ritual, and she added "There are hardly any Christian tragedies in plays as such. None in Shakespeare, one by Marlowe. Otherwise, I was breaking new ground in these plays."
One wonders if she knew what lasting impact the plays would have, any more than George Orwell might have guessed that an impact his *1984* would have, when shown on Television. As a book, it was remarkable enough. As a TV production, it created some of the public reaction to Orson Welles's radio programme, in the 1930s, of the Martians landing in New Jersey, when people ran screaming into the streets.
A characteristic final note from Miss Sayers's preface: "It is irresistibly tempting, but not kind or Christian, to mention the Lord's Day Observance Society and the Protestant Truth Society, who so obligingly did all our publicity for us at, I fear, considerable expense to themselves. Without their efforts the plays might have slipped by with comparatively little notice, being given at an hour inconvenient to grown-up listening.... Let us record the plain fact—the opposition did us good service and let our gratitude for that go where all gratitude is due."
There is an additional point, which must have been discussed in detail with Val Gielgud, as producer, about the dialect in which the characters were to speak. "All the Galilean people," she wrote, "ought to talk in the strong local dialect, and the Jerusalem people in another, while the Romans would have to be distinguished as to whether they were talking Latin to one another or striving to express themselves to the local inhabitants in bad Aramaic, or possibly colloquial Greek."
She added: "I don't want to land myself with Jesus and the disciples consistently speaking broad Scots, Irish, Welsh, Somerset or Mummerzet. It would be trying to the listener. We decided that Jesus and His mother should speak standard English, but that the multitude should be allowed to speak rough." The question then arose, "should the Disciples be allowed to speak standard English?" Sayers said, "in that case, they might sound like a University's

Mission to the East End! Or should Jesus appear to have a monopoly of refined speech, at the risk of appearing among his Disciples like a BBC announcer lecturing to the Workers' Educational Association?"

The expedient adopted was to "step up" the Disciples from the multitude, and also to "step up" among themselves, John and Judas, for example, speaking standard English, Peter being kept rougher, and Matthew being given a Cockney twang, to distinguish the county minor official from the country fishermen.

The cast-list for the first production was impressive, for any *Children's Hour* programme. In addition to Speaight, there was Cecil Trouncer as Herod, Valentine Dyall (as one of the Wise Men, but not in black), Stephen Jack, Gladys Young, Brian Powley, Abraham Sofaer, Lillian Harrison—the sort of cast one would have expected Val Gielgud to assemble for such an occasion.

But the most haunting memory of this famous series is, we think, the choice of the signature tune. A signature tune for the Passion of Christ? Yes, and not Bach this time. It isn't quite clear, at the moment, whether it was Gielgud who originally decided on a passage from Maurice Ravel's "Introduction and Allegro for Harp and Strings," but it became, with its mixture of peace and pity, an essential part of the production. Many radio shows have been built up on signature tunes, but no melody has introduced such a fine drama production of the most famous story in the history of mankind.

Very little is known about Dorothy Sayers's life. Like her fellow female writers of popular thrillers—Agatha Christie, Margery Allingham and Ngaio Marsh among them—she kept out of the limelight and just wrote her stories. But in 1959, Vera Brittain, another of the bright jewels in Somerville College's crown, recalled in her book *The Women at Oxford*[1] the "lasting impression" Miss D. L. Sayers made both on her contemporaries and the outside world in the years immediately preceding the first World War. In 1912 she was "a bouncing, affable, exuberant young woman, with a vivid and somewhat crude taste in clothes, which at least could not have been described as 'dowdy.'" A Miss Farnell, a contemporary, told how she "appeared at breakfast one morning, previous to an early lecture at the Taylorian, wearing a three-inch wide scarlet riband round her head, and in her ears a really remarkable pair of ear-rings: a scarlet and green parrot in a gilt cage pendant almost to each shoulder and visible right across the Hall." Her father was Headmaster of the

[1] G. Harrap & Co. Ltd, 1960.

Cathedral Choir School at Oxford and, Vera Brittain recalls, he created a quality in the Bach Choir which influenced its conductor, Sir Hugh Allen. Later, typically, she parodied Wimsey in a college revue sketch. But after 1935—and this is where the BBC comes into the picture—she gave up writing detective fiction and devoted herself to Theology and Anglo-Catholicism. Vera Brittain also points out that her first religious play, *The Zeal of Thy House*, preceded *The Man Born to be King*.

EASTER IN EUROPE

One other religious programme on the grand scale is worthy of attention, partly because it was broadcast under the banner of the Features Department. The Dorothy Sayers cycle came under the Drama Department—neither was under the control of the Department of Religious Broadcasting. This—probably the most ambitious and diverse religious broadcast BBC radio ever made, was entitled *Easter in Europe*, and was first transmitted, over a period of two hours, on Easter Day 1948. (A repeat performance, in a shorter and revised form, was made at Easter two years later.)

The original idea came from that voluble, enthusiastic, knowledgeable and popular interpreter of music, Alec Robertson. There have been a number of radio speakers who have been able to bring music home to the listener in a familiar and likeable way. Most would agree that Walford Davies began it, and his name must be linked with Percy Pitt, Filson Young, George Thalben-Ball, the celebrated organist, and others, through the years, to Anthony Hopkins and Joseph Cooper. The contribution of that incredible team, way out of this workaday world, of Anna Instone and Julian Herbage will be described under *Music Magazine*. Each contributed in his—or her—own way. No one will ever forget, in the Proms, the peculiar affection enjoyed by Sir Henry Wood and Sir Malcolm Sargent. They were not so much held in awe, as were men like Toscanini and Beecham and Furtwängler and Stokowski, as personally admired by people to whom good music had never previously meant anything at all. It was till then just "highbrow" stuff.

Beecham bridged the gap to some extent by his "Lollipop" arrangements. He would willingly play Sibelius's *Valse Triste* with the same attention he would pay to one of his symphonies. He would revive ravishing themes from little-known music of the eighteenth century. He was a showman, a wit, a raconteur, a man whose gusto for life and music was legendary. But they were the great ones: it remained for the BBC to bring music—through any medium from the Gersholm Parkington Quintet and Sandy Macpherson at the organ, to Toscanini conducting an electrifying performance of the *William Tell* overture.

Robertson had a wide variety of musical tastes. He was a Roman Catholic convert from the Anglican side, which made him particularly susceptible to Palestrina and plain-chant, as opposed to the robust old Wesleyan chants. But the initial impetus which gave *Easter in Europe* its attraction was the Lutheran J. S. Bach's *St Matthew Passion*, probably the greatest musical work ever achieved by man. Alec had the idea that the "Matt. Pass.," as we came to call it (in working days) could be used to tell the story of the Crucifixion. The events which led up to it were interleaved by the Gospel story, spoken, and the singing of choirs of many denominations at Eastertide in various parts of Europe, all specially recorded for the occasion.

This was the element in the idea which particularly appealed to a man like Gilliam, recently appointed Head of Features in his own right. Feature producers and reporters were already known as world travellers, from the time they became war correspondents. Gilliam and Alec Robertson got together. The European scene in all its magnitude and magnificence began to build up in their minds, and the programme, which had begun as little more than a performance of the St Matthew Passion, recorded on discs by the Philharmonic Choir in Hamburg, a city Bach often visited, with musical notes and readings, grew into one of the most ambitious programmes of all time, destined to be carried, in full, to most European countries, and across the US and Canada.

When an idea is basically good and tenable, anything can arise from it. When enough people believe in the idea, they can move mountains. This is what happened over *Easter in Europe*, as it had happened in *The Man Born to be King*. There were, of course, divisions of opinion as to the denominational importance of certain parts of it, and the team eventually responsible was probably the most remarkable variety, literally as well as liturgically, which ever attempted—and achieved—such a unity.

Alec Robertson and Barsley (who was an Anglican, with a father a Canon and Precentor of Liverpool Cathedral, a brother a Vicar, a cousin a Bishop) immediately found themselves at odds, from the sectarian point of view. Yet, with patience, all was sorted out. Laurence Gilliam brought in an Irish Protestant poet, W. R. Rodgers, to write a verse sequence throughout, varied with readings from the New Testament by Cyril Cusack, another Irishman. Knowing the strong Irish element in the Features group, colleagues were somewhat surprised to find that the whole production had not been handed over to Louis MacNeice, relative of the Bishop of Killaloe.

But, like Topsy, the programme just grew and grew. It became—like most of Gilliam images—a sort of Cecil B. de Mille production of Eastertide. Recordings were made, regardless of cost, at places like Ste Gudule in Brussels, where the conductor of the 200-voice choir argued about the price until a few seconds before they began Handel's Hallelujah from the *Messiah*; at Salzburg, where the choir of Mozart's own church sang his *Ave Verum*; at St Paul's in London, at St John Lateran in Rome, at the kirk in Kinlochleven in the Highlands of Scotland, at the Russian Orthodox Church in Paris, at the Greek Orthodox Church in Bayswater, at the Cathedral of Dijon in France, at a refugee camp of Latvians and Lithuanians and Poles in Schleswig-Holstein, at the Catholic Cathedral in Utrecht, Holland (where, under persuasion, the choir sang a Protestant setting of one of the Psalms of David), a choir in Denmark, the famous choir in the Royal Chapel at Windsor, and another in the village of Kidlington, Oxford. Thousands of voices were raised in honour of Easter.

The most remarkable contribution came, perhaps, from the Kuhn Choir in Prague. The Communist take-over of Czechoslovakia had just occurred, and the Kuhn Choir were scheduled to record the opening of Dvořák's *Stabat Mater*, live for the BBC on Easter Eve. The Russians were in charge of communications with Czechoslovakia from the moment of the *coup*. Without refusing the broadcast, they asked, as occupying powers, for the text or script of the broadcast. The following telegram was sent from the BBC to the USSR commandant, in Prague.

"Text reads: Stabat Mater dolorosa juxta crucem lachrymosa, dum pendebat filius. Message ends."

The Russians sat on this information for about four days, no doubt thinking it to be in code instead of Latin. Eventually permission was granted, and the last recording on direct line from Prague to London took place. At the end of it BBC control room called Prague. "Excellent reception. How are things?" Reply: "I used to be in BBC during the war. Good luck to you. I can say no more. Goodnight from Prague."

This is perhaps as dramatic a way as could indicate what can go on behind a programme of the calibre of *Easter in Europe, 1948*.

Barsley continues:

"The verse-sequence was in the predictable style of W. R. Rodgers. It had the rhymes and runes of the Celtic, Anglo-Saxon style of poetry. Rodgers was a strange character: he had all the compelling, Irish, here's-a-story approach. In his soft brogue he would hold you, even if you had other business to attend to. So when it came to the verses he wrote, you couldn't do other than accept—with exceptions. The exceptions were what the story was about, but all was solved at the time when Stephen Murray, that superb but shy actor whose voice is like a trumpet-call, read his lines. In many ways they were diffuse and diverse: they weren't what was expected, and will never live as great poetry in the style of Eliot. Cyril Cusack introduced his biblical texts, never faltering over a phrase, though we could have done with a man with more body to his voice. At one time it seemed that the Catholics and the Celts had taken over in what was one of the really great European programmes.

Transmission took place in Studio 4A at Broadcasting House. It was hard from a production point of view, because the cue-in, as we call it, from studio to disc, within the production end, was as split-second as the conducting of a symphony.

Probably few of those in the studio were Christians in the true, traditional sense, apart from one or two of the organizers. This was a Big Programme, scheduled from 2 p.m. to 4 p.m., Home Service, with network lines overseas. It was a complex job of work to be done. Once again the Panel Engineer was "Laddie" Ladbrook, the man known for many years in the BBC as the master-mind technically of the intricate, round-the-world Christmas Day programmes, which, for their time, were as complicated as landing men on the moon. For a total of four hours or more, his fingers never left the control knobs—a physical feat in itself—and though the cast was small and well experienced, to balance voices and music is one of the most difficult things in radio. Perhaps "Laddie," one of the cheerful, beer-loving boys, never imagined he'd get to know the St Matthew Passion so well.

Two of the most moving passages were the motet "O Vos Omnes" ("O, all ye who pass this way, behold and see, if there be any sorrow like unto my sorrow") sung by the choir of St John Lateran in Rome, and by contrast, a fresh, almost dainty, mediaeval "Alleluia" which brought to this country, for the first time, from Hilversum, the voices of the small Nederlands Kamerkoor, conducted by Felix de Nobel, a brilliant man from Amsterdam, who was to bring his Chamber Choir to England several times in later years. Perhaps equally poignant were the voices of the young refugees in Schleswig-Holstein, who sang "There is a Green Hill"—in English. They had only one copy of *Hymns Ancient and Modern* in their D.P. camp, and learned it from that.

The programme received a message of thanks from the American Forces' Network, which reported good reception, not only in Germany, but in the United States. Among listeners who sent letters was a factory worker who wrote: "Thank heavens some things can rise above national ideologies" and another who began "I'm a hard-bitten pressman, but this programme really moved me."

Before the great closing chorale of Bach, came W. R. Rodgers's final poem in the sequence:

> "Lord of the open tomb
> Resume and reimburse our silent wood
> This Easter Day, elaborate its saps
> Bid the bare tree burst into bloom, and fill
> With leaf the hungry gaps
> And in its head set the heart's singing-birds.
> And you who sang this day
> With such divine consent
> Employing every play
> Of art and instrument
> May all your ways be blessed and all your hearts content
> In Him."

VARIETY: THE *ITMA* STORY

The story of how Tommy, Ted and Francis came to work together has often been told, with variations. Let us accept the fact. But the most successful (and likeable) triumvirate in the whole history of broadcasting was made up of very diverse elements: Tommy Handley, already well-versed in radio sketches, with a wit as quick as his delivery, and a background of Liverpool, church school, voice in the choir and modest theatricals; Ted Kavanagh, with a background of New Zealand: a Roman Catholic but a radical with an admiration for G. K. Chesterton and an interest in medicine; Francis Worsley, son of a Canon, Public School, Oxford undergraduate at Keble College, BBC West Region producer with a sardonic smile—however did they combine?

Ted had already written scripts for Tommy, who had become well-known, particularly for his sketch "The Disorderly Room" and for his double act with Ronald Frankau. Francis had been asked to produce a documentary on the subject of Cheddar Caves, and considered that a bit of light relief might be obtained by including a comical tourist, so he obtained Tommy. That the three should get together was therefore largely an accident—and what a happy one for the public!

There was Tommy's sense of humour. His "Disorderly Room" act wasn't really what he wanted, but he couldn't find anyone to adapt themselves to his particularly English form of humour. There was Ted, who had a fabulous memory. He would sometimes, in his slow, indolent way, appear not to be taking an interest in what people were saying, rather be lost in thought. What he did was store away some chance remark or joke, which would somehow suddenly fit in on a future occasion: an invaluable asset to the eventual *ITMA* script. Nobody, in fact, knew just what Ted was thinking. So much the better. It all came out in the wash. Francis—well, Francis was the saturnine, apparently cynical one of the three, shrugging off an idea as beneath comment, then suddenly laughing—or rather, giggling—at another. His laugh was a great contrast to John Watt's shaking schoolboy-howler outburst, and when Francis gave a giggle, it usually meant he'd thought of something.

Each of them was necessary to the other two. When Tommy died, the show died with him. But it probably couldn't have carried on without either Ted or Francis. True, Francis, officially, was simply the BBC staff man who produced a weekly show called *ITMA*. But he was very much more than that, as Ronnie Waldman, who took over when Francis was ill, would agree. Many were the spectacularly successful individual parts in the show, but all were written by Ted, given pace and life by Francis—and they all revolved round Tommy, who gave them, in turn, their chance, never smothering them. No one was just a leg-man, a side-kick, a foil in *ITMA*. One line—two words —one catch-phrase, and they could be famous. Some, like Jack Train, already had reputations, but to be in *ITMA* in the great days was a thing all artists desired and never forgot.

To see the Triumvirate, the Trio, in conference was an experience in itself. They didn't shoo you away. They never tried their jokes on you. They were lost in their private world of fantasy, perhaps in the Paris Cinema in Lower Regent Street, London, or in a church hall at Clifton, Bristol. It was all the same to them. Francis might bring up a situation: Ted would pour a few puns over it: Tommy would sharpen it up into lightning phrases, like verbal machine-gun fire, and another piece of the weekly jigsaw puzzle would be temporarily in place—never permanently, until the red light went on for the show.

To read the first script of *ITMA*, after the series had re-established itself in wartime Bristol, is to realize one of its supreme virtues—topicality. Tommy immediately appears as the Minister of Aggravation and Mysteries, in the office of Twerps, just at the time when new Ministries were being formed by the dozen. Dickens would have loved that touch. There were not only Tommy's usual phrases like "Well, splash my spats" and "Butter my Bath bun," but Hitler going to the moon—"the higher the Führer." After all—Hitler had given the show its title. He was originally That Man. When Ronnie Waldman first took over the programme, he was puzzled—and it was Ronnie's job *not* to be puzzled, but to create puzzles—when Handley had a habit of disappearing just around 6 o'clock on the day of transmission. Then he found him in another room, listening to the News. There was always a chance that something might catch his ear, to be turned into a last-minute topical allusion.

A Snagge memory of Tommy's impromptu quickness took place in the comedian's other weekly programme *Handley's Half Hour*. "He had a way of pulling your leg unmercifully—and then getting you out of it. I was taking part in this programme: just a brief appearance, a line or two. Well, I said them, but I forgot to wait for the effects-boy to make the sound of a door opening, and Tommy said at once, 'How did you get in without opening the door?' and I was completely flabbergasted and stung by it, and then Tommy went on, explaining to the listeners, 'Oh, they haven't repaired the door properly this week. There's a gap, and I saw you crawl underneath it!' He'd do this—make a joke of it, and get a laugh."

Snagge calls attention to his kindness—this was well known to many people—but also to his aloofness. "He'd come and have a drink with you willingly, yes, and greet you in the hall, but he never, to my knowledge, invited anyone to come out with him. He'd just do his disappearing act. His favourite recreation, according to Francis Worsley, was reading; his favourite subject, crime and detection."

Another landmark came in 1942:

"I remember the delight—and awe—with which an invitation to Windsor Castle was received, for Princess Elizabeth's birthday. A royal command performance—the first for a BBC show! But for John Watt, it presented a problem. *ITMA* was a radio programme, and nothing else. Ted, Tommy, and Francis had never harboured any ambition for it to be anything else, and indeed, it could never succeed in any other medium. But with his usual instinct, John hit upon the right formula—that the performance should seem to be put on exactly as it always happened. No props, no fancy costumes, no scenery, no learning of scripts. The effects team to be there in action, famous door and all. Done that way, it really *was ITMA*, and would fascinate our royal hosts, as such. They knew the programme well.

"It wasn't always that way. The normal waiting-list for the public to see *ITMA* ran into tens of thousands. I was often asked for tickets, and could sometimes give them, but with them I gave the advice, 'If you've got any illusions about it, I wouldn't go, if I were you, because you'll probably be disappointed. There'll be no dressing-up. Tommy will appear holding a script: Jack Train doesn't look a bit like Colonel Chinstrap: the effects look like a lot of old iron'—and so on. But they still wanted to go. Perhaps they'd heard about the royal visit, or the warm-up Ted would give to get the audience in the mood before the red light flickered and went steady. It was often as funny as the script."

At Windsor Castle, Tommy had been in typical form. The party called, as requested, at a side door, which was opened by a royal flunkey. Handley peered around and asked "Have you got any good digs here?" This was taken in very good part, and in the room where a buffet lunch was served, Tommy looked round at the array of royal servants (most of them in service uniform) who had been called in to serve the party, and said to the late Eric Miéville, the King's Private Secretary, "What happens if nobody eats *anything*?"

The script was, of course, studded with royal allusions. When Mrs Mopp said the traditional "I brought this for you, sir," Tommy asked "What's that? It looks like the Crown Jewels covered in custard!" The show, of which the *ITMA* performance was the climax, proved a great success, and when, five years later, the royal party visited the

Concert Hall at Broadcasting House for the twenty-fifth Anniversary of the BBC, *ITMA* was performed again, this time being televised into the bargain. Tommy, looking at the orchestra, all in evening dress, made the typical remark "I wonder what the waiters at the Athenaeum are wearing tonight?" On that occasion, to show he hadn't forgotten, King George VI said he was sorry to have missed the previous broadcast show. Tommy replied "Oh, but there was that wedding, wasn't there?" and the King said "Yes, you know how it is with weddings. . . ." The marriage was that of his daughter Elizabeth, and the first royal *ITMA* had been part of her birthday present. His Majesty also caused a laugh by asking if Mona Lott was any relation to Gordon Crier, and the Queen asked Horace Percival, "Did you bring any of your saucy postcards?"

We have not mentioned any of the catch-phrases which were a famous feature of the series, but they were known to all, from the King downwards, and we all had our favourites, from "I go—I come back," "Can I do you now, sir?" "It's being so cheerful as keeps me going," "Good morning—nice day," "TTFN," and "After you, Claude," followed by the inevitable "No—after *you*, Cecil."

Tommy Handley was universally liked: certainly not only in Liverpool, that cradle of so many comedians, from "Almost a Gentleman" (Billy Bennett, star at the famous Argyle theatre in Birkenhead, across the Mersey river), Robb Wilton—remembered particularly for his monologue beginning "The Day War Broke Out" —Ted Ray, Ken Dodd, to favourites of today like Jimmy Tarbuck. Barsley, a fellow Merseysider, adds:

"The mother of 'Mrs Handley's boy, mother's pride and joy,' lived all her long life in the suburb of Garston, near the gasworks, and whenever he came to Liverpool Tommy never failed to visit her. He had cause to be her pride and joy. After a broadcast, he would put a call through to her, and to his wife, singer Jean Allistone. Every year Tommy would take his mother to the Liverpool pantomime at the Moss Empire Theatre. On one occasion the Dame, comedian Dave Morris, spotted Tommy and introduced him to the audience. He stood up in response to the applause, and his mother, who in later years had become extremely deaf, pulled at his coat and said: 'Sit down, Tom, everyone's looking at you!'" There were, too, many Liverpool references in the script. I remember, as a schoolboy, making a family trip by ferry-boat up to New Brighton, perhaps on the

Iris or the *Daffodil*, ships given the proud title "*Royal*" after the part they played in the attack on Zeebrugge during the First World War. On the pier stood a one-legged diver, who made his plunge into the Mersey just as the boat berthed. He would be up at the top of the gangway, cap in hand, saying hoarsely "Don't forget the diver, sir—don't forget the diver!" This, exactly imitated in accent by Horace Percival, became one of *ITMA*'s great catch-phrases.

Tommy's accent had a northern sharpness, but it was not "scouse," a word which has now become a household one (there is the Scouse Press, a publishing house which has even translated parts of the Bible into the Liverpool dialect, and it is familiar with Liverpool "pop" musicians like the Beatles, who talk unaffectedly about "jam butties"). Scouse is hardly a mellifluous way of speaking, but it has its students, who would appreciate the remark of one woman about another in a Liverpool tram—"It's not fur—she's wearing fairs."

But it was the *ITMA* team which first made it famous. Tommy recalled that, after staying the night at Liverpool's mournful Stork Hotel, he was woken by a tousled head suddenly appearing round the door, saying in scouse "Was you the gentleman what wanted to be woken up at seven o'clock with a cup of tea?" "Yes, that's me," Tommy replied, and the voice went on "Well, it's eight o'clock and it's coffee!"

Derek Guyler, who had been at Liverpool College with Barsley, seemed the ideal choice, and entered the *ITMA* scene, with the words "Well, fancy that! They don't tell nobody nothing nowadays, do they?" His name, Frisby Dyke, delighted the whole listening public, not least those who had known, in pre-war years, Frisby, Dyke and Co., gentlemen's outfitters (called the "Sunshine Store" because it was the first to use natural daylight illumination). After one of the raids on Liverpool, nothing remained of it except a white notice, like a tombstone on the rubble, announcing that here had been Frisby, Dyke and Co. Walking past it one day, down shattered Bold Street, Tommy, Francis and Ted came upon the notice. The name was enough to christen the new character. Derek still has one of the firm's catalogues in his possession—a precious relic indeed.

Tommy made many friends outside the *ITMA* circle and radio itself. He was much in demand for public appearances, though he had none of the smooth, fulsome charm that some famous figures adopt for the occasion. It was as natural a style as that of his fellow-Liverpudlian Ken Dodd.

BILLY SMART

One of the more bizarre of Handley's occasions was the opening of the first circus of showman Billy Smart, at Southall on 5th April 1946. Barsley can claim to have "discovered" Billy, and broadcast a brief obituary on his death.

The discovery was made during a series called *People's Pleasures*, which investigated the return of show business and popular entertainment after the deprivations and austerities of war. It ranged from the big Holiday Camp in Clacton to a village fete at Cassington, near Oxford, and one obvious subject was dealt with under the title *Swings and Roundabouts*. The Big Wheel, the Gallopers, the Whip, the Swirl, the Ghost Train, the Dodgems, the shooting alleys and the booths of "grafters" with their "swag"—tea-sets and giant dolls and real enamel saucepans which were hardly ever won—all were returning. Advertisements crowded the pages of *The World's Fair*, the showmen's own paper.

During their researches they found a firm making fairground machinery, Lang Wheels and Co., who told the BBC men "Look for a bloke called Billy Smart. He's pulling on at Putney next week, and he's the coming man in the trade." On the big field at the top of Putney Hill, the travelling show was already in full swing (and roundabout) when they arrived. At the side stood the huge waggon of the man who came to be known as "The Guvnor." (These opulent vehicles are never called caravans by fairground people.)

Built of handsome wood, with a roof like an American railway car, it had two doors, but one was approached by a flight of steps and flanked by hanging baskets of flowers. The door handle was of crystal glass. Inside, painted scenes which represented Venice and Egypt, vases in hectic colours, ornaments in mother-of-pearl contrasted with a plain kitchen range and a big black kettle on the hob. In a chair of honour sat a big burly man of about eighteen stone, his cigar jutting upwards like the mainsprit of a sailing ship, a black homburg on the back of his head. He looked remarkably like Ernie Bevin.

"Automatically speaking," Billy Smart said, "welcome all." The BBC were offered eels, whelks, and milk-and-whisky by his wife Dolly. On a tour of the show, he told how he laid out a fairground.

"Automatically speaking," he began, "it's done by footage. I takes it by the yard. With me little whitewash brush. Then the waggons make a ring, see, with the grafters, so as to keep the public inside, once they get in. And outside I 'as the Flash. [This is apparently a separate act, such as a juggler or high-rope walker, seen free of charge, as a sample of the standard in the show.] I once had a high-wire man got stuck on the wire. Fright, see? And when he fell and came off, and we went over, we didn't know if he was dead or indifferent."

By now Producer Peter Eaton was getting to know Billy's style of talking, which is what a radio interviewer or producer must know. He referred to one of the machines as "automental" (and it was, in fact, automatic and ornamental) and when we came to record him later that summer evening, his first reaction to the round microphone was "take that f——ing frying pan out of my face!" But there's one of his summings-up on being a showman which represents a rare gem in a style no script-writer could have made up.

"Me being the most enterprising as regards on the road," he said, "I say there's no such thing as a wet Saturday. There can't be. The kind of patrons we actually depends upon solely, they can't 'old their money. They can't 'old it till the Monday. So if we haven't it to come Saturday, we don't 'ave it to come Monday, definite, no." He paused and then added: "I'm highly strung in that direction."

Billy Smart's first radio appearance was in *People's Pleasures* on 10th September 1945. Another fairground character in the programme was a maker of Dodgem cars, Jack Shillan, again an out-of-this-world character who also built speedboats. He, too, made a fortune, and later invested in an hotel in the Bahamas. But on that day, in between rehearsals for a radio show (the BBC budget for which was about £120), Jack did a deal with Billy for about £10,000 worth of Dodgems. It was quite an occasion in its own quiet way.

So was the opening of the Circus less than a year later, at Southall, and this is where Tommy Handley comes in, literally. It has always been a tradition in the circus world that no one can create a successful ring unless the circus is in his family. Billy Smart proved this to be wrong. He had never been content to be a travelling showman based on Ealing, though he claimed "I am an Ealing-ite and I've been out ragboning." His ambition was to build up a mammoth circus in the country, and he succeeded, putting the Mills Brothers and Chipperfields out of the business on the way. At the time, the ambition seemed as vast as Billy's own bulk. "What do you think of my Bill?" his mother asked Barsley, in the waggon on the opening night, ostrich plumes nodding in her hat, "he ain't bad for one of my twenty-two, is'e? But he was the only one who was in the show business, 'e was, and the only one which pulled on and drawed off on the commons, 'e was." At the end of her speech, Billy, who was visibly moved, thrust two pound-notes into her hand, and said, "That's it, me old dear, that'll make you feel better." And automatically speaking, as it were, he shouted to his faithful henchman, "Sid! Bring over the Daimler for mother."

Billy's whole family, in the showman's tradition, had worked with him on the fairground: Ronnie with the diesels, David, the all-purpose charmer, young Billy, already presenting the "high school" horses, as Billy called them, Dolly on the Swirl, Hazel on the Whip, Rita on the Big Wheel, Rosie, pretty, dark Rosie, on the Dodgems, and so on. Mrs Smart was always with them.

Within a few months, plans for the first circus were already in being, and Billy said to Barsley "You've had your eyes to work in that radio business. There's some big names. 'Ow about getting the biggest—'ow about getting that Tommy 'andley and his gang to open the show with an act? Automatically speaking, I thought of you, like, to sound them out." Barsley contacted Francis Worsley, who, when he heard about Billy's cheek in challenging a world hitherto dominated by the Mills Brothers with their Lords and Ladies at the annual Olympia lunch, seemed highly amused and genuinely impressed. A meeting was arranged between Francis, Tommy, Ted and the unknown circus pioneer and as a result, a deal was struck, after several subsequent negotiations. Billy agreed to pay £400 for a ten-minute show, including all the main *ITMA* characters, and a handshake between Tommy and Billy was photographed. In 1946, £400 was a lot of money, but after that night, despite pouring rain and primitive conditions, Billy never looked back, and came into his full triumph, thanks largely to the patronage of BBC Television. He ended up a millionaire, but on that first business deal he paid his deposit in the traditional showman's way, with two of his sons carrying sacks of silver coins into an astonished Ted Kavanagh's office—a touch worthy of *ITMA* itself. Billy Smart was certainly highly strung in that direction, too.

DEATH OF HANDLEY

At the memorial service in St Paul's Cathedral—the first ever to be held there for a comedian, Dr Wand, then Bishop of London, said this of Tommy Handley (who on the first announcement of his death was described as *Thomas* Handley!).

"He was one whose genius transmuted the copper of our common experience into the gold of exquisite foolery. His raillery was without cynicism, his nature without malice. Who could tell how great a benefit he conferred upon the nation in the days of its grimmest endeavour, as he brought week by week to millions a flow of irresistible laughter, and the iridescent froth and bubble of the professional jester? From the highest to the lowest in the land people had found in his programmes an escape from their troubles and anxieties into a world of whimsical nonsense."

Sir William Haley wrote, in the *Radio Times*:

"He had that rare gift which few are born with—and most never acquire—of being able to broadcast sincerity. As you listened to him you felt the personality of an essentially friendly and good man."

JACK TRAIN

Jack Train always wanted to join *ITMA* as soon as he realized, in Bristol, what an inspiring show it was going to be. It wasn't that Jack was just looking for a job: he had no need to. But gleefully in his autobiography this talented Devonian, who was putting up with things like the rest of them at Bristol (he shared digs with Francis Dillon and his wife Tanya, which meant he had good food and good fun) relates how he created Fünf the spy. He had visited the local cinema and seen a film with the sinister Akim Tamiroff in it. After this, he dropped into a local pub, and found a group discussing the same film, which centred round espionage. They were having a go at imitating Akim's accent.

Just at that moment, by sheer chance, Francis Worsley came over to Jack and said "I want to put a spy into *ITMA*. Would you like to do it?" On an impulse (Jack's beer-glass was empty) he put it sideways to his mouth, and spoke to Francis that way. We can just imagine that Worsley laugh. The idea, the spy-voice, was taken at once, but the welter of suggested names stopped when Francis heard his son counting in German, "Ein, zwei, drei, vier, FÜNF . . . !" Mission completed: a new part and a new laugh. Jack also took half that pantomime-horse act of Claude and Cecil.

Colonel Chinstrap, Snagge declares, came later, and the character was based on one of Snagge's elderly cronies, a true Major, ex-Indian army, in the great tradition. The alcoholic pun is said to have come from a cartoon in a *Punch* of 1880. The scene is a train at a station:

"*Guard:* Virginia Water!

Old Man: Gin and water? Dash it, I don't mind if I do!"

To the Colonel was later added Major Mundy, played by Carleton Hobbs, and Ted Kavanagh's outrageous sense of Blimpish humour did the rest. Not for nothing was cartoonist David Low a fellow New Zealander: he and Ted knew their Blimp stuff, and Chinstrap came to be one of the few *ITMA* characters to soldier on after Tommy's death.

Jack was equally pleased with *Twenty Questions*, in which he played an entirely unpredictable but intuitive part. His guesses were not always wild or wide of the mark. He recalls a royal occasion—the Buckingham Palace staff party, when a piece of paper, with the name of the object on it, reached the King's hand. George VI burst out laughing, and on an impulse Jack cried "The Privy Purse!" He had got it in one. At the time of the BBC's Silver Jubilee in 1947, when the royal party visited Broadcasting House, young Princess Margaret said to him "You're in *Twenty Questions* too, aren't you, Mr Train? Actually, I like it better than *ITMA*, but I daren't tell my parents so!"

Jack had more than his share of ill-health, but after one bout of illness he was allowed to return to just one part—Chinstrap. This insistence was partly caused by a royal remark on another occasion, when the King asked "Where's Jack Train these days?"

He will be greatly missed, particularly by the Savage Club, and by sinistrals, of all people, for Jack, like Ben Warriss, had been President of the Left-Handed Golfers' Club.

PETER DUNCAN

In Town Tonight will always be linked with the portly, flamboyant figure of Peter Duncan, who revealed something of the self-confidence which Alan Whicker has shown on television. Introducing his radio story[1] he declared:

"I have been intimately concerned with stars of every nationality and from every branch of the profession. I have started young artists out on their careers. It is my concern to entertain the audience who are, in fact, the life-blood of show business."

Duncan joined the BBC in 1934, and was assigned to work on *In Town Tonight* during his first year, but not until twelve years later did he become boss of the programme, and as well publicized as its signature tune by Eric Coates. He will go down to history in some people's minds as the man who sacked Gilbert Harding, the regular

[1] *In Show Business Tonight* (Hutchinson, 1954).

interviewer, for John Ellison, who was equally expert but more amenable. Gilbert anyhow would have been off after higher things, as it proved. Peter Duncan did his training in several of the wartime favourites, including *Band Waggon*, *Happidrome* and *Workers' Playtime*, but not until he ran *ITT* did he produce show-business stars by the hatful, until his book reads like a continual Royal Command Performance—Bing, Bob, Danny (Danny Kaye's first interview, in which he took over the production and the final announcement, is a classic), Anne Shelton, Joy Nichols, Elsie and Doris, Robb Wilton, Emlyn Williams, Michael Redgrave, George Formby, Errol Flynn, Patrice Wymore, Linda Darnell, Richard Todd, Tallulah Bankhead, Frances Day, Rock Hudson, Sir Arthur Bliss—he had everyone except royalty, and in this modern age of monarchy no doubt that could have been arranged.

In the last chapter of his book, entitled "The Show Must Go On," he writes: "To go into entertainment is to turn life into one vast game of chance. A career becomes, at best, nothing more than a game of poker. . . ." Well, as we know, *In Town Tonight* did not go on, nor did Peter Duncan as its editor. But that, as he would be the first to admit is, if not Show Business, at least BBC business.

RONNIE WALDMAN AND OTHERS

One experience we have gained in meeting so many radio characters during these years: partnership need not spoil real friendliness, not only towards partners but towards the general public. Think of the Hulbert/Courtneidges, the Lyons, the Bradens, the Warner/Waters, the Murdoch/Hornes. There have been notable break-ups, such as Tony Hancock and Sid James, but many team programmes have continued through thick and thin.

Jack Warner can look back on one of the happiest of careers. He started a double-act with Jeff Darnell, a Sutton schoolmaster, as long ago as 1935, but it was the war which gave him his chance, in *Garrison Theatre*, with "beanpole" Charlie Shadwell, and his orchestra. Jack had never considered himself much of a writer, and didn't originate his role as the Tommy chatting up his "Little Gel" (Joan Winters) the "chocolates–cigarettes" girl in the show, but he wrote all his own personal material such as the celebrated letters to Brother Sid, and his job as "bunger-up of rat-holes." He joined the Huggett family in their radio series, and then Ted (Lord) Willis, as unlike a Lord as Lord

Vintage '47

"Do You Remember?", the BBC's 25th Birthday Programme, 14 November 1947, produced by Francis Worsley and Michael Barsley, introduced by John Snagge. Left to right: The late Sir Harold Nicolson, Wynford Vaughan Thomas, Mabel Constanduros, Stuart Hibberd, John Snagge, the late Ted Kavanagh

BBC Copyright Photograph

John Snagge commentating at Henley (1949)

Radio Times Hulton Picture Library

Oxford Sinks! (exclusive)

The only close-up picture of the Oxford crew sinking in the Boat Race of 1951 was taken by a BBC Television camera. Hopeful press photographers were further upstream

BBC Copyright Photograph

Christmas Day Round the World

At the panel: Peggy Lupton, Secretary, Laurence Gilliam, Head of Features, and "Laddy" Ladbrook, Senior Studio Manager

BBC Copyright Photograph

Michael Barsley, with portable tape-recorder and local hat called "The Dome of Discovery," interviews Trevor Howard on location for the film *Outcast of the Islands* in Ceylon, while on the Christmas Day programme (1951)

Times of Ceylon

This drawing by Michael Barsley was sent out from the War Report studio to all BBC War Correspondents in the field for New Year's Day, 1945

Barsley Sauce

One of Michael Barsley's many drawings made during BBC programmes. This one depicts the studio during the South Africa "Royal Tour" series in 1947. John Snagge (right) introduced the series

"We're only here for the Beer-match."

An unofficial BBC cricket team arrives at Cassington, near Oxford, in style. Try and pick out George Colouris, R. D. Smith, Ronnie Waldman, Michael Barsley, Leigh Crutchley, Alan Burgess, and—can it be Hugh Carleton-Greene bringing up the rear? (1946)

Crown Copyright

Early recording-team on location on the Norfolk Broads, with E-type disc gear (1946). Group includes engineer "Jumbo" Jackson, John Bridges, Michael Barsley, John Lane

"Under the command of General Eisenhower, Allied naval forces, supported by strong air forces, began landing Allied armies this morning on the northern coast of France."

This ends the reading of Communique Number One from Supreme Headquarters, Allied Expeditionary Force.

D Day Announcement
Originally intended for two voices, one American, the final announcement was made by John Snagge alone

Drama and Variety 145

(George) Sanger, chose him for the lead as a policeman in *The Blue Lamp*, since when Jack has been almost continually on the beat. His policeman's lot has been a happy one; so have the careers of his sisters, Elsie and Doris Waters, whose "Gert and Daisy" rank among the immortals and who can still draw capacity houses.

Kenneth Horne, who died so unexpectedly at a Producers' and Writers' Guild Ball, was a man who combined boardroom and bawdry, partly in business, partly in show-business. He found the perfect counterpart in Dickie Murdoch, and there was always about him the air of a man who lived in two worlds and liked both of them. No one had a better sense of timing in comedy, not even the split-second Tommy Handley.

Looking back on the great days of radio Variety Department in retrospect, Ronnie Waldman admits to being taken by surprise on joining the BBC.

"I belonged to the theatre, working every night. I'd hardly heard any radio, but I was conscious that there was something new and different the moment I entered the place—the growth of the creativity hadn't gone very far, but it was there, all right."

His call had come almost perfunctorily. One hears of so many examples of chance meetings, luck, the old-boy word passed round, nepotism, frontal assault, careful campaigning, in joining the Corporation that Ronnie's entry seemed almost too easy. John Watt said he'd heard of him and would like to meet him at St George's Hall, Variety Headquarters. Ronnie thought John wanted to buy some songs he had written, so he took them along with him. "But instead, there was this little elf of a man peering at me over his desk and saying 'D'you want to be a producer here?' So I picked myself up off the floor, and said 'Yes, please.' "

Sancta simplicitas! But obviously, an elflike John Watt already knew something about Ronnie's background. He had been at Snagge's college at Oxford (Pembroke)—but in Barsley's years, and the latter remembers him chiefly as a pianist, playing tunes like *A Little White Gardenia*, as well as being a member of the OUDS. He had also written two revues. The fact that he knew nothing about radio variety, or producing, wouldn't have mattered at all to his future boss, who had brought into the department an atmosphere very different from that of Eric Maschwitz.

"John," Ronnie sums up, "was primarily a journalist, with a journalist's approach, and he wanted to hit the headlines with it. He knew the Press, and exactly what time the evening papers went to bed every day, and therefore exactly what time to release a story about a new radio show. But that didn't mean he ignored impresarios like George Black when it came to finding artists: in fact, he learned one great thing from him—the art of construction."

With John Watt's name must immediately be connected that of "Pep"—Harry S. Pepper—whose name in turn was associated in those days with Doris Arnold, presenter of one of the most popular record programmes, *These You Have Loved*. The melody certainly lingered on in her case. In comparison Watt always gave the impression of representing a pugnacious side, fighting administration as his variety predecessors had done, with Pepper the more gentle, easy-going type. Ronnie disagrees, by reminding us of the day Harry Pepper, who had been an outside contributor to variety for years, in series like *The Stage Revolves*, and in concert parties, was invited "inside," for an interview with Admiral Carpendale.

"He was shown into his office, and Carpendale seemed very busy at his desk, and didn't even look up. Well, Pep didn't like this at all, so he pushed aside a few things and put his umbrella and bowler-hat on the desk, sat down, and opened a newspaper. This rather shook Carps, who put away his fountain-pen, and said, 'Now, Mr Pepper, I understand that you've applied to join us,' whereat Pep replied, 'No, no, that's not it at all. I understand that you've applied for me to join *you*, and after what I've seen this morning, I'm not sure that I want to.'"

This shot across the bows roused the Admiral's sense of humour, and Pep was duly enrolled in the ship's company. The partnership of Watt and Pepper went on, in Ronnie's phrase, "like a steam-roller."

Each relied heavily on the other, for each had a particular role to fill. Pepper's great contribution lay in the fact that he had worked with so many of the artists in show business. He'd been one of the original party of the *Co-Optimists*, and had spent years at Drury Lane, for instance. So the stars, the troupers whom the BBC wanted, knew him and trusted him. "They didn't know John," Ronnie adds, "but once they'd met him, they took to him, because he made them laugh." The primary object of both of them was to make contact with the radio listeners, something hardly ever attempted before. Not the contact of *In Town Tonight* which Maschwitz started, or of *Billy Welcome* and *Have a Go!*, which conquered the North with Wilfred

Pickles. Not, in other words, direct audience participation, but indirect.

Waldman, though a comparative newcomer, could see this happening very clearly in the development of a magazine programme, out of what was originally *Monday Night at Seven*. Maschwitz had bequeathed to the department the idea of an hour-long show divided into four separate performances. It didn't work. Watt and Pepper sat down to try and make it work, and Pep came up with the suggestion for the first-ever radio Quiz in the programme (it was to develop into Ronnie's well-known *Puzzle Corner*) and a detective serial—Inspector Horneleigh, with Ernest Dudley writing a weekly episode for S. J. Warmington to act, and for listeners to solve.

Down in the basement of Broadcasting House is a large space in which, during the War, the control-room was housed. Above is a gallery, from which visitors on a conducted tour of the building can look down on the engineers at work. On pre-war nights, this gallery looked down on two studios, BA and BB, where the Monday night programme was produced. The hour of seven was first chosen because artists were often free at that time, since theatres started at half past eight or later (see Noel Coward's *Tonight at 8.30* and Herbert Farjeon's revue *Nine Sharp*). Studio BA became a sort of club, with stars like Jack Buchanan, and Bea Lillie and Cecily Courtneidge, perhaps not even in the act, but dropping in for a chat. The show eventually became *Monday Night at Eight* and was broadcast from Bristol, but the pattern remained the same. Even when, in the end, an audience was allowed in, there was to be no laughter or applause. The real audience was listening at home.

One series to have an uncertain start was *Band Waggon*, a fact which may seem incredible to those who remember the Arthur Askey–Richard Murdoch partnership, with extraordinary events taking place in an imaginary radio flat, and the non-participating but ever-menacing figures of Mrs Bagwash and her daughter Nausea. John Watt had been in and out of the tiny office which Ronnie shared with that burly, amiable character Gordon Crier, discussing this and probing that and in particular doubting the assumption that a dance-band programme was all the public wanted. It was apparently one of the first pronouncements of the newly-fledged Listener Research Department that this, on inquiry, was not necessarily so. Which new ingredients were, then, required? To liven things up, John Watt tried a compère, also a comedian, and a linking script by Vernon Harris, later a producer. This, Ronnie admits, was a near disaster. It was only when Harry Pepper was called in that, with his deeper knowledge, the problem was solved. Comedian and compère were to be complementary. The engagement of Arthur Askey is part of his life story. With Murdoch, discovered by Gordon Crier in the early television days, as his foil, *Band Waggon* reached a high place in what we would now call the Top Ten, and gave to the listening world one of the first of the radio catch-phrases which were to be repeated by people in all walks of life, Askey's "Ay-thang-yew!"

Failure to success: a pleasant thought, but not achieved without hard thinking. Pepper, says Waldman, didn't like individual scriptwriters as such, working alone. "He believed in a sit-round. You had to have brains bouncing off each other: this is the way the sparks flew. So we all used to sit, six or seven of us in a tiny office at the top of St George's Hall, and somebody would say, 'Well, what shall we do next week?' and somebody else would say, 'Well, let's ... let's ... let's launch a battleship!' OK, so everyone started talking at once, mad ideas raining down, with little Penny Worth, the secretary Gordie and I shared, sitting there and writing down what she thought was funny —and that was the script. We didn't know we were creating the first situation-comedy ever, nor—and this is where Harry Pepper's genius for construction came in—that out of the entire one-hour show, Arthur and 'Stinker' Murdoch never appeared for more than sixteen minutes, in separate episodes."

It is worth dwelling at length on this partnership of Watt and Pepper because between them they both provided a stimulus and set a pattern. This is in no way to suggest that other popular shows were an imitation, or used the same ingredients. *ITMA*, everyone admits, was in a class by itself, for the reasons we have already given. Ronnie Waldman is proud of the months in which he produced it during Francis Worsley's illness.

JOHN WATT

John Watt's resignation from his Variety job came as a surprise. Many thought he would have made another famous name for himself on television, but he never repeated his earlier efforts. When he died, his friends particularly remembered the John Watt who had lived simply at his country house in Essex.

Arkesden is a picturesque village. The local station, with a convenient and much-frequented pub outside, is Audley End. It was from this station that his wife Angela saw John off for the last time. The telephone number of "Watt's Folly"—Clavering 200—was easy to remember and very often used. Angela and John had found their "dream cottage" as long ago as 1934, and John had tossed the innkeeper landlord for the price—£140 or £150—and had won. But one tenant, paying a rent of only 2s. 9d., wouldn't budge for a long time. Ask anyone in Arkesden about the story of "Watt's Folly," and they will tell you in a variety of ways. Ask, particularly, the writer C. Gordon Glover, whose monthly programmes on the countryside have graced —there is no other word—the radio for many years, with his narration colourful but never exaggerated, with the art concealing the art, as in Harold Nicolson talk. Gordon Glover found in the BBC Variety Chief a quality which the showbiz world knew nothing about.

The Glovers—his wife Modwena Sedgwick writes children's books and sells antiques—were near neighbours of the Watts; and though they were not in exactly the same branch of the BBC, they were often together. It was Gordon who wrote the introduction to Angela's book and this tribute to him in the local paper.

"There were two John Watts and I knew them both—the hard-driving BBC Director of Variety in the spotted bow-tie with the intuitive talent for shaping great entertainment, and the other one in corduroys and neckerchief, who played with trains and was a baby at Christmas. The John whom I shall remember with deepest affection was the one who, on Christmas morning, paid a call upon each of his village friends, who lighted his house like a stage-set and was fain to weep when shepherds watched...."

Unknown though he may be to the new generation, Gordon Glover is probably right in describing him as a "one-hundred-per-cent radio man, probably the greatest all-rounder within his field which broadcasting has ever known, or is likely to know again." Should we, then, quarrel with the dictum he laid down, when appearing on his own *In Town Tonight*?

"No one ever discovered anybody; if they've talent, they'll get there in the long run. No one who isn't any good ever made good."

ARTHUR ASKEY

It is not fair to say of Arthur Askey that he has small feet (size six) and a big head: though he might well say this about himself, having been quoted as saying "a comic gets his biggest laugh when the laugh is on him."

With Arthur Bowden Askey the Liverpool background of Toxteth Park must be included, and the connection is with Tommy Handley. They were born not far from each other, Tommy six years before Arthur. Both sang in choirs, Arthur's being the more remarkable career. Barsley adds: "My late father was the first Precentor of Liverpool Cathedral, the third largest in the world. It was intended, by Bishop Chavasse, to be a great centre for preaching, but the edifice the City Fathers decided on—altering Giles Gilbert Scott's original, more graceful twin-towered building—was so vast and empty and echoing that in the earlier years, before the study of acoustics developed, preachers found great difficulty in being heard at all. The echo duration was then seven seconds. Now, with the nave, it is ten. The Cathedral therefore became the setting for great choral services, and the choir one of the finest in the country."

Among the choirmen was Arthur Askey. He had begun his singing career as a boy, being the first soprano soloist at the opening of the Lady Chapel in 1910, before a distinguished gathering, and he calls this "my most memorable performance." He remembers Barsley's father as "the man who said he went bald at the age of thirty." Harold Wilson, our local MP at one time, said the same thing, so it must have been one of Canon Barsley's favourite stories. What is puzzling is how the now adult Askey (five foot three and a half inches) managed to see over the choir stalls. Perhaps he stood on a hassock. Another member of the choir was TV producer Dennis Vance.

"Big-Hearted" Arthur went to Liverpool Institute school, took a job in the Education offices of the Corporation and made his first stage appearance in the Electric Theatre at Colchester. He had previously toured with Tommy Handley in concert parties during the First World War. Various other engagements followed. The Little Fellow with the Big Glasses (he had begun with pince-nez as a gag, and got a laugh out of losing them) joined a company touring Shanklin, Hastings, and Margate. At one of these he was spotted, in 1938 by Ronnie Waldman and Gordon Crier. "We spotted *two* naturals, in fact, in Shanklin," says Ronnie. "One was Trinder, the other Askey. We were asked 'Which one would you like?' We said 'We don't know. It's a toss-up. Try Trinder.' Well, Tommy Trinder wasn't available, so we invited Arthur Askey, and we couldn't have made a better choice."

The measure of his programme's popularity can be judged by a wartime remark made in the House by a Minister (it is attributed by one source to Sir John Simon, by another to Sir John Anderson, Home Secretary): "Things are getting back to normal—*Band Waggon* is back on the air next Wednesday."

Though Askey never made the success in films of, say, a Norman Wisdom, he made an unforgettable impact on Television, and the use he made of the intimacy of the medium for the knowing aside to the audience (both seen and unseen) has been imitated ever since. Like Tommy, he has always been a great favourite with the Royal Family. Robert Hirst quotes a meeting in the interval of his wartime pantomime at the Palace Theatre in London in 1941.[1]

"The Princesses (fifteen-year-old Elizabeth and eleven-year-old Margaret) had produced their own pantomime at Windsor that Christmas. Proudly they told 'Big-Hearted Arthur' about it. 'It was a good pantomime, wasn't it, Mummy?' they asked. The Queen smiled indulgently. 'Yes, it was—but I am afraid there were a lot of old jokes in it.' The faces of the Princesses dropped. But 'Big-Hearted Arthur' came to the rescue. He endeared himself to them with the remark 'But you see, Ma'am—a good pantomime must have old jokes.' "

Another of Hirst's examples, and a less mawkish one, is the meeting between Askey and George Bernard Shaw, who had told him his radio performance was "a lot of schoolboy rubbish." Arthur's reaction was to ask Shaw if he might have permission to impersonate him in his new show *The Love Racket*. He received a one-word postcard in reply (an achievement in itself and worth more than Arthur's autograph). Askey immediately went round to see him. Exactly what happened has never been explicitly told: Arthur described it airily as "a meeting between man and superman," refusing to say which was which. But the permission was tacitly granted, and Askey appeared on stage dressed in Norfolk jacket, knickerbockers and Shavian beard. The dialogue was predictable.

"Are you Shaw?"

"No, I'm certain."

---

[1] For two interesting accounts of his life, see *Three Men and a Gimmick*, by Robert Hirst (World's Work Ltd, 1957), and an interview in his seventieth year by Geoffrey Wansell (*The Times*, July 1971).

From choirboy humour to schoolboy humour to—Askey humour. It is all part of what *The Times* calls "Forty-six years in the business of making people laugh."

HENRY HALL

The pattern of dance-music, dance-bands and dancing itself has changed out of all recognition since the 1930s. Only one type is really honoured in its original form: the traditional, Basin-Street blues of the 1920s. Let us now, as Humphrey Lyttleton might say, praise famous musicians, and they would be the Jack Teagardens and Red Nichols and Ellingtons of that world, and the greatest mourning would be for the late maestro, Louis Armstrong.

It is possible that group therapy—that is the influence of a group of three, four or five persons playing and singing in harmony or disharmony—is on the way out. We ourselves sincerely hope so. Mass adulation has perhaps passed its peak, and the idea of just sitting around in amorphous multitudes, rather than dancing to the music, may become boring in time. The days of Scott Fitzgerald's ballroom in the 'twenties, where "a thousand pairs of silver shoes shuffled the shining dust" and when Lew Grade was The World Charleston Champion, no longer have any meaning. When two or three thousand young people are gathered together now they seem alternately in a frenzied or a drugged state (real or imaginary); when only two or three dozen are gathered it will probably be in troglodyte state in an underground discothèque. Their vocabulary will be strange, their motives obscure, their apparel a grotesque parody of the generations they despise.

Let us compare such a scene with the appearance of a natty, well-spoken young man, immaculate in white tie and tails, and fresh from the swank atmosphere of the lush hotel at Gleneagles, Scotland. He is Henry Hall, conductor of the BBC Dance Band, "the only man," wrote critic Collie Knox, "who has got out of that extraordinary organization what he wanted."

We could have chosen his predecessor, the more florid and flamboyant Jack Payne, who first saw the possibilities of a radio dance orchestra, and made such a success of it that he decided to go into music hall and show business. But since Henry coined the phrase "Hall Marks" then it's permissible to say that he remains the hallmark of BBC dance-band leadership in the golden age of radio. The fact that, as he claims in his life-story,[1] his was the first voice to go out from the new Broadcasting House in 1932, was in itself an omen. His signature tune was composed by the BBC man who had encouraged him, Roger Eckersley. His voice was quiet but authoritative, his private life was exemplary, his arrangements orthodox. It was all frightfully BBC and all that. And yet, on that night of 15th March 1932, in Studio 8A, the only operational one in the new building, he confesses to having been a bundle of nerves.

"The first programme words ever to go out were: 'Hullo everyone, this is Henry Hall speaking. . . .' Outside, millions of listeners waited in a defensive mood, and inside, every newspaperman and every member of the BBC staff, it seemed, waited with fingers crossed. We were two minutes late, because the preceding programme over-ran, and I think my band would agree that those were two of the longest, most nerve-racking minutes we ever had together. . . ."

Here's to the next time, but there's always a first time, even for seasoned types like Henry Hall. He quotes the *BBC Year Book* for 1933 laconically: "It is pleasing to reflect that many listeners chose to be encouraging to this new enterprise." Hall was accustomed to executive duties: as Director of Dance Music for London, Midland and Scottish Railway Hotels, he had control over more than thirty bands.

What he may seemed to have lacked is "personality" (on the assumption that a dance-band leader should be twice as large and twice as loud as life) but Henry soon made up for that. At first he was, unlike Val Gielgud, awestruck at the atmosphere of the new Broadcasting House:

"It had the effect of making you feel you must walk on tiptoe and talk in whispers—I thought it was probably because one realized the power of radio, the terrific sweep of its influence, the area and people covered by a few wireless waves. . . ."

He was right. If you don't get bored by your medium, you're likely to make a good job of it.

Snagge was the first member of the staff Henry Hall met next day, introduced by Harry Pepper and Doris Arnold. It is a temptation to quote Henry's reaction:

"He epitomizes the BBC. His manner of delivery is calm, unruffled, without urgency, and yet never for a moment can you stop listening. He put me completely at ease and continued to do so for the rest of my stay there. With his aid that first morning I entered the

---

[1] *Here's to the Next Time* (Odhams Press, 1955).

'contained' life of a studio broadcaster. If the hotels had been a world unto themselves, the BBC was an island community, remote, and self-sufficient, and like an island it had its own tribal laws and customs, and its hierarchy of upper and lower castes."

The last observation is shrewd and wise. The radio world is not one to be taken for granted. It is even more "contained"—admirable term—than the world of television, which uses two of the senses. To be at home in a radio studio: to put yourself across easily and expansively, or tautly and relentlessly like the Ancient Mariner, is a natural gift, even though it may be acquired. The most difficult demand of all is to establish a connection with the unseen listener, with nothing but the sound of one's own voice or the quality of one's own performance to go upon. With people in the world of music, like Walford Davies, Eric Robinson, Alec Robertson, Christopher Stone, Sandy Macpherson, Anthony Hopkins, there is a certain flair difficult to define. For theirs is not the performance. It is the music which matters. The best of them know when to shut up, and are modest about their contribution, and always anxious to improve it. "Contained—but never contented." That might sum it up.

It took some time for the clipped, at first apparently perfunctory introductions of Henry Hall, with the occasional strange inflexion which made him almost say "The BBC Dunce Band," to find favour with the public. There was little showmanship about it, but there was the subtle magic of the letters "BBC" about it. This much, as we know, was realized by George Black, and no doubt Henry Hall was sincere when he expressed surprise at eventually topping the bill, like Wilfred Pickles, at the London Palladium, and partly for the same reason. It was July 1934. Orchestra stalls, as a Leslie Baily would have noted, were 5s. and 4s., and balcony nine old pence. Also on the bill were Elizabeth Welch, Ted Ray, Forsythe, Seamon and Farrell, and Scott Saunders, but lo! "Ben Adhem's name led all the rest." By contrast, he could present Leslie Henson and Richard Goolden in *Toad of Toad Hall* in the theatre under his own management, and to his radio "Guest Nights" he invited all the top names in show business, from the Crazy Gang and Gracie Fields to Max Miller, Fred Astaire, Irving Berlin, Laurel and Hardy—and Michael Redgrave, as a singer in naval uniform!

He was to accompany his "epitome of the BBC" on the famous maiden voyage of the *Queen Mary*. But that is another story, and it can be found on page 70.

GERALDO

Many of the Vintage-Years Dance Band leaders found their own performances and recordings sufficient for their careers. Bert Ambrose, Roy Fox, Lew Stone, Charlie Kunz, Carroll Gibbons, Harry Roy—they often broadcast, but rarely became involved in programmes. Exceptions included Henry Hall, Victor Sylvester, Charlie Shadwell, Billy Ternent, and Gerald Bright, better known as Geraldo. Bright was a great favourite with the BBC, a simple-hearted but expert co-operator in the studio. Bruce Wyndham, as the "Mr Music" of the day, acted as interpreter of Geraldo's rather inarticulate introductions, which often had to be rehearsed word by word. Snagge worked with him over long periods in *Handley's Half-Hour*, Tommy's special series for overseas listeners.

There is one Geraldo story which he could enjoy against himself. Having acquired the trappings of a successful band-leader—a Rolls-Royce, top-hat, astrakhan-collared coat, rings, and cigar, he decided to pay a visit to the place of his birth, Whitechapel Road. He was stalking in some magnificence through his old haunt, when a little man came up to him, and said "You're Gerald Bright, aren't you?" Geraldo graciously admitted it. The little man said "You were the bloke who was going to go up to the West End and run a big show with a top band and all the stars, so you told us—weren't you?" The great figure nodded again. "Well," said the little man, "wot 'appened?"

7
Talk, Talk, Talk

THE answer to the question "When is a Talk not a talk?" is one which has, for many years, worried the life out of the BBC. The two short answers (1) "When it's News" and (2) "When it's a Feature" may now appear to be very much out of date, but the borderline was at one time as hotly contested as anywhere in Ireland during the troubles. Definitions might be drawn up, only to be bypassed or diluted. This is Asa Briggs all right, and anyone who follows the Professor's mighty history of broadcasting will find no subject more fully discussed than the BBC Talk, and the convolutions of its Department.

Some say the BBC Talk was born the day John Reith interviewed a young woman called Mary Somerville, and told her to go and get a University degree before trying again. Others may argue that, if there had been no World War II, Talks and News would have remained separated for ever (the division was created by Charles Siepmann in 1934). Indeed, at the outbreak of war in 1939, the BBC planners made the incredible miscalculation of cutting down on Talks more than on any other Department—a draconian decision reducing output by no less than 77 per cent, the unkindest cut of all. In the event, the mistake was soon realized, but unfortunately, it was the Ministry of Information which recognized it and insisted on putting the BBC's house in order in its own fashion.

To cover the whole field of Talks is not our objective. One may single out individual Heads—Hilda Matheson, a name which echoed along many a BBC corridor, and Sir Richard Maconochie, whose sole experience before his appointment in 1936 seems to have been a prolonged period in India—but the Talk as such took a long time being recognized for the enormously valuable element it was in broadcasting. Miss Matheson's early idea for *Conversations in the Train* was one of the first attempts to present informal talk—indeed, Felix Felton, as much an actor as a producer, and a man whose versatility and knowledge have remained underrated by the Corporation, hit on the key to the matter with the title *Casual Conversations*. "Good chat" is now a steady BBC standby on radio—it's lively, and it's cheap at the price. But in the pre-war years it was difficult to come by. The Fireside Chats of Baldwin were as studied as those of Roosevelt. It was left to Churchill and J. B. Priestley to bring the single voice to its most illustrious status, and there had to be a lot of history to go with it.

There have been exceptions. The equally memorable talks by Max Beerbohm were, like those of Harold Nicolson, both studied and casual, and needed no occasion. Indeed, one of Wynford Vaughan Thomas's stories relates how, as he was about to record the Incomparable Max in the quiet of his garden in Rapallo, the local shooting season began—at that precise moment. But when Wynford raced across to the shooting party, and explained what he was doing, the guns were lowered and fire withheld, in the name of art and culture!

Two aspects of Talks in the Vintage Years are well worth mulling over. One, the *Brains Trust*, which was too good to last. The other, the Third Programme, alternately the glory, jest, and riddle of the BBC world.

It still seems almost incredible that the BBC could have invented such a title as DIRECTOR OF THE SPOKEN WORD.

The thing has almost an Oriental ring about it. One could imagine Gilbert using it in The Mikado as a variation of the Lord High Everything Else. Or it might have appeared in *Omar Khayyam*:

> "Awake! For in the morning I have heard
> The new Director of the Spoken Word...."

The man on whom all this title eventually fell, George Frederick Barnes, possessed none of the oriental splendour we might associate with such an office. Barnes had previously been appointed, by Haley, as the first Controller of the much-discussed and often-maligned Third Programme. The idea, apart from an early preciousness and exaggerated emphasis on erudition, was an admirable one. Here was at least a programme relieved of the strait-jacket of exact timing, and of the temptation of large listening figures. The Third offered a great new opportunity for a Poet's Corner of writers, a postgraduate course for lecturers, and in music the invitation to broadcast whole operas and the work of *avant-garde* composers. There was no concession to popularity and no dilution of original style and standards. The Reithian tradition could be seen at once in the immediate intention to prepare a series of no less than eighty-six broadcasts on one theme—the Victorian Age. In one sense, the Third seemed to put the clock back—a grandfather clock. In another, it encouraged that sort of modern clock which has no numerals on its face. It made the most of both these timepieces.

About lighter, humorous material, it was a little less certain. The first week contained a scintillating "How" programme later described by Joyce Grenfell, but it is a pity that various attempts to introduce political satire, on continental lines, failed to win favour. This was partly because George Barnes, an ex-schoolmaster, was no Hugh Carleton-Greene, a man who had studied the technique in pre-war Berlin. Barsley attempted a musical satire based on his wartime character Colonel Bogus, and was encouraged, as many a sanguine scriptwriter has been, by a Listener Research report giving a high rating both in figures and in appreciation index. He prepared a memo, suggesting a parallel with continental cabaret on the lines, not only of German theatre but of the *Theatre des Dix-Heures* in Paris, and the Christian IV Theatre in Copenhagen. Alas for aspirations! The Controller gave him audience, and referring to Listener Research, said "We're not seeking popularity. Why not do this sort of thing on the Home Service?" The fact that the Home had recommended the programme in question for Third merely confused the issue. The Controller then outlined the idea for a straight series developing the history of satire, from Chaucer onwards, causing Barsley to reply "This seems to me like a University extension course. Listen to the Third and you'll *get* a Third."

"Beastly Barsley!" Barnes exclaimed, and that was the end of the matter.

Other authors found greater favour. The programme turned out to be ideal material for the historical, belles-lettres type of radio essay. W. S. Landor's *Imaginary Conversations* were brilliantly brought up to date by Rayner Heppenstall, and producers like R. D. Smith and Raymond Raikes had a rare time delving among long-forgotten Elizabethan plays. Louis MacNeice turned to the classics, and his *Golden Ass* made history in one way by introducing the word "piss," which had never sullied microphone before, yet which was not vetoed. Douglas Cleverdon made a major impression with David Jones's *In Parenthesis*. Lionel Salter, among musicians, brought forth little-known operas. Talks lasting forty-five minutes or more could be scheduled without flinching, and one Third Programme announcer achieved such a sombre and reverential air that, as one wit remarked, he seemed always about to follow any name on the air with the words "—who has since died."

If John Watt's favourite word for his type of show was *panache*, George Barnes might have applied *cachet* to broadcasts on the Third. It became fashionable to have one's performance done under his wing, to find a fit audience though few. Only a BBC cast in the mould of Reith, continued by Haley and canonized by Barnes could have maintained such a service, and it is greatly to its credit that it did. To be able to say "The time is three-and-a-half minutes past nine" without apologizing was to breathe the heady air of freedom.

Under Milk Wood was not finally broadcast until 1954, but Cleverdon's production set the seal on the Third's reputation. The temptation to transform Dylan Thomas's script into the media of the theatre, television, and the cinema is understandable, but it betrays the original purpose, which was a theme for radio.

One oft-discussed topic, among BBC staff, has always been that of credits. It seemed to many inequitable that, in production, a man working for Drama or Features or Variety should have his name printed or announced, while one working for Talks should remain anonymous. True, a straight talk cannot be "produced" by anyone but the speaker, whereas in the other departments there may have to be elaborate treatments and rehearsals. But a Variety producer with, say, a number of professional acts following each other in his programme needs little more than an air of hospitality and a stop-watch, while a Talks producer may not only have needed much persuasion to secure his speaker (the exception is always an MP) but may have to give reassurance to a nervous one and professional advice to a faulty one.

One notable Head of Talks, John Green, was quite against any credits at all, and held a rather lofty view of his job. According to Elizabeth Rowley, who graduated from Schools broadcasting to become Senior Talks Producer, he once said "The sort of discussion I like to hear is what the Athenaeum would like to hear," and no matter how implausible the programme sounded, it was all right if it suited the Athenaeum. There was, too, the problem of producers not liking certain speakers, and having the right to refuse them access to the air. Miss Rowley cites Lady Violet Bonham-Carter as one victim, adding that "Although her Appreciation Index in a previous programme might be over 80 per cent, Controller Andrew Stewart simply wouldn't have her, because he said she preached." It needed a change of Controller to bring her back again. One wonders whether her original vote, as a Governor, against the appointment of Sir William Haley as Director-General had anything to do with it.

Miss Rowley cited another example of interference, when she was producing the famous series *The Critics*. One of the items chosen for discussion—the radio one—happened to be a Reith Lecture, and every critic slated it. Orders then came from on high that this edition of the programme must not be broadcast. The news leaked out, and there was, we're glad to say, an unholy row. On a later occasion, when the subject of Lesbianism arose, the idea for any discussion of it was turned down by Frank Gillard, then Director of Broadcasting, on the grounds that it presented "no problem." "Let the women soldier on," he said. What would Women's Lib have said?

At no time has the BBC Talks Department been short of speakers. Indeed, it has been said that more people invite themselves than are invited, and this was particularly noticeable at the beginning of the war. But there was a chorus of press disapproval of the paucity of broadcast material and Bernard Shaw supported this view—Shaw, who will be remembered by the BBC, not only for his help with committees on pronunciation, but for the opening words of his talk in the series *Whither Britain?* in 1934:

"Whither Britain! What a question! Even if I knew—and you know perfectly well I *don't* know...."

Other speakers in the series had included H. G. Wells, Ernest Bevin and Lloyd George. During the Second War, Shaw was invited to submit another talk, but the idea was turned down by the ever-officious Ministry of Information. Most listeners would agree that it was J. B. Priestley who redressed the balance during the long-drawn-out summer of 1940—few will forget his talk after Dunkirk about "the little holiday steamers that made an excursion into hell and came back glorious." But Priestley's "social and political views" did not recommend themselves to the Director of Talks, Sir Richard Maconachie, and the envious howlings of right-wing MPs, who could not themselves find a speaker to equal Priestley's calibre, further weakened his position. It was not really "done" for the BBC to admit more than a certain degree of popularity, that is, power, to any one speaker. The Corporation's policy was what it has always been in such a case of individualism: either divide and rule, or dilute.

One of the criticisms that can be levelled at BBC Talks throughout this period of its existence is that it discouraged delegation and yet would rarely give a direct and quick decision. This was particularly frustrating for its producers, who were not only denied their names in print, but also their responsibility in programmes.

HOWARD THOMAS

One of the men who realized that good conversation could provide good entertainment on radio was Howard Thomas, who now runs Thames Television. In his spacious office overlooking Bloomsbury, he likes to think back on those early, formative years. He had been working in Manchester before the war, and his first radio play, *Beauty Queen*, was written for the BBC North Region. One of his comedy series, *A Lancashire Lad in London*, a vehicle for George Formby, brought him in touch with Cecil McGivern, then a producer at Newcastle, but soon to become deeply involved in war programmes. Howard Thomas began to make his name as the author of what he calls "Radiobiography Musicals," one-hour shows about celebrities like Ivor Novello and Noel Gay.

"My most successful series was 'The Showmen of England'; the second of these was a very starry show written around C. B. Cochran, and was referred to kindly in his autobiography. The BBC producer, Roy Spear, was taken ill a day or two before the show went on the air and I was asked to take over. This became my first-ever production as a BBC producer/director."

When war came, and he had been rejected by the Army owing to defective eyesight, John Watt offered him a job as Variety Producer in Bristol, at £1000 a year. Howard accepted, giving up his commercial radio post.

"When I went into commercial radio, I started a department for one of the biggest advertising agencies, The London Press Exchange, and I also wrote and directed hundreds of programmes. I was highly paid, head of a department as well as writing as a freelance for the BBC; so joining as a £1000-a-year producer was hardly a step up. But I was delighted to be back in broadcasting and to feel I was doing something useful in wartime. I had found the pre-war BBC in London highly departmentalized, dominated by executives who knew little about broadcasting and entertainment, and altogether stuffy. I had turned to commercial radio because I was given authority and freedom to do almost anything I liked, subject to satisfying our advertising clients, from Cadbury's to Kruschen Salts.

"The atmosphere in Bristol was totally different because whole programme units like the Variety Department and the Features and Drama Department had been moved away from the heavy load of top brass. Broadcasting conditions were difficult: Bristol was under nightly bombardment by the Luftwaffe and the nine parish halls we had equipped for studios offered no protection against air-raids. There was also great difficulty in persuading artistes to travel there, so the Corporation was thankful to get any programmes at all. They didn't care overmuch about what we did, so long as the service kept going.

"Everyone worked hard and felt extremely free, and learnt a great deal about broadcasting by trial and error. At one time I was writing and producing four programmes a week. In fact, I produced 500 programmes, during three years with the Corporation. It was a very creative period, out of which, as you know, sprang such programmes as *ITMA* and *The Brains Trust*. All the BBC staff got along well together and the barriers of departmentalization disappeared. Soon I had to journey to London every fortnight to record two *Brains Trust* programmes at a time, but I found the atmosphere at Broadcasting House still rarefied. However, at outposts like the Variety Studio in Lower Regent Street and the Overseas Entertainment programmes in the Criterion, the environment seemed more congenial.

"Communications with London were mostly terse teleprinter messages between the programme people in Broadcasting House and departmental heads like John Watt in Bristol. We all gained from the fact that in a city like Bristol, BBC people were living, eating and drinking with the ordinary public in their bars and cafés. Everyone felt directly in touch with the listening public. The producers in Bristol soon began to feel that they knew more about the audience than the desk men in Broadcasting House, and they shrugged off the odd criticism that might trickle down. You must remember, though, that the Bristol BBC was very much a centre of entertainment, and therefore not directly concerned with the news and documentaries which were more directly linked with the war effort. The public had become bored with the orthodox light entertainment formulae and in Bristol the awareness of this encouraged some of us to seek new patterns."

Now enters, as one might expect, a key figure who was to support Howard Thomas's interest in what might be called an entertaining information programme.

"John Watt, as well as being a very skilled broadcaster, had the gift of leadership and he could inspire ideas and hard work. He was very receptive to anything new and he was always prepared to do battle with the programme planners. He was fiercely loyal to his staff and one of the best executives I have known. He was an enthusiast and a man of great drive, and he would have enjoyed very much being in television today." So *The Brains Trust* idea gradually came into being. "Programme planners had become aware of viewers' complaints about the lack of enterprise in programmes and they decided that they would like to have some new programmes which could be informative as well as entertaining. John Watt returned to Bristol from London and called me into his office. He asked me to work with Douglas Cleverdon, a local bookseller who was in the Talks Department, to see whether we could come up with a new slant. We could never reconcile our ideas because Douglas was wholly a Talks and Documentary man, and he became very good at this, whereas my training was in entertainment. We submitted two quite separate reports and my suggestion was the one John Watt adopted.

"However, when *The Brains Trust* became a success and our questions and choice of guests was widely discussed and criticized by everyone, from the newspaper critics to the Board of Governors, John Watt found himself out of his depth. He grew tired of being the postman handling daily teleprinter messages between me and the top administrators in London. It was all the more difficult for him when some of the Governors began to telephone me personally, to give me their opinions on people I should or should not use in the programmes. The situation became even more acute when, because of the controversy, the BBC made that famous rule—no more questions on religion or politics. John Watt was relieved and delighted when Benjie Nicolls, BBC Controller of Programmes, decided that the programmes should be withdrawn from the Variety Department and that I should work directly to him. I think this was the first time (and perhaps the only time) that a programme producer had been singled out for this dubious distinction. I was moved up to London and occupied a so-called suite (the maids' quarters) in the top floor of the Langham Hotel, opposite Broadcasting House.

"From there I was in daily touch with Nicolls. He insisted on approving every question and every person used in the programmes, and there were long argumentative sessions. There were also many occasions, when the Director-General intervened and I was hauled up before him."

They must have been interesting meetings, between Nicolls, the brilliant double-first from Oxford, an Establishment man, and Thomas, the Entertainment expert who had come from the commercial world. Although he worked direct to Nicolls on *The Brains Trust*, Howard Thomas was still employed by the Variety Department and continued to produce additional weekly programmes like *Shipmates Ashore*, and series like *Under Your Tin Hat*. It was at this time he started *Sincerely Yours, Vera Lynn*, which elevated a dance band vocalist to a popularity which is still with us, thirty years later. But to return to the later history of *The Brains Trust*:

"John Watt believed, as I did, that the only way to attract a mass audience was to produce a conversation piece between brilliant men in a relaxed mood, rather than have a panel of erudite professors pontificating to the public. He fought very hard to maintain this concept and eventually got it through, although at first the planners would not accept the title 'The Brains Trust" and adopted my alternative title of 'Any Questions?'. The series was booked for six weeks but during that time we planted the label of 'The Brains Trust' so heavily in the programme that listeners seized upon this, and it was a good example of the public getting its way. Beyond that exhilarating beginning, John had little influence in the development and let me do exactly what I wanted to do with it. He offered suggestions for people to participate, but his main interest was that above all the programme should be entertaining and avoid boredom."

However, it didn't work out quite as Watt and Thomas had envisaged. While Bristol was virtually cut off, there was a certain freedom. Admin. was more obsessed with keeping programmes on the air than with considering their contents in detail. However, the *Brains Trust* had attracted so much publicity, first in the headlines and secondly in the House of Commons, and eventually through the springing up of Forces' Brains Trusts and the duplication of the idea at gatherings all over the country, that the administrators realized they had a problem child in the family. "The first restriction imposed by them was to limit the range of questions and, agreeing with Nicolls, they would not permit this discussion of politics and religion, a far cry from today.

"They also tried to control the selection of guests and objected, for instance, to the use of controversial figures like Professor Haldane. Then there came the conclusion that the trio of Huxley, Joad and Campbell had become too powerful an element, exercising too much influence on the nation, and particularly on the Forces.

"It was demanded that the trio should be diluted. I was instructed to use only one or two of them at a time and to find other people whose influence would be less dominating. This was the beginning of the end of the popularity of the programme, because my original concept was that the three key figures should be, respectively, a brain, a tongue, and a heart. I was lucky in my original choice of Huxley, Joad and Campbell and I found it difficult to select a substitute for the knowledgeable Huxley, the gifted teacher (if slightly charlatan) Joad, and the Munchausen-like Campbell. Similarly, I was told to find alternatives for the Question Master (a title I had coined) and Donald McCullough had to alternate with others who were more efficient but less witty.

"Complaints from interested bodies about controversial questions were treated far too seriously. For example, when Doctor X [who happened to be Charles Moran, Churchill's doctor] criticized patent medicines, the Proprietary Medicines Association protested so fiercely to the BBC that the Director-General sent for me and I sat in his office with his Press Officer, one Kenneth Adam. Mr Robert Foot, who was then Director-General, wanted me to cut this answer from the recorded programme when it was repeated a few days later but I argued against this on the grounds that such action would be criticized by the Press as a grave weakness on the part of the BBC. I won my point but it did not endear me to the administration.

"The beginnings of the programme were so insignificant that the men in London were not very interested. I recorded the pilot programme at Bush House in the studio where J. Walter Thompson used to produce their commercial radio programmes. The pilot was such a torrent of undisciplined words that it was unbroadcastable and I scrapped it. But I learnt enough from it to achieve a formula which gave us a clear-cut and successful first programme on the air. As the series was limited to six programmes early in the evening it had no impact on the administrators but it was seized by the public as something they wanted. Only when the programme became a national institution did the administrators muscle in on it."

The final question then arose: why did the Brains Trust idea fail on BBC Television, when it had proved such a success on radio, and when discussion programmes on TV had made reputations for such men as Lord Boothby, Michael Foot, A. J. P. Taylor and Malcolm Muggeridge?

"The Brains Trust," said its inventor, "was designed purely as a radio programme, and to be heard under particular conditions, in wartime, in blacked-out homes, and by men of the Forces sitting together round radio sets. My main target was to get in touch with these two types of audience, so that listeners could feel they were actually taking part, trying to answer some of the questions themselves, expressing their opinions to each other, and writing to the Brains Trust.[1] I did not regard any one of the sessions as being successful unless it was fiercely argued about next day in buses and trains and places where men and women met together. We soon attracted a mail of 3000 letters a week.

"When television was resumed at Alexandra Palace after the war, the BBC tried to make a visual Brains Trust, but it did not succeed. Then in 1955 Cecil McGivern decided to have another try and ask me whether I would be willing to produce a Brains Trust series. I did not believe it could be done, because to me it was essentially sound broadcasting and little was to be gained by having the talkers in vision. However, he persisted and even accepted my high price which I thought would put him off. It was many times my old £1000-a-year salary. With John Furness as producer we tried out a Brains Trust formula, with the added attraction of a good-looking secretary sitting next to the Question Master Norman Fisher (and also being fed on-air with instructions from the director). But the impact was not very good.

"Part of the success of *The Brains Trust* on radio was that, as the producer of the programme, I could sit with the Question Master and the members of the panel, and I could act as a guinea-pig listener sensitive to boredom and guiding the development of a discussion. I was able to steer the Question Master in nominating people to reply, cutting short the bores, persuading the more interesting people to continue, and above all switching the subjects by bringing forward a sparkling question following a sequence of dull answers.

"Again, radio made demands on the imagination of the listener and, just as in *ITMA* they could envisage those taking part almost as Disney cartoon characters, so each listener had a Brains Trust concept of those distinguished people talking not only among themselves but also to the listener in his home. All this was destroyed when *The Brains Trust* were draped around the inevitable coffee-table and were so busy trying to impress each other that the viewer at home never joined the 'family circle.'

[1] One letter, quoted in the *BBC Handbook*, from Madeleine Shaw, age six. "I do not think it is fair that the Brains Trust is on at the same time as Children's Hour do you? Because both Mother and I want to listen at 5.15. Would you alter it please so that we are both satisfide?" Later, the programme was put forward to 4 p.m.

"It should also be remembered that resulting from the tremendous success of *The Brains Trust* when it was No. 2 to the brilliant *ITMA*, we produced a series of three half-hour films for the cinema. The first did fairly well, because of its novelty value and its 'star appeal,' but the second and third in the series lacked audience attraction. Again, the static nature of a group of rather elderly people trying to outshine one another created a barrier which alienated the audience."

It is surely significant that a man like Howard Thomas should continue to hold the opinion that this programme was pure sound broadcasting and gained little from camera coverage.

ALISTAIR COOKE

Alistair Cooke's *Letter from America* is another triumphant vindication of radio as a medium. Who can imagine that this unique, informative, tender, illuminating series could possibly have been improved with the addition of real pictures to the word-pictures? His talks ought to continue at least as long as the BBC Charter, for Cooke has an affection, not only for the Old Country, but for the Old Firm. The former may partly be because he isn't by birth or upbringing an American, but a sparkling product of Cambridge University, where he edited the undergraduate magazine *Granta*. A glimpse of the United States on a scholarship, however, settled the matter. Cooke stayed on as our unofficial ambassador. He can evoke a scene or a situation as few can, even among the masters of the radio talk. Listen, and hear in this example of the Cooke technique, how he leads his audience gently to his theme:

"Gud evening [he always had this familiar clipped intonation of 'good.'] It is the day when the summer is put away, the swimming-trunks squeezed for the last time, the ash-trays in country cottages filled with mouse-seed and rat-paste, the doors hammered into place, the lock turned for the last time on your private world of sun and sand and picnics and the pride of growing children. Labour Day [and now he shifts his theme almost imperceptibly] brings you back to the world of schools and offices, to sniffling colds and insurance policies, to taxes and radio commentaries, to dark nights and the dark horizon of politics." So, in another of his masterly introductions, Alistair Cooke gets you ready to listen to some subject which might not otherwise have held your attention.

Cooke is an acknowledged authority on the American scene in

every aspect, from the White House to a fat White Woman whom nobody loves, the sort of American matron with hair rinsed "in Purple Dawn or Marmalade Surprise." Hot news or hot pants: he is interested in the effect of both. He is an admirer of the original New Yorker set—Dorothy Parker, Robert Benchley, Donald Ogden Stewart, James Thurber—of the legendary film figures, the Marx Brothers, Marilyn Monroe, Orson Welles—but also of the American types, the commuter, the con man, the cop, the West Side kids and the Wall Street tycoons. Above all, as in that brief picture of the end of summer, he paints the American scene, and gives to mere names like Nevada and Wisconsin and Baltimore a background which makes America real. The formula, it need hardly be added, is not achieved without infinite care and genuine affection. When the final record of radio comes to be assessed, the place of Alistair Cooke will be a very high one, and yet, whenever we have met him, in war and peace, in a flurry of activity (his documentary for BBC Features in 1940 on the role of the US President was superbly timed) or relaxed and amused by the latest British fad, he has always been his unassuming self, not "desiring this man's art and that man's scope," in the words of another American who loved England, T. S. Eliot.

QUESTION MASTERS

The role of Question Master is an ancient one. Perhaps the Host in Chaucer's *Canterbury Tales* is an early example. Guessing games, so popular in Victorian times, needed a cool, alert, unflappable leader, especially for the over-eager young. Radio, and later television, exalted the Question Master to a figure of great importance, and some became masters of the delicate art. Donald McCullough on *The Brains Trust*, Richard Dimbleby, Lionel Gamlin, Stewart Macpherson, Freddie Grisewood, Gilbert Harding and Lionel Hale on *Round Britain Quiz*, the ever-urbane Roy Plomley, Macdonald Hobley, Franklin Engelmann—each brought personality as well as law and order into the parlour games.

Two men specialized in the younger generation: the late Robert Macdermot, and John Ellison. It takes perhaps greater sensitivity to get the best out of boys and girls, without being schoolmasterish. Results with programmes like *Top of the Form* were remarkable, and became an accepted pattern of life. At one time, John (whose wife Diana Morison once took the part of Miss Hotchkiss in *ITMA*, with her stentorian cry of "Mr Handley!") teamed up with the late and well-loved Kenneth Horne in a book of questions—six hundred of them—which race on like the Charge of the Light Brigade.[1] Some are quite straightforward, others tease. No. 84, for instance, asks "Who was the first Yorkshire Captain to go to Australia?" and this could not be answered in terms of cricket! To the question "Who is known as a troglodyte?" the editors add, sardonically, "Pop Groups excepted."

AUDREY RUSSELL

In these days of Woman's Lib, it would presumably be dangerous for the BBC to run the risk of being prejudiced against women at the microphone. But what of the vintage years? There has never been quite the equivalent, in the VIP and upper-age bracket, of Eleanor Roosevelt and Her Day, but the long run of Woman's Hour is something of which the Corporation can be justly proud. Marjorie Anderson's story is told elsewhere, but there have been others whose voices became a familiar part of the radio scene—Georgie Henschel, Joy Worth, stalwart among announcers, Jean Metcalfe, whose true love-story (in this "dismissive" age, as the BBC's music man, Antony Hopkins, so perceptively described it) with Cliff Michelmore was literally an example of "whom the microphone hath joined, no man has wanted to put asunder." Barsley is proud that two of his Oxford contemporaries, Marghanita Laski and Honor Balfour, have been in constant demand by listeners.

"Marghanita was the first girl to be co-opted on to a university magazine, *Cherwell*, and subsequently became its first female editor, alternately winning and waspish. She was married when still *in statu pupillari* and publisher Peter Howard is still her husband. During my years as Editor of *Panorama*, when we had lost a speaker, on whatever subject, my director John Furness and I would say "There's always Marghanita...." As for Honor Balfour, she has always been a human dynamo, careering around in a career on *Time and Life* which must be infinitely exhausting, but inexhaustibly fascinating. Recently they were both together on one of those excellent ring-up programmes, and I had the pleasure of calling them."

The first lady of the microphone as far as reporting is concerned is undoubtedly the determined but modest Audrey Russell. We irreverently nicknamed her "Tawdry Bustle"—the sort of nickname

[1] *Quizzically Yours* (Macdonald, 1969).

only applied to people we really like. Audrey had the right qualifications, including training at the Central School, and a Gold Medal from the Poetry Society in 1934. Though often a mass of nerves within, she appeared unflappable. Though constantly reporting on royalty, she has never taken on those awe-struck tones some speakers use. Her greatest trial and greatest triumph was during the prolonged Royal tours of 1953, when the number of her "airline tickets to romantic places" would have made a small book. But Audrey takes her own atmosphere with her. She is as much at home in Brunei as in Brummagem. Moreover, when describing what those quick-change artistes the Royals wear, she has never adopted the glacé voice of the catwalk commentator. It's probably true to say that the BBC has never produced anyone like her. Ask the programme engineers: they always know. It was a fitting triumph that Tawdry Bustle should be made a Freeman of the City of London in 1967. Why not, if Queen Juliana can be a Liveryman of the Company of Carpenters?

8 The Organized Jungle

THE BBC Features Department, which was formerly a branch of the Drama Department, obtained its independence during the war. Val Gielgud, as Head of both, felt sad at losing half his empire, but had a great admiration for his second-in-command, who took over.

LAURENCE GILLIAM

Laurence Gilliam was a Londoner, born in 1907 and educated at the City of London School and Peterhouse, Cambridge. After a brief period on the *Radio Times*, he joined Features and Drama in 1933. He was prematurely retired in 1964, and died in 1967. With him died "The Organized Jungle," as he called his Department. His staff called him Lorenzo, and the comparison with the Magnificent Medici was not a bad one. He was certainly the most dynamic figure in the BBC during the war years and after, and brought the documentary technique to its highest pitch.

Gilliam was a big man, both physically and in ideas. "The physical type is a strange one," wrote one of his producers, Rayner Heppenstall.[1] "The colouring was fair, the complexion pale. There was something negroid about the crinkly hair and the regular but somewhat flattened features in a broad face.... His middle name, Duval, is certainly one which occurs among South Africans."

No man inspired more loyalty in the men and women who worked with him. As Wynford Vaughan Thomas put it to us "His great gift was that he could tolerate near-misses. Some of us have been ashamed of near-misses, but Laurence was prepared to see through that, and encourage us to continue experimenting. He had a great gift for words: he himself was no mean writer. And the other thing is, of course that he was one of the only Heads in the BBC who really did feel that the artist had a right to exist. We always somehow felt it was the habit of Administration to regard the artist as a necessary evil, who got in the way of tidy Administration—tidy is the word."

Wynford found that it was always an adventure to work with

[1] *Portrait of the Artist as a Professional Man* (Peter Owen).

Laurence. "You'd go into his office, and he'd say 'We're going to send you to Borneo, my dear boy. It's all right, we've got the thing fixed, and you leave on such-and-such a plane.' This enormous, almost Falstaffian figure would wave all difficult details aside, with that laugh that echoed as you entered the room. And he meant it: to Borneo you'd go. To enter that room often meant a passport to some marvellous liberating adventure."

"If you had to pick out three or four men," he summed up, "who were shaping radio in its heyday, you'd pick out 'Lobby' on the OB side, and for the development of Features, of course, Laurence Gilliam. There were others who developed news, drama, variety— yes, but there were probably only four or five who did this from within the central structure, and one was certainly Laurence. He excelled at the big programmes, naturally, like the Christmas round-up, which took months of preparation, but he could also handle the sudden emergency programme on a grand scale, and with perfect judgement."

We have described the Christmas programme and the royal and national occasions in a separate section of the book, because they were team jobs, involving a whole host of different personalities and techniques and countries. Gilliam showed what could be done, given a free hand and the sort of teams with whom he loved to work. His great quality was equality. He would listen to the suggestion of a twenty-year-old Junior Programme Engineer as closely as he would to the opinion of a Controller. You have only to ask any of the "Jeeps" or other technical types who spent long and trying hours with him. They never got the brush-off for interrupting: Laurence admitted he always had something to learn, and he knew how to pass on what he had learned. The only people he *would* brush off were the faceless ones, with initials instead of names, who got in his way. He'd be busy talking in the control room or at a production panel if a Jack-in-office wanted a formal meeting, or to argue about some dereliction in his Department. When the appropriate time came he'd take up the matter briskly and brusquely, and get back to work.

Scripts were read closely, not taken for granted; he would have made a first-class chief sub-editor on a newspaper. He once gave this advice: "Write your script and put your recordings in—then take out most of the things you yourself like best, and you've got a programme." He was too busy to write a book about his methods and experiences, and at the end of his life too disillusioned. The only glimpse is a brief chapter at the end of an anthology of programmes he edited:[1]

"The search for material, the living contact with what he is writing about, is the heart of the matter. That keeps the vision fresh and renews the inspiration. This is no mechanical word-spinning, but distillation from personal experience. The first and last rule of good feature writing and production is—go to sources. . . . Good documentary brushes aside secondary sources, dismisses the hearsay witness."

Here too is a principle on radio which he could equally have applied to television:

"Broadcasting offers to the writer of our time a form of expression, and a method of publication that demands discipline, flair in the use of language to be spoken, and the ability to hold the attention of a vast miscellaneous audience by words, sound and music. In the last resort all are exercises, in the most modern of techniques, of that most ancient of all crafts, the art of telling a true story."

FEATURES

The example of Louis MacNeice proved one of the characteristics of the Features Department: that most of its members could write their own scripts as well as produce them, and sometimes could narrate them as well. This one-man-band ability might have its drawbacks—if, for instance (as MacNeice put it) writer A disagreed with himself, as producer A. It could also lead to a sort of introvert, inbreeding, house-joke approach, but Laurence Gilliam could soon detect this and quietly discourage it. In general the versatility led to a wide range of programmes, from light musical satire to the sonority of the great verse-play, and from the real-life hustle of a topical documentary or travelogue to a quiet reconsideration of some neglected poet.

Departmental borders were as ill-defined as they are today. No one could say where Features ended, and where Talks or Drama or Variety began. Talks, with its more clear-cut brief, became the most doctrinaire of the three. Its anonymous producers, according to Features men, rarely went anywhere beyond the office or studio, except for taking speakers out to lunch. By the same token, according to Talks men, Features producers were very rarely to be found in their

[1] *BBC Features* (Evans Brothers, 1950).

offices, preferring to spend their time swanning to exotic lands at vast Corporation expense. Several were, indeed, widely travelled, and Features men were the first to have experience of the new portable tape-recorders for foreign visits. Producer Peter Eton was a pioneer in testing one, on a trip to the Midi by the Blue Train. His recording of a train at speed was considered good enough for the Recorded Effects Library. It was made simply by dangling the tiny "crystal" microphone over the open pedestal in the *toilette*. Barsley recorded the rhythmic sound of being massaged in a saloon in Bangkok and the wail of a Chinese sing-song girl in Saigon. Eddie Ward and his wife Marjorie Banks went in search of the elusive rasp of the cicadas. A whole new world of "snapshots in sound" awaited the alert reporter. This was Gilliam's "distillation from personal experiences" put into practice, and the use of the miniature tape-machines was eventually adopted by other Departments.

Features escaped some of the "centralized" feeling by being housed, in the vintage years, not in BH, but in a block of flats, Rothwell House, two minutes away. They had their own pub, "The Stag's Head," and if official departmental meetings were few and far between meetings at "The Stag" were frequent, and many programme plans were discussed there, with the figure of Gilliam (who, like Hugh Greene, liked to drink with his lieutenants) looming over them.

If one did not know the workings of the BBC's Admin. mind, one would have been astonished that such an assortment of talents could be disbanded so ruthlessly—but perhaps, when the blow fell, many of the personalities and much of the glory had gone, never to be replaced.

> "Whither is fled the visionary gleam?
> Where is it now, the glory and the dream?"

Where indeed? The Features Department was born and flourished in wartime, and kept its reputation until television cameras began to rob its real-life programmes of their impact. The more imaginative, dramatic features remain inimitable. There could never be a television *March of the '45* with such width of scene and depth of feeling. The television programme on Culloden made its name for its raw and realistic brutality.

The specialists in Features included such people as Jenifer Wayne, an ex-school-teacher with a modest smile who, with her husband-to-be

Bill Hewitt, presented the intricacies of the British legal system with superb simplicity in the series *This is the Law*: Nesta Pain, whose willing and lucid victims were often distinguished doctors or psychologists: Maurice Brown and David Woodward who professed a love of the sea and all things naval (and Maurice added a passion for Kipling's tales); Terence Tiller, Rayner Heppenstall and Douglas Cleverdon (producer of the original, immortal *Under Milk Wood*) whose handling of the literary feature set a new standard in radio; Leonard Cottrell, whose early interest in motor-cars was abruptly and most beneficially transferred to a survey of the Ancient World, on which he is now an acknowledged expert; R. D. Smith, whose heart lay in the gaudy, bawdy scene of the Elizabethan dramatists; Joe Burroughs and Tom Waldron, who would combine to take a topical subject and submit it the bright glare of inquiry; these, and others beside them, had their favourite neck of the woods, but most were versatile enough to take on the "standard" Feature which might be ordered for some anniversary, or that perennial and dubious act of devotion, the programme for St George's Day. "Who's got any fresh, *new* ideas?" Laurence would ask his unwilling group of producers, and no one ever had any.

The *Country Magazines* of Francis Dillon were in a category by themselves. Dillon, a hoarse, haranguing Irish version of Groucho Marx (if such a person can be imagined) combined a deep love and understanding of history with a keen appreciation of bucolic life. David Thomson, his helpmeet, looked, by contrast, as pale and bald and studious as a clerk in holy orders. Together they made, with men like A. G. Street and Ralph Wightman to unfold their stories, a unique rural ride which has never been surpassed—and there are villages today that remember, with ribald pleasure, the time when Jack Dillon and his crew descended on them, bringing an entirely new concept of the BBC.

Many famous personalities appeared in Features, or had programmes written round them, and few would refuse.

There was an axiom among interviewers that "the higher you go, the easier it is." The minor officials, the Deputy-Ministers, the Assistant Directors, the friends of royalty—these are the ones who kept one waiting, demand scripts and stick to protocol. Barsley recalls the first time that Prince Bernhard of the Netherlands broadcast after the war, as part of a feature:

"I was in Holland in 1948, making recordings of tributes to Queen

Wilhelmina for the fiftieth anniversary of her reign. There were comments from Resistance Leaders, State Governors and the man in the street. It then occurred to me that, logically, they should end with a tribute from the man in the Palace to his mother-in-law. 'Why not ring him up?' said his private secretary Jan Tomassen, whom I met at a party in Hilversum. 'But,' I replied, 'You can't just ring up Prince Bernhard.' 'Why not?' he answered, 'his number's in the phonebook.' And it is: Soestdijk Palace, Baarn 2841. Eventually Tomassen put through the call himself, returned and said 'O.K., but he wants to do it in England when he's over for the Olympic Games, so can you fix that? He says paying tribute to a mother-in-law sounds rather like an English music-hall joke—but he'll do it.'

"So, at 9 o'clock one August morning, an athletic figure in a sports jacket and flannels scrambled out of a BBC car and strolled into Broadcasting House, smoking a Dunhill pipe. I had arranged for no one to meet him but the Duty Officer, and had not told the press. This seemed to please him very much. 'Then you can keep your word, and "do" me in half-an-hour,' he said. He threw a script on the table of Studio L1, where so many wartime broadcasts had taken place: 'Being BBC, you'll want a script,' he added with a laugh. I shall never forget the rattle of the cup in the saucer as my secretary tremblingly brought him coffee. He looked at her appraisingly, evidently liking English prettiness (she was actually half Scottish, half Irish). 'Is this from the canteen?' he asked. 'It was, during the war.' 'No-o,' she replied in her Scots voice, 'I think it's something special.'

"Prince Bernhard went through an excellent piece at first go, without rehearsal, voice-test or fluff. He had said 'I make this five minutes dead' and after the broadcast, I went into the studio and said 'I'm sorry.' He looked up and said 'What happened?' I said 'It's five minutes and two seconds.' He was away back to the car and the Games well within the half-hour, and in thanks for such a brief, workmanlike session he invited me over to spend a day with him, plus Queen Juliana and the daughters, on their yacht *Piet Hein*. I have known them ever since, and he has usually been willing to appear on television as well as talk on radio, when the subject interests him, and that has been my experience for over twenty years."

Features people came from many different backgrounds, as did their nearest counterparts, the Outside Broadcasters. One, John Bridges, had been a sergeant in the Grenadier Guards; Douglas Cleverdon had sold antique books in Bristol; John Glyn-Jones had been "doing his own thing," in the Players' Victorian Theatre, and a very amusing thing it was; Alan Burgess, before he joined the year following the war, had sailed on the famous barquentine *Cap Pilar* to New Zealand, been a mountain guide, and had wandered and hoboed from Tahiti to the Panama Canal. The series *The Undefeated*, in which true stories of personal courage were dramatized, was his special care. One of these, the tale of Gladys Aylward, missionary in China, became a book, and then a successful film under the title *The Small Woman*. Alan—the Jack London of Features—has written of the beginning of the story:

"It all started with a slender clue in a newspaper. A few lines of print saying that Gladys Aylward, who had once worked as a parlourmaid in London, was back home again after seventeen years in China as a missionary. We rang up the reporter and got her address. We went to a small house in a small street in Edmonton and interviewed her. She was small and dark, and was dressed in Chinese clothes. She was not shy after our first explanation, but she was a little uncertain if her 'story' was good enough for our purpose. So were we."

But as the story developed, Burgess sat, fascinated, for three hours, and later, after many hours of discussion about the children she had cared for, he decided "we had stumbled upon a story of courage and fortitude with few—with very few—equals."

The success of the programme goes back to Gilliam's dictum on a good Feature writer: "The search for material, the living contact with what he is writing about, is the heart of the matter."

The demise of the Features Department (which had provided the BBC with a number of notable demises) comes well outside the heydays of radio. It was, as one might put it, on one of the grey days of radio, in 1964, that the axemen set to work. They were, as Heppenstall notes, men in neat suits of clerical grey, and on 16th February they summoned an Extraordinary Meeting of the Department, without announcing the agenda beforehand. But, with an introduction declaring that the palmy days were over and radio was in the red, the intent, apparently, became obvious. The Department, as such, was to be disbanded. This did not mean that Feature programmes were to be thrown out—far from it. There would be plenty of scope for Featureproducers, even though they would be absorbed elsewhere. Gillard, the Director of Broadcasting, who appeared as the only speaker, was clearly embarrassed by the task he was undertaking. He paid a warm tribute to Laurence Gilliam, as well he might, since Gilliam had more or less created his name in *War Report*. But Gilliam, of course, was what the meeting was really all about. His Features empire, so far-flung during and after the war, had shrunk, and its revenue was reduced. Laurence, who planned on the grand scale, had been left with little to plan. It was therefore necessary to force upon him premature retirement. Gilliam *was* Features, and it was necessary to topple him in advance, in order to break up his organization.

This is a method the Corporation Establishment often employs. For a programme or a Department to belong solely to one man (unless it be a vehicle in Showbiz or Variety) is anathema to the Establishment. So the end of Gilliam, on that occasion, was coupled with the scattering of his followers. Heppenstall recalls the scene:

"The silence may perhaps be described as stunned. The reader [Gillard] removed his spectacles and picked up his papers. He and the very tall thin man [Michael Standing] departed ... leaving us there with our unspoken questions. Laurence told us that his official date of retirement was in three years' time. ... The least sympathetic of us must, I imagine, have found him in that moment a noble, a dignified, almost a tragic figure."

A report by a correspondent on *The Sunday Telegraph* eventually announced that Gilliam was to be prematurely retired and added "demoralization at Broadcasting House is now complete. A decision has been taken, and the staff of the Features Department do not know what is happening to them."

They still do not know.

9 The BBC Faces War

THE Day War Broke Out, in comedian Robb Wilton's simple words, to preface his immortal monologue, was not the same day for the BBC as it was for Britain. Friday, 1st September 1939—the date when Germany attacked Poland—was the occasion for broadcasting to take up its wartime positions, for all the BBC Regions to disappear, as separate entities, and to be merged into one Home Service. A new second service was to appear in 1940, in the shape of the AEFP (Allied Expeditionary Forces' Programme) which became the Forces Programme. Finally came the Triple Expansion, resulting in a greatly increased BBC staff and service combining Home, European and Overseas programmes. The latter increased its languages from six to fourteen.

Hugh Carleton-Greene, later Director-General, claims to have been probably the first journalist in Warsaw to let the Polish Government know that fighting had started. As he recounts, his "stringer" Clare Hollingworth, in Katowice, rang him at 5 a.m. on the morning of 1st September, to tell him that bombers were over the town, and he called the Polish Foreign Office just before the sirens began to sound in Warsaw.

But though war at home was for months the "phoney" war, the BBC took immediate steps to carry out the planned dispersals to Bristol, Manchester, Evesham and other places. Every personal memoir and every relevant history of the BBC has its own stories of the upheaval, with its discomforts, but also its opportunities for experiment. Leslie Baily's *Scrapbook for 1939* recalls that one of the few survivors on deck at the BBC, London, was Sandy Macpherson, who filled in hours of waiting between news-bulletins and Government instructions and advice. "There was always Sandy" became a well-known, affectionate phrase. On 6th September, a programme began "Who is this man who looks like Charlie Chaplin?" It turned out to be Hitler—and Tommy Handley.

War News from abroad came largely through news agency sources, and was reflected from the first by such stalwarts as Ed Murrow of CBS, whom Stuart Hibberd recalls as working in the BBC Newsroom all night on 3rd September. Ed, one of the best radio friends Britain ever had, was to be in London a year later, to record the siren-wail and patter of feet down into an air-raid shelter in Trafalgar Square, and to tell American listeners:

"The long-range view of London in close-up must command deepest respect for the morale and sturdiness of its people. The slightest imagination can conjure up how terrifying must be the war of nerves right on the scene of action."

The most sensational eye-witness outside broadcast before D-Day was made by Charles Gardner, as he watched the bombing of a convoy from the cliffs above Dover in 1940, and he was lucky enough to see a German plane shot down before his eyes. This broadcast, which, like Churchill's speeches and Quentin Reynolds's *Dear Schickelgrüber* and *Dear Doctor*, was made into a commercial recording, though at the time it was attacked for being "inhuman."

Recording-engineers in the days of the early discs have their own way of describing memorable trips. Here is Reg Pidsley's account of a raid over Berlin in 1943, told specially for this book.

"On these epic occasions, you couldn't afford to make mistakes. One little slip, and you'd lost the show: the disc might be too cold, or the cutter might be blunt, and that was it, so you had to be well prepared. I didn't know when I volunteered for an operational flight with Vaughan Thomas, that it was going to be Berlin. Well, I was allowed to install my stuff—frig about with the intercom. and so on. I broke all the rules, even taking a photo of the Big Cookie (the 4000-pound bomb) as they were putting it in. What people perhaps don't realize is that we were in the air for altogether eight and a half hours and out of these we were shot at for about six and a half. We were even shot at when we came back over Sweden, but that was just to keep us up, I suppose!

"Well, we had the luck to produce one of the best recordings ever. You might say the disc was *too* good: the whole crew played up, did their jobs properly—the best crew we could have had. Wynford and I were the amateurs. I hadn't even got a flying-suit on. I made some terrible mistakes on the trip. They gave me some of that foil to push out from the flare-chute at the rear, the foil to confuse the radar. There it was, lying like Christmas paper-chains, with the aluminium backing. So I stuffed one lot out, and then opened the flap of the chute to put out another, and the first lot blew back! I'd taken the rubber bands off, and the plane looked like Christmas decorations.

"Wynford started his recordings but unfortunately, in the end, his voice didn't really sound like him, because he was moving about and if you move about under oxygen your voice sounds slurred. But the effects recordings were OK. Anyway, Wynford was talking, and one of the crew said 'I'd hold your adjectives till we get over the Big City,' so Wynford held his adjectives. Then at last we were on the bomb-run, and this recording I'm talking about, it was a miracle. I got the cutter going, and everything was nice, and they were counting the bombs going away. (I'd been keeping the discs up my battle-dress to keep them warm.) Then there's a shout—'Big Cookie away!' and with the release we went up like going up in a lift and the needle dug hard into the acetate right up to the aluminium backing, but I managed to lift it and get it on again and carry on cutting."

The original disc lay on his desk at Broadcasting House, with its red label, and there in the middle was a distinct furrow. Pidsley had, in fact, been sitting amidships right over the bomb, and had been able to touch it "nice and close" through an opening in the floor. But there was more trouble to come.

"Some rat-tatting started then, and it seemed a Jerry was sitting nicely on our tail, and he'd fired, but because of the bomb going away, we weren't where we were supposed to be, owing to the going up. Otherwise I wouldn't have lived to tell the tale. Then the crew got to work to get him, and you know, *this* is where it was as if they'd all acted their parts and all done what we wanted them to do. 'Come on,' says the Australian skipper. 'What happened, rear-gunner? Did he go down? Over to you.' 'I can see him,' says the rear-gunner, 'and he's going down and he's burning.' 'Bloody good show!' shouts the top-turret-gunner, and so on.

"Then we started on the homeward run and began weaving, to get out of the flak and the searchlights. The German searchlights were very efficient. They had one master-light, a blue job operated by radar, which the others used to follow, and once you got in that light there wasn't a hope, you were shot down for certain. Then came Sweden, and *they* shot at us, as I told you."

Pidsley said there were more than thirty aircraft shot down in that raid, but even the smallest detail doesn't escape a recording engineer at the end of his job.

"The last indignity was when we came into breakfast. They had eggs on, that day, and we queued up, and when it came to me, the chef said 'No eggs for you,' and I asked why, and he said 'You haven't been on Ops.,' and I said I had, I'd just come back, and he said 'You can't have been, you haven't got a flying-suit on.' "

We imagine that Pidsley got his eggs after all, but the chief concern of Wynford, elated by the success, and BBC men Michael Standing and Rooney Pelletier, who had turned up at the aerodrome, was to hear the recording played, there and then. "But I said 'No. No play disc.' They were put off by that because they were so keen to hear it, and Wynford was twisting my arm, and they all said London wanted a report, but I said, 'No' again. 'No disc. We play disc when we get back to Portland Place, and then we copy disc at same time,' I said. And that's what happened. Otherwise, we might have lost it for good."

The outbreak of wartime Variety programmes was soon to cheer up the home front and the forces so much that a naval officer was able to write from somewhere in the Mediterranean: "Please let us have more Tommy Handley at breakfast time. We find it so good for the Captain's liver." The BBC Forces Programme was stepped up considerably when it was discovered, after a poll, that most of the BEF was listening to Radio Normandie.

Non-military wartime programmes are dealt with in various parts of this book, and the range is very wide, from *ITMA* to *The Man Born to be King* and *The Brains Trust*. As for war-reporting itself, this was only put on a regular footing, with all BBC resources involved, after D Day, 1944, with the nightly *War Report*, but early in the struggle, some correspondents were in the thick of it. Godfrey Talbot always seemed to be reporting in blazing desert sun in North Africa, with Richard Dimbleby, while in the far north, in Finland, we heard the familiar voice of Edward Ward.

EDWARD WARD

Eddie, whose title—the Rt Hon Viscount Bangor—was, financially, a considerable embarrassment, owing to the death-duties imposed on the crumbling estate of his father's castle in Northern Ireland, never looked like an heir to a title. He always assumed an air of unassuming nonchalance. He has a vague military air about him, but it is far more akin to the mess than the battlefield. He seems to have been rather frightened by war and puzzled by it. When a prisoner, he much preferred being treated as one of the troops, where he organized entertainments, than as an officer (the British Foreign Office finally conveyed to the Italians that war correspondents were, in their eyes, to be regarded as having officer status). When everything was organized for him, Eddie felt bored.

The official BBC war-chronicles wrote little about their reporters until the unit was in full swing, and Eddie had to put the record straight about his earlier exploits in his own book,[1] which deals, among other things, with his early life and the fabulous years he spent in China in the 1930s. It all has the laconic ring of an Evelyn Waugh novel. Extraordinary events happen to Ward—to his mild surprise. At the moment of his capture by the Afrika Korps in the Western Desert, he could only say to his fellow-prisoner and press colleague Godfrey Anderson "this is the kind of thing that happens to other people, but not to us."

At the beginning of the war, Eddie felt he had come to a dead end as an announcer, after some criticism of his rate of speaking, and a decision to send him to the West Region seemed like being sent to the salt-mines. He told Snagge he'd rather resign, and went immediately to the News Editor, R. T. Clarke, and asked for a job as a reporter. This was equally and immediately granted by Clarke, who knew Eddie spoke some Russian.

"What do you want me to do, R.T.?" asked Ward. Clarke smiled. "I was thinking about that last night," he said. "I was wondering if you'd like to go abroad."

"Good heavens, yes. Where to?"

"I was thinking of Finland," said Clarke.

As one of the first BBC war reporters, Eddie put it "there were no rules. You had to make your own." There were no engineers or recording teams, either, and his voice usually came through live from a local Finnish station. Even air-raids were a novelty in his baptismal time of fire. He teamed up with Geoffrey Cox[2] of the *Daily Express*, and together, in Lapland, they coined the phrase "It is reported in well-known Arctic Circles." Together, too, they witnessed the massacre at Suomussalmi, where two Russian divisions lay dead in the snow.

"Never, I should think, has there been such a scene of frozen horror," Eddie reported, "since the retreat of Napoleon's Grand army from Moscow, and even that cannot anywhere have been so concentrated. Some of the best war material had been taken away, but the bodies were there—the ground was far too hard for them to be

---

[1] *Number One Boy*.
[2] Later Diplomatic Correspondent of the *News Chronicle*, TV broadcaster on Panorama, Editor of ITN and the architect of its success, and now, as Sir Geoffrey Cox, CBE, Managing Director of Yorkshire TV.

buried—they were there in their thousands, frozen as hard as stone in the ghastly attitudes in which they had fallen. There was a terrifying unreality about these bodies. Somehow they didn't look human. The terrific cold had made them look like rather badly executed waxworks. They were a curious brown colour and when, once, I stumbled and hit a dead man's hand, his finger snapped off as if it had been made of plaster. The bodies were everywhere: on the sides of the road, in the makeshift shelters and dugouts where they had tried to escape the relentless fury of the Finnish ski patrols. They didn't seem even to have attempted to resist."

At Lake Ladoga, Ward and Cox saw equally horrible sights during the initial German campaign. But the Finns, though lavishly praised by the Allies, were in a hopeless position. The famous Mannerheim Line was to be of no more use than the Maginot Line. Eddie was back in England when he got wind of a possible Finnish surrender. With the typical acumen of a reporter, he flew to Stockholm instead of Helsinki (with Virginia Cowles, representing the New York *Herald-Tribune*) and got a news scoop, from Mr Erkko, Finnish Minister in Sweden, on the end of the war, and contrived to file it.

He then began reporting from France, and anyone who knew his liking for good food and wines will not be surprised to learn that, in the distinguished company of journalists Sefton Delmer and Quentin Reynolds, he had what was to be the last lunch served to the Allies by Maxims, in a deserted Paris. The stupendous meal, reported Eddie, came to seventy-five francs—eight shillings—a head. The Head Waiter regretted that he could not give them dinner. His next guests were to be the German General Staff. It is also typical of Eddie that he chose the celebrated *Chapon Fin* restaurant in Tours during the fall of France, and found half the French Government lunching there, with "Laval at the next table" and Georges Mandel, a Jew, assuring him in an interview, that he would remain in France as long as he could. In the same way, on the British boat bringing him home, he found Baron de Rothschild, surrounded by tins of caviare, which the refugee millionaire was only too willing to exchange for Eddie's humble sardines.

The other theatre of war in which his reports made valuable history was the Western Desert. The Evelyn Waugh touch creeps in as he describes the splendour of Richard Dimbleby's way of living in Cairo, in a houseboat surrounded by servants, and a big Chrysler "with a chauffeur who looked like a Turkish admiral."

Both Richard and Eddie liked the good things of life—and yet some of their most memorable despatches came from places like Suomussalmi, Belsen and Buchenwald, as well as the names well-known in the Western Desert—Tobruk, Bardia, Benghazi, Halfya (Hellfire) Pass, Sidi Rezegh and Sollum. Twenty-five years later, when Barsley made a television film in the area, to record the present-day appearance of the battlefields, he described himself privately as going "Dimblewards through the Desert." Tobruk was still half in ruins, with Libyans suspicious of any photography being done at all. Bardia looked very like the shell-shocked port Eddie Ward had seen, after the bombardment by sea from the Royal Navy.

But to Edward Ward, everything was there, and it was all happening. He and Chester Wilmot took the road through Cyrenaica and, understandably enough, found the seaside town of Derna so delectable they wanted to stay there. However, Benghazi was the immediate objective, a town taken and retaken five times. The Australians, Ward found, were amazed and disappointed that Benghazi boasted no trams. "To them, trams were a status symbol." Later Ward was to re-enter Tobruk by sea, during the fruitless siege by Rommel, in a minelayer-cruiser which successfully re-garrisoned the town under cover of darkness.

His next objective was Greece, which the British—probably unwisely—were attempting to defend against a particularly successful German onslaught. Eddie didn't spend long in Greece but headed, predictably, for the King George Hotel in Athens, one of a long list of "correspondents'" hotels which dotted the wartime world, from the Scribe in Paris to the Marounuchi in Tokyo. On a bombing raid over Benghazi, Ward found his plane was filled with bottles as well as bombs. The procedure, apparently, was to drop the bottles as well, since they "made a screaming noise through the air which terrified the natives."

There followed trips to Addis Ababa (where he failed to get an interview with Emperor Haile Selassie), Jerusalem (where Dimbleby's car stood as a sign that Richard had taken up residence in Palestine) and a glimpse of the lush life in Beirut, before Eddie was back in the Western Desert. There, still disbelieving it, he was captured by the Afrika Korps and put "in the bag."

His subsequent adventures as a prisoner are highly entertaining—indeed, as he rather indignantly remarks, war correspondents were assigned to the Prison Entertainments section—and his fluent German helped him to get reasonable treatment. But we take up the story in what we called "Ward Report," during the BBC series. Eddie was flown back soon after his release from a German POW camp, and Dimbleby brought him to Broadcasting House in time for the usual evening programme. He looked thinner than usual, but otherwise was his normal, debonair self; so normal, in fact, that we found it difficult to believe that he had undergone such bizarre adventures. Then back he went, this time to the Eastern front, to become the first BBC man to report the link-up of the American and Russian armies at Torgau on the Elbe.

The story of the party which followed is legendary. The only faintly coherent record of it—and it is literally a record—must still be somewhere in the archives of the BBC Recording Library. It reached *War Report* marked "Edward Ward. Party at Torgau. NOT TO BE BROADCAST." Eddie has described the superhuman efforts he and Reg Pidsley, his recording engineer, a man with a suitably sardonic sense of humour, made in order to fix any recording at all, so full were they of vodka, and so deafened by brass bands of balalaikas. Eddie's voice loomed out of the din:

"Hullo . . . BBC. . . . This is Edward Ward speaking from Torgau. It's a bee-ootiful day, we've had a bee-ootiful lunch, and everything's absolutely BEE-OOTIFUL!!"

It was when, after attempting to describe speeches by General Zhadov and General Hodges, and to translate parts of a Hitler-Goering comedy act, he introduced a Russian press colleague, that Eddie got really tangled up. His colleague was a correspondent from *Izvestia*, not an easy word to roll round your tongue anyhow.

RICHARD DIMBLEBY

Of Richard Dimbleby it's very difficult to say anything that has not been said before. The Dimbleby we knew during the war was an ace correspondent, far ahead of his time in the first year or two, with the Western Desert as his field of operations. The best way to get the measure of a man in his sort of job is to ask the recording engineers who worked with him, and by that yardstick, he emerges, as did Chester Wilmot, as a real professional. Being a journalist helped: there's a tough streak in that profession which moves mountains but never forgets detail. He was self-centred, admittedly. "Heaven knows who will knit things together after I've gone," he cabled, on leaving

Paris headquarters. We drew a cartoon of Richard as an old woman, knitting below the guillotine. He loved it.

He recorded the take-off of the first paratroopers at 0800 hours on D Day, and was soon up in a Mosquito. We called that "the flight of the Dimblebee." "We flew on south-west," he reported, "and I could see France and Britain, and I realized how very near to you all is this great Battle of Normandy. It's a stone's-throw across the gleaming water. I saw it all as a mighty panorama, etched in all its detail. . . ."

As an example of a flying reporter, Richard had no equal. He was on more than twenty bombing operations over Germany, and as liaison with Bomber Command brought many a hero-pilot into the *War Report* studio, and helped to calm his nerves with a drink and a smile. Richard was rightly proud of his own reporting and fought for his own stuff. The climax came when he went into Belsen concentration camp with the British 11th Armoured Division. His unforgettable report, however, lasted for fourteen minutes, and on that night, with war news pouring in, we could only take an extract from it. Richard was furious, but being a working journalist at heart, he saw our difficulty, and it was broadcast in full later on. Radio was still not flexible enough to have it put out as a special item, which obviously should have been done.

There may have been only one Chester Wilmot and one Ed Murrow, but there were several Richard Dimblebys: the Dimbleby of *Down Your Way*, described by his colleague John Shuter as a lightning operator who didn't believe in repeat-interviews, but got results first time; the Dimbleby of *Twenty Questions*—the nimble Dimbleby, an apt foil for the have-a-go spontaneity of Jack Train and the bright persistence of Anona Wynn; the Dimbleby remembered above all as A Man for All Occasions, the greater the better. Television viewers will think of him as the Dimbleby of *Panorama*, though in fairness it should be added that in this he took over, from Malcolm Muggeridge and Max Robertson, a series which was already well established, with five million viewers.

At times he was accused of being pompous, but the accusation is wide of the mark. It is possible to put it this way: Richard enjoyed, and excelled at, a scene of pomp and circumstance. In a run-of-the-mill, routine interview he might appear bored or impatient, but television exaggerated this trait. It was never evident, for instance, in *Down Your Way*, where his patience was proverbial. As for being a good man to meet—well, again, ask the engineers. He took them at their true value. Shall we say, he walked with kings, and only occasionally lost the common touch? The word he would like above all to have associated with him is the humble word "homework." To this he devoted infinite attention. Perhaps the best summing-up is the final tribute, in a book compiled by his friends, from Wynford Vaughan Thomas.[1]

"Ours is a transient art; our words and pictures make a powerful immediate impact, and then fade as if they had never been. But Richard brought a permanence to our impermanent profession. . . . We knew him as a simple man, a good man, and in the end a very brave man."

D DAY: BREAKING THE BIG NEWS

The date: 6th June, 1944.
The time: 0932 DBST.
The place: SHAEF Headquarters, London.
The announcer: John Snagge.

There are two interesting points about the historic D Day announcement, the moment for which the world had been waiting. In the first instance, Snagge did not speak from Broadcasting House, but from a small underground cubicle beneath the Senate House of London University in Bloomsbury, which was the wartime Headquarters of Eisenhower's Supreme Command. In the second, it was nearly not Snagge's voice but that of an American which made the announcement. The battle which took place behind the scenes, about the appropriate voice, was known only to one or two members of the BBC, Government officials, and representatives of SHAEF.

This is what listeners heard, at 9.32 Double British Summer Time:

"This is London. London calling in the Home, Overseas and European Services of the BBC and through United Nations Mediterranean. This is John Snagge speaking. Supreme Headquarters Allied Expeditionary Force have just issued a Communiqué and in a few seconds I will read it to you. Communiqué No. 1. Under the command of General Eisehnower, Allied Naval Forces supported by strong Air Forces began landing Allied Armies this morning on the Northern Coast of France."

"I had begun broadcasting many years before," says Snagge, "but

---
[1] *Richard Dimbleby, Broadcaster*, edited by Leonard Miall (BBC Publications).

in all those years, this was the most dramatic announcement I had ever made. It had an electrifying effect. The tension had been building up and increasing month by month, day by day, and finally hour by hour. As I read the announcement, from a pink card which had been handed to me at 9.15, I sensed the excitement, and knew what it would mean to the people at home, and especially to the resistance movements of the occupied countries of Europe."

The story behind the pink card is also, in its own small way, dramatic. For the card had been written to be spoken by two announcers, and contained indications for Voice A and Voice B. The words were identical, but the announcement for Voice A had been crossed out in red pencil. Moreover, when Snagge went into his cubicle that morning (the broadcasting room was immediately below the Press Room, where the D Day news was given simultaneously and verbally) he realized that beside him in another cubicle was the American military correspondent, Colonel Dupuis. His Voice A announcement went out only to the troops waiting to go across to France to reinforce the initial landings.

What exactly had gone on, during the night hours, to make the change?

Snagge takes up the story:

"We have to go back a bit. The date of the opening of the Second Front must have been one of the most closely guarded secrets of all time, and within the vast and intricate organization necessary to mount such an assault, the BBC was destined to fulfil a special role—and to fulfil it according to the BBC's method, that's the important point. All the secrets have been out for years now—the last-minute postponement, the fact that the BBC Overseas reported the Invasion two hours earlier, by quoting an Occupied Europe broadcast from Holland, and so on. But perhaps the victory of the BBC in insisting on the use of a well-known BBC voice first—which happened to be mine—has never before been properly emphasized. The man who won that victory was William Haley. As Director-General, he declared that the use of an American voice first would cause confusion, and that Voice A must not only be British, but be one of the regular, named announcers. I have never to this day been able to estimate the amount of pressure he and his colleagues were under—his right-hand man on this, as on so many other wartime occasions, was A. P. Ryan, who led the BBC War Reporting Unit—but they never wavered. It's a tremendous tribute not only to Haley, a man often underrated by BBC staff who had hardly met him, but to the strange power of the BBC to go its own way. It was not so much the Nelson touch: it was the Reith touch."

The actual card of the announcement, with Voice A eliminated, was taken by Snagge back to Broadcasting House that day, and now hangs framed in his house. At one time, his friend Ed Murrow asked if he could borrow it, and when it was returned, the card was signed "To John Snagge, who first spoke these words on the air: Dwight D. Eisenhower." Underneath are the confirming signatures: "Winston S. Churchill" and "Tedder" (Lord Tedder was then Eisenhower's Deputy).

There were several more vitally important personnel involved in the D Day broadcasting story. As Head of Presentation, Snagge's first job was to contact the Senior Superintendent Engineer, Leslie Hotine, and the man who put out European Service programmes, Gibson Parker. That was about three weeks before 6th June. The equipment was to be installed at SHAEF, not at BH. All programmes were to be faded, and linked with United Nations Radio. European transmitters would then put out an Alerting Period, with an initial call in English, followed by recordings made by Heads of State in their own language—Queen Wilhelmina, King Haakon, General de Gaulle, and so on. Snagge had to write out all his instructions in long-hand, without secretarial help, until Senior Controller, Basil Nicolls, was later able to supply his own personal secretary, who was within the magic circle. Frank Phillips recalls that he was in charge of Overseas announcements from Bush House, but said to Snagge "I don't know what my instructions are." Nor did Joseph Macleod, who was detailed for the Continuity announcing. The instructions were, of course, in longhand—in the safe.

So to 5th June, and Snagge continues:

"I had not been allowed to leave Broadcasting House for days. I couldn't even leave the office—not even to make necessary physical calls—without informing Duty Officer. On the 5th, I went to bed as usual, with no indication that we were on the verge of D Day. But looking back, I remember that the engineer in charge, Leslie Hayes, had a habit of saying, knowingly, 'You can sleep tight tonight,' or something similar. He said it on the night of the fourth, but *not* on the night of the 5th! At about 4 a.m. my bedside phone rang. Jim Forte, the Duty Officer, said: 'You must report to SHAEF headquarters at once.' I rang Frank and Joseph, and told them to take up their positions. With Pat Ryan I walked the ten minutes or so over to Malet Street. I don't remember what we talked about. At 6.30 a.m. Macleod opened up the Service normally, and according to programmes in the *Radio Times*. We sat and waited. We knew we had dynamite to announce—at last.

"A sergeant brought me a slip of paper at 9.0 a.m., headed *Topflight Zero* 732 *GMT*. This meant that 0932 Double British Summer Time was the deadline. I contacted Joseph, to transfer from BBC to me at SHAEF. To Frank Phillips I said 'Get the keys of the safe from Gibson Parker,' and gave him zero hour. I had to scribble my own introduction to the Announcement on the pink card. Colonel Dupuis started his broadcast first, but only to his limited audience. The moment I heard him announce the Invasion of Europe I went ahead too. After reading the momentous words, I repeated them, and again many times during the day, to the first *War Report*.

"To while away the time of waiting, some of the high-ranking British and U.S. officers around that tiny studio organized a two-shilling sweepstake on the exact hour. I won eight shillings with my estimate of 9.0 a.m., and still have the odd scraps of paper on which we wrote down our estimates. Such is radio history."

WAR REPORT

Today, Studio LG1 (lower ground one) in Broadcasting House is a genteel, tastefully-decorated room used for genteel, tastefully worded talks. The producer's cubicle is carpeted and calm, and full of shining tape-recording gear. There is—and it is a regrettable omission—no small plaque on the wall saying "*War Report* was broadcast from here." Along the lower ground corridor, within sprinting distance, and on the way to the Concert Hall, is LG14, once the Green Room for artistes appearing before the audience. Between D Day, 1944, and VE Day, 1945, it was the most important single room in the whole building—also the untidiest and the most amusing. Here, 235 nightly programmes were prepared, organized, edited, and, in the phrase used by French radio, "*foutus sur l'air*"—in other words, rushed to LG1, where the production staff were waiting, as the BBC clock hiccupped the minutes up to 9.15 p.m. Only on one occasion did the programme get a rehearsal—and that, if memory serves us, was rather a dull night. The series—the most prestigious, inventive and expensive BBC radio has ever mounted—had an audience estimated at between ten and fifteen million listeners, as large as *ITMA*. It met its inevitable ups and downs, but for anyone to be able to say, "I worked in *War Report*" is the civilian equivalent of having served at Agincourt, in the Peninsular Campaign, or with Monty at Alamein. Moreover, since the first German V1 flying bomb fell on London within ten days of the series starting, the production team was often as much in the front line as the war correspondents whose dispatches they presented.

The Green Room, during the earlier blitz, had been the underground headquarters of the News Talks Department, so it was already fitted up with bunks, which were often used when news was flowing in all through the night, or when doodlebugs were active. The most important item in the room was a large box which we would have called Big Brother if George Orwell, who had been working for BBC Overseas service down the road, had written *1984* by then. It wasn't watching you, but talking to you, continuously. Connected with the transmitters in Europe, it gave us every dispatch, every service message from correspondents (messages to wives or otherwives, requests for money, rude remarks about the BBC, outbursts of spleen and occasional congratulations) at any hour. On one famous occasion, when we awaited the fall of Paris, a voice suddenly spoke up, in the middle of a sleepy afternoon, saying breathlessly "Hullo, BBC, hullo NBC, hullo Blue Network—hullo *anybody*—this is Herbert M. Clarke, and I'm speaking from *Paris*!"

War Report went out each evening after the news, for fifteen minutes (we could often have filled up sixty). Apart from the correspondents and John Snagge, the usual presenter, it was, quite rightly, entirely an anonymous production. This had always been the tradition of the Talks Department, and although there was a majority of Features men in the team, it would have been invidious to single anyone out. This could have been done when the official story of the monumental series came to be published, but it turned out to be merely a selection from correspondents' dispatches, rather a history of the war than a history of War Report.[1] This "great BBC adventure," as William Haley described it to Snagge, was as much a backroom job as a front-of-house presentation, and it seems strange that the official account should have been edited by a writer who had had no first-hand experience of the programme at all, and should have omitted the

[1] *War Report:* a Record of Despatches, with foreword by Field-Marshal Montgomery, (Oxford University Press, 1946).

names of two out of the three men who were the great figures behind it. It is, of course, possible that A. P. Ryan, that odd, leprechaun character who ran the War Reporting Unit, didn't want to be mentioned in dispatches. The same may be true of the late Laurence Gilliam, whose editorship gave life and colour to the correspondents' stories, and vast encouragement to the Green Room gang. It was the first time that Feature treatment had been given to this type of programme, and the effect was electrifying, particularly to the Americans, whose war correspondents turned in such exciting material. The *New York Times* summed up: "The service of the BBC was not less than superb ... exemplary in its presentation and especially fine with its actuality broadcasts. Time and again throughout the day they came over bringing a sense of reality and on-the-spot realism beside which the contrived studio programme seemed virtually static."

If the War reports seemed to flow easily as well as excitingly, this was because of the teamwork behind the scenes. The Green Room story has already been told,[1] but here briefly was the set-up. Under the all-over control of Ryan were two editors, Gilliam of Features and Donald Boyd of Talks. They were entirely different types of men, but both dedicated to the job in hand. An expert could probably tell if it was a Gilliam night, or what we called "Boyd Songs at Eventide," but the advantage of the change was that the series didn't often suffer from monotony. One radio critic called W. E. Williams wanted the whole thing stopped—"liquidated" was his curiously fascist phrase—because of the noises-off, which he likened to "old iron, cracked gongs or tyreless vehicles." These were, in fact, authentic sounds of battle, often uncomfortably close to the microphone, and the very stuff of the programme. Who at that time, for instance, could forget the sound of the murderous mortar fire at Arnhem, as Stanley Maxted heard it, the roar of the Buffalo craft which swept Wynford Vaughan Thomas across the Rhine, or the voice of a Soviet soldier calling into the night, in Russian, on the banks of the Elbe, as he waited with Edward Ward for an answering call from the American troops?

The two main producers who led the team at Broadcasting House were, in the first stages, the late Cecil McGivern, writer of *Mulberry Harbour* and later to be Controller of BBC Television, and John Glyn-Jones, a former actor, and the delight of the *Late Joys* Victorian music-hall at the Players' Theatre. Glyn was to stay the whole course,

---

[1] "Here is Tonight's War Report," from *The Wolf at the Door*, by Michael Barsley (Michael Joseph, 1946).

to the delight of the staff. The Girl-Friday producer was a sumptuous blonde, Brigid Maas, who had scored a success with her series *Into Battle*. Scriptwriters included the distinguished Scottish playwright, the late Robert Kemp, Gordon Boshell, then "Bee" of the *Daily Mail*, and freelance John Cheney, who had already lost an arm in war service but made good use of the other, in writing.

In due course, we got to know the war correspondents very well, not only personally, for they always dropped in for a drink when on leave, but by their work. We were their lifeline, and as Stewart Macpherson told us, on a visit to Britain in 1971 from Canada, "all the reporters in the field used to listen to the programme whenever they could, and of course there was a feeling of disappointment if you'd sent in something and it wasn't used. I even kept a box-score, and I think it was thirty-one (if Laurence Gilliam were here with us he'd know) thirty-one I once had in a row. I remember Chester Wilmot once saying 'There he is again,' giving me the needle. But it was fiercely competitive out there, that news-getting, something that doesn't exist in radio today, and I told myself, well, thirty-one consecutively—I must be doing something right! As for the series itself, undoubtedly it has to be inscribed in the annals of broadcasting as a masterpiece—no other word for it—if only for the fact that I could see Americans out in the field listening to it regularly, even though there was only an occasional reporter from the States like George Hicks or Larry Leseur or Bill Downes, bless him. Yes, Americans listening to 'Auntie' BBC from London, whom they'd all laughed at. How was that for a tribute?"

Stewart admits that he deliberately went out of the way to look for the lighter side of certain war stories, and that this approach paid off, and made him popular. He counts *War Report* as his greatest stepping-stone to success, as indeed it was with a number of other correspondents after the war ended. Perhaps this was something to do with his style—his quick-fire Canadian approach, the ice-hockey angle—but by contrast, Stan Maxted and Matthew Halton, both Canadians, were much weightier, more authoritative broadcasters.

As programme followed programme, and the series began to build up into this unique sound-picture of nations in the full fury of war, the birth-pangs of production died away, and we feared neither God nor man in our daily task. The one type of person we discouraged was the visitor. When Lady Violet Bonham-Carter was due to call (she was then a Governor) we only remembered, just in time, to take down a cartoon of her as Lady Violet Network (the American networks were named after colours). Probably she wouldn't have minded! On another occasion, the DG brought a party of foreign journalists round to see the BBC's dynamic programme in action. Haley threw open the door of the Green Room. It was empty, except for a rather attractive secretary stitching rather attractive underwear, in a corner. We were all in the studio, listening to discs. The programme went out nightly, in liaison with its vigorous counterpart, *Radio News Reel*, which shared some of our material for Overseas, and *Combat Diary*, for the Forces' Programme. There was only one long gap, between 4th February and 23rd March 1945, when the Allies crossed the Rhine for the final phase. During that gap we didn't know what to do with ourselves, having become so accustomed to the shift-system and the Green Room's private world. But War Report made a triumphant return, the covering of the Rhine battle being, as we could now professionally assess, well up to standard. It was, within the production team, quite a reunion, for several members continued right through the series, including John Lane of recorded programmes, and two stalwart hussies who handled discs with the skill of conjurors, Joan Wilen and Mona Dinwiddie, under the benign gaze of programme engineer "Laddie" Ladbrook, who was in charge of the big programmes in the life of the Features Department.[1]

One name not to be forgotten in our own roll of honour was our Messenger, who had the most inappropriate name of Sleep. Few men of his age could cover the ground between Broadcasting House and SHAEF Headquarters as quickly and tirelessly as Mr Sleep. We regarded him as far more important than any Head or Controller, for until our scripts were passed for censorship (the recordings from the battlefront were usually censored on the spot) the programme couldn't go on. Later, a brace of SHAEF censors was assigned to BH, so great was the volume of material. They were tall, mild, kindly sort of chaps, who looked at us, a Dirty-Dozen sort of crew, all cigarette-ash and beer-stains, in faint astonishment, as we bustled visiting Generals out of the way, and sped glum heroes up the line—not to death, but to the microphone, which they often seemed to fear more than death. "I'd rather bomb the *Tirpitz* again than go through this," as Wing-Commander Tait put it.

[1] There were, for the record, six babies born to the wives of reporters or War Report staff, among them David Dimbleby and Margaret Barsley. There was only one casualty: John Snagge. On 24th September 1944 he fell off a ladder while picking apples in the garden of the Controller of Programmes, and was off the air for two weeks.

In course of time, we got to know our correspondents very well by nature as well as name. The one disadvantage of the Big Brother loudspeaker in the room is that we couldn't answer back (service messages were exchanged in a War Reporting Unit room upstairs). So they only knew what we thought of them and their dispatches when they were on leave. Some wily radio reporters know that the way to get by with a long report is to make it difficult to cut, not only on the page but in voice. It is messy to end in mid-sentence, with an upward inflection. A necessary ingredient to most programmes was a "Sit. Rep." (Situation Report) from a particular Army Group, though these could be very dull compared with a combat piece, thudding with gunfire. It was a very difficult formula to achieve, this blend of information and—well, it will have to be called drama or entertainment, because that's what gave us such an enormous following among listeners.

It was certainly real "live" drama, from the moment when we heard the voice of Howard Marshall, normally the deceptively-lazy chronicler of cricket-matches, late on D Day:

"I'm sitting in my soaked-through clothes with no notes at all; all my notes were sodden—they're at the bottom of the sea, as it's only a matter of minutes since I stepped off a landing-craft."

This was the real thing: Our Man on Our Day—and what a time he'd had getting ashore on the Normandy beach.

"Our craft swung, we touched a mine, there was a very loud explosion, a thundering shudder of the whole craft, and water began pouring in.... We were some way out from the beach at that point. The ramp was lowered at once, and out of the barge drove the Bren gun-carrier into about five feet of water, with the barge settling heavily in the meanwhile. We followed, wading ashore.... There was no sign of any confusion."

The reports sent back on the first few days made astonishing listening: Air-Commodore Helmore flying over the battle-scene, talking into a midget recorder; Guy Byam jumping with the paratroopers (he was to repeat this at Arnhem, and to be lost in action a week or two afterwards); Chester Wilmot following up the progress of the Sixth Airborne Division; Dimbleby in his Mosquito; Robert Barr with Ike: Frank Gillard with Monty; the Admiralty revealing absolutely nothing. All this was the beginning of a familiar pattern to us. "Censor-ships that *don't* pass in the night," we commented on the paucity of naval information, and that was to be our irreverent attitude throughout. There were times when we ourselves came under fire—or rather, our two gallant Editors did—from correspondents, the press or the High-ups. But we were usually too busy putting the programme together to listen to them.

There were unforgettable moments, too. Arnhem was one. We had already filled programmes with stories of the Nijmegen Bridge battle, when Chester Wilmot flew to Brussels, and tried to get through live to *War Report*, by contacting listeners in Britain on a medium wavelength, begging them to ring up the BBC—which they did in hundreds —to tell us he had the story. But more dramatic still, when our men had finally to pull out of the hell that had been Arnhem for more than a week, was the appearance, that night, of our two correspondents, Stan Maxted and Guy Byam, in the studio, still in their mud-caked battle-dress, Byam young, handsome, eager-voiced, Stan, once an actor, grey-haired, talking in slow, gravelly tones (he claimed to be the oldest BBC war reporter of them all). One of the first things he had done, when meeting the advance striking force at Arnhem, was to make a few inquiries, single out a paratrooper, go to him and shake hands and say "Hullo, son."

The Arnhem paratrooper was, in fact, his son.

Almost the first thing Maxted asked, before broadcasting, was how *we* were getting on in London. It had, in fact, been a bad week for doodlebugs, but we hadn't thought of it that way. All of us will remember how Stan, in Studio LG1, twirled his beret in his hands, and said:

"About five kilometres to the west of Arnhem, in a space 1500 yards by 900, on that last day, I saw the dead and the living . . . those who fought a good fight and kept the faith with you at home, and those who still fought magnificently on. They were the last of the few. I last saw them yesterday morning as they dribbled into Nijmegen . . . I walked up to one lieutenant to ask him about his sergeant, and he started to explain what had happened and then turned away. Then he turned again, and said 'It's hell to be pulled out when you haven't finished your job, isn't it? It doesn't occur to them that if they hadn't held that horde of enemy force at Arnhem, that force would have been down at Nijmegen upsetting the whole apple-cart.'"

How different was gallant Guy Byam's voice as he continued the Arnhem story—a young voice charged with emotion:

"They came out because they had nothing left to fight with except their bare hands, maybe. . . . The men had been fighting without food, and practically no water, fighting an enemy whose growing strength was always in our midst, fighting with small-arms against armour. Every brick, every wall, every house was a part of the battle that ebbed, to and fro, a yard here and a yard there. . . . And yet the men found time to laugh. Oh yes, they didn't look much like men by now: many were wounded, and many were so tired that when they smiled, they smiled as if it hurt them to move their mouths. . . .

"Then the Division heard that they were to be evacuated over the Rhine. They hated to go, because they were not beaten, but they got ready, smashed their equipment, the meagre equipment they had left. They put sacking over their shoes, and prepared for the last ordeal."

Then there were the recordings they had made on the spot, during the battle. Byam had swum the Rhine holding them. We played them all, including the despairing moment when Stan saw the supplies fall out of reach. Finally, we had a Dutchman in the studio with us, the well-known author Johann Fabricius. He had rung up, and asked if he could pay a tribute on behalf of his countrymen. It was a very moving one, and ended: "Some of these brave young men will stay behind in our country for ever. They shall not rest in cold foreign soil. The soil of Holland, which, in the course of our long and glorious history, received so many heroes for their eternal sleep, will proudly guard your dead as if they were the deeply mourned sons of our own people."

Near Arnhem today, on the banks of the quiet river, there is a special museum devoted to those men, containing momentoes, forged money and passports, weapons, photographs, and a large door taken off its hinges and propped against a wall. The Dutch are very proud of this, for on the door are boldy chalked the words: "F—— the Jerries."

Among the "regulars" on *War Report*, those correspondents who could turn in a "sit. rep." as well as a spectacular, we got to know, particularly, the dispatches of men like Wynford Vaughan Thomas, Frank Gillard, Robert Dunnett, Robert Reid, Robert Barr, Robin Duff; and for the Commonwealth, of course, Stewart Macpherson, Douglas Willis, Colin Wills. Pierre Lefevre was our most consistently good French reporter, and Bill Downs of CBS was probably the best standby among the Americans, with a wealth of good material.

Then there was Chester Wilmot, who survived all the many hazards of war—and he and his engineer, the grave, unflappable Harvey Sarney, were usually well in advance of the advanced striking force of the military—only to be killed, tragically, in the Comet explosion over

Elba. Chester was perhaps in a special category, since he was a writer as well as a journalist and radio reporter: his *Struggle for Europe* was one of the best books to come out of the war period. A burly, ebullient Australian with the hide of a rhinoceros, he took the measure of his job early on, and made it into one of the triumphs of the series. His notable contributions were many, from D Day, when he "jolted, lurched and crashed" his way in a glider on to French soil, to the surrender of the German forces to Montgomery at Lüneberg Heath, and the recording he made with the British sergeant who tried to forestall the suicide of Himmler, with its haunting final words: "And then we threw a blanket over him, and left him."

Probably the truest adjective to apply to Chester was authoritative. It sounds a dull word, but in his case it could be satisfying as well. In the Green Room on a dull afternoon, one of the staff might ask Traffic Control, who handled all the messages, "Anything happening?" and the reply might be (we always hoped it would be from one gorgeous girl with a flirty voice) "Wilmot's coming through at 5 o'clock," and we'd know that at least three minutes of programme time would be well and truly filled.

But such are the fortunes of war in broadcasting that Wilmot's greatest moment of triumph at Lüneberg Heath was also *War Report's* greatest moment of disaster. Wilmot had achieved the apparently impossible for our programme on 4th May 1945, four days before VE Day. Montgomery had agreed to let Harvey Sarney record the actual surrender of the German generals that afternoon inside his tent, as a BBC exclusive, to be played into *War Report* the same night. Case-hardened though the production team was with war news, we were on our toes, with that electric feeling which accompanies a big occasion. There was even a thrill in Chester's normally level voice as he set the scene, ready for Montgomery's dramatic entry. "It's now twenty past six. The discussions have been short and to the point. Admiral von Friedeberg has stepped down from Field-Marshal Montgomery's caravan. He is now walking over to the tent where the signing ceremony will take place. . . ."

Wilmot continued talking as the party entered the tent, and we heard Monty's cold, sharp voice begin: "Now we've assembled here today to accept the surrender terms which have been made with a delegation of the German Army."

Then the line went dead.

Sounds emerged which, when one later came to think of it, might have been Norwegian sailors celebrating the end of the fishing season. There was, for the first time in over 250 programmes, panic in Studio LG1. An Editor gesticulated. The announcer (who shall be nameless, and was not the usual one) must have taken it as a cue, and calmly said "That is the end of tonight's *War Report*." "That," somebody said quietly, "has torn it." It would have been so easy for the announcer to have said something like "I'm sorry, we seem to have lost the line, we're trying to get it back," holding the audience, for indeed the line did come back shortly afterwards, but by that time *War Report* had closed down in shocked, traumatic silence, preceding a babel of blaming. The BBC naturally, was besieged with telephone calls. What had happened? Had Montgomery been blown up? Having recovered from the shock, and having recorded the whole act of surrender, we demanded a break-in to programmes, so big was Chester's scoop. The request went higher and higher, reaching the Director-General, who granted it, and an hour later the whole story went out. Chester himself, on his final broadcast from MCN, Mike Charlie Nan (another of those hard-working-girl transmitters), said "We were sorry to fail you at that critical moment," but the failure was not his. The break was only half a minute: and we panicked.

Frank Gillard, another stalwart, was perhaps not in the same category as Wilmot, Dimbleby or Vaughan-Thomas, but he had no disasters in his long list of dispatches, and his great moment—the official link-up between the Russians and Americans at Torgau on the Elbe—went without a hitch. We had been calling it The Missing Link-up for several days, but the day came, and the time—eighteen hundred hours, nought minutes and fifteen seconds—and this time it was "live" into the News, not into the *War Report* programme. Gillard spoke first because he'd won the toss as to who should begin (as on D Day, the Americans lost the lead, and it was their link-up). Meanwhile Edward Ward, who had been around in the area for days, was getting ready for his famous party.[1] Frank was always a model of accuracy, making no concessions to emotion. Some thought his style too dry and earnest (someone nicknamed him "The Boy Scout of Radio") but he gave very good value.

Among other sensational moments, we had memories of Robert Reid in Paris, who was recording a description of General de Gaulle entering Notre-Dame under a hail of bullets, when he was knocked over, still talking, by the surging crowd. There was a second's pause,

---

[1] See page 186.

then his engineer plugged in his lead, which had slipped out, and Bob went on, in his ringing northern voice, "Well, that was the most remarkable thing that ever happened to me!" This commentary was so sensational, in fact, that it was carried on the entire American network later that night. If only Bob had been on contract for the Ed Sullivan Show! Previously that afternoon, we had heard Robert Dunnett, recording the same rifle-fire, lying under his recording truck. It was nearly the last time *either* of them saw Paris!

Robert Barr's note of warning before the last big German thrust in the Ardennes in December 1944 led to some vivid commentaries by him, representing Scotland the Brave, since the situation suddenly became very menacing. It was notable for the famous reply by the American commander of Bastogne to the Nazi demand for surrender. General A. C. McAuliffe didn't use a reporter, but recorded it himself:

"The German commander had the effrontery to send us a surrender command. When we got it we thought it was the funniest thing we ever heard. I just laughed and said, 'Nuts.' But the German major who brought it wanted a formal answer, so I had it written out: 'To the German Commander: NUTS. Signed, The American Commander.'"

McAuliffe was a man after our own heart. So too, in that area, was Cyril Ray, the well-known connoisseur and writer on wine, who was, so we thought, masquerading as a BBC war-reporter. At Bastogne, he asked the Americans "What sort of Christmas did you have?" It was rather a feeble joke, but it was replied to promptly—"Splendid," they said "Splendid—that was the day we got twenty-eight German tanks."

Humour and war, oddly enough, are inseparable companions. We laugh that we may not weep, and "To move wild laughter in the throat of death" is one of man's unaccountable characteristics. Everyone joked during the Blitz. There is the story of a British officer telling his men: "We shall attack immediately after the Tommy Handley programme." The Green Room also contained a blackboard, on which the running-order of the day was chalked, and rubbed out, and re-chalked till the last minute, and a notice-board, on which, as in messes and ops rooms and factories, we made fun of everything. Who but the Americans could have thought up, for the initials of transmitter JESQ, the title Jig Easy Sugar Queen? She became our Pin-up Girl, drawn as a Barsley Blonde. Her rival was JELG1 (Jig Easy Love George One) but the most consistent voice was that of MCM3 (Mike

Charlie Mike Three) As calls for MCM3 droned on, day after day, Mike and Charlie seemed to us to become real gremlin people.

Other people's house-jokes are usually tedious and soon fade, but we had messages from some correspondents which were hilarious in themselves: the correspondent in Algiers who found a man saying "I am a moderate terrorist"; the request by Stewart Macpherson, in the middle of the Arnhem battle, to return "for dental repairs, which are becoming urgent"; a description of Frank Gillard, by a Belgian newspaper, as "*un garçon élancé, à la figure ouverte*"; John Nixon's inquiry, from an Athens studio during the ELAS–EAM civil war—"Shall I keep the window open, or have you had enough gunfire sounds?"; and perhaps the best report of all, in the style of Evelyn Waugh's *Scoop*, from Alan Melville, until then a debonair writer of sophisticated revue. Melville eventually became a valuable regular correspondent with the 2nd Tactical Airforce, but on D Day, he was with the navy, somewhere off the Isle of Wight and well out of any combat area. While other BBC men were flying, parachuting and pontificating everywhere, Alan was left, with nothing but four racing pigeons to look after, "not the sort of encumbrance one really wants to be lumbered with when liberating Europe." His report went on:

"The quartette were christened Blood, Sweat, Toil and Tears. Blood was released when we were halfway across the Channel with the stirring message that we were halfway across the Channel. It occurred to me that if the bird flew in the wrong direction, it would give the whole thing away, but fortunately it went belting back to Angleterre. Sweat, who had a turn against me—it was mutual—gave one of my fingers a vicious peck when I was filling its drinking tray with fresh water. It was the only time I lost blood in the entire campaign, and the bird was despatched at once without any message at all tethered to its limb, in the hope that he/she/it would be in disgrace for having lost his, her or its little bit of rice-paper before homing. Toil and Tears were both released as soon as we landed on the beaches, both with rather hysterical reports saying that we *had* landed, as if by then everyone didn't know. They circled over the sand-dunes once or twice and then made for home. Considering what was going on at the time I didn't blame them and indeed would have been glad to join them...."

This classic dispatch, recorded and labelled, won our private Award, perhaps for unconsciously explaining why we won the war—but can you guess what happened to Melville's masterpiece? It was turned down by a surly Editor as being "trivial," and we had to wait for a decade (when the Editor in question no longer mattered) before we could include it in the D Day Tenth Anniversary Programme.

The night the final *War Report* ended, we sat in the Green Room in a dead, stunned silence. On the notice-board, the messages, the memos, the cartoons were pinned like dead moths. The famous blackboard in the middle of the room, on which so many names had been scrawled for the nightly menu, was swept clean. As we lingered there, as survivors linger in a dug-out, a "brown-coat" cleaner entered, a little Dickensian figure.

"Excuse me, gentlemen," he said hesitatingly, "But have you got a bit of chalk for the darts?" One of us got up and looked.

"I mean," went on the brown-coat, "*War Report's* finished now, isn't it? You won't be needing that board no more."

We nodded. There were two pieces of chalk left. He accepted both gratefully.

"It was a good programme, War Report was," said our visitor. "With Dimbleby and Chester Wilmot and all them. And the night they all come in from Arnhem. That was good, really good. Well, good-night, gentlemen, and thank you for the chalk."

The door closed. We sighed. So War Report really *was* over.

10 Some Radio Personalities

CHARLES HILL

The *vox humana*, which, apart from music and other sound effects, is the be-all and end-all of radio, is a remarkable instrument, and it's fascinating for a professional to study its effect on the listener, because this is the important thing. It may be what we call the Ancient Mariner approach, the inescapable voice. Although we admit that it was first the visual, glittering eye that affected the Wedding Guest, the listening follows:

> "He holds him with his glittering eye—
> The Wedding Guest stood still,
> And listens like a three year's child:
> The Mariner hath his will.
>
> "The Wedding Guest sat on a stone:
> He cannot choose but hear...."

How many radio speakers wish they could be as compelling as that Mariner, and in their different ways some of them have been.

Once upon a time there was a man who became known as the Radio Doctor. What he said made commonsense: he was BMA-trained, forthright, authoritative, outspoken—and plummy. How he seemed to exult in his own richness of tone! But he was not reciting Milton: he was prosaically saying something like "a pathologist is a man who sits on one stool and examines those of other people"—a phrase which brought forth protests. He would say "belly," and despite more protests, people would listen to what he would say about that part of the body he had described with anatomical correctness. "Stomach speaking" he once said to the children on Boxing Day—and they all listened, parents as well as children, because good old-fashioned advice followed.

Now, this same Radio Doctor became, not a mariner, but an Almighty Figure, astute and prestigious enough to be made, successively, Chairman of Independent Television, and Chairman of the BBC.

Some Radio Personalities 205

Yet his pronouncements on high policy are not listened to by the millions who heard him in his prime. By now the voice itself no longer matters.

When he first arrived at the BBC, Hill was met by George Barnes (then on his first day of duty at Broadcasting House) and producer Janet Quigley.

"This gentle and intelligent man, whom I came to know well," he wrote of Barnes, "died all too early. Miss Quigley, whom I was to know and admire until her retirement in 1962, made an immense, if unspectacular, contribution to her side of broadcasting."[1]

Hill started by giving four talks on the Nutrition Report, and contributed to Freddie Grisewood's programme *The World Goes By*. Later on he appeared in *Kitchen Front* with Howard Marshall, whom he congratulated on his "rich plummy voice"—like the plum calling the apple red! Throughout his broadcasting he was known simply as "The Radio Doctor"—an anonymity he thoroughly enjoyed. Listener Research once put the number of his listeners as high as fourteen million.

He describes his method of preparing a script as falling into three parts: one, brooding; two, tramping round dictating; three, trimming the draft for length. Often, he said, to be in a hurry produced the best results. Once, a female producer queried the use of the word "fairy" in a script. He was puzzled, until she explained. "She must have known more than I did in those pre-Wolfenden days!"

One cause of snoring he described as "too much booze, causing you to flop down in bed like a sack of potatoes, usually on your back with your face to high heaven, and your beautifully expired air ascending to a heaven you'll never reach! Remedy obvious—the water wagon."

Though he broadcast before the war for a fee of five guineas, he was never offered more until 1950, but never complained. Snagge was often in charge of him in the early morning, and they would have breakfast at a café near the BBC. When asked how he could get away with such apparently outrageous remarks, Hill replied "It's quite easy my dear chap. All you've got to do with the BBC is to put in two dirty ones, and if they find one they won't even look for the other!"

Hill also told him about the local gardener who used to go about saying "That there Doctor: he be going to say f—— one Friday."

Hill had great administrative ability, which began with his secretaryship of the BMA, with its importance in public relations. But his

[1] *Both Sides of the Hill* (Heinemann).

voice played a large part in creating his image. It was a distinctive voice, like Gilbert Harding's or Malcolm Muggeridge's, and he could talk forthrightly to the man in his own home, never making a public pronouncement, even on his own subject. This was to aid him as a politician, when he stood as MP for Luton. In that General Election he made a Party Political Broadcast on behalf of the Conservative Party, which had a great effect on the election itself, because of his popularity with listeners, not as a politician, but as the old GP of radio. The Tories were lucky to possess such a verbal weapon.

After chairing the Governors of both BBC and ITV, how much higher can the Hill rise? There is no need. BBC faith can move mountains, and has at least moved its Hill.

There are others whose voices themselves do not draw the listener, so much as what they are saying: among these we would include Richard Dimbleby (whose actual voice was unassuming, but whose style and cadences and flashing phrases riveted the attention), H. G. Wells (who could outline an absorbing line of thought, but in a high-pitched squeak) and Frank Phillips, whose clarity of diction was unsurpassed, but whose delivery gave no indication of his appearance, background or personality. It is perfect anonymity, though on occasions, such as when presenting a light-hearted programme, he could make delightful asides of his own.

GILBERT HARDING

When most people heard the name Gilbert Harding, they thought chiefly of the massive, shaggy, angry figure on *What's My Line?* or the growling but supremely authoritative voice on *Round Britain Quiz*. To those with longer memories within the BBC, Gilbert was already a legend long before he had uttered a word on radio or television in this country.

He has written of his life in smouldering prose,[1] and many tributes have been paid to him, rightly praising his kindness and compassion as well as his usually understandable wrath. But we remember the earlier Gilbert, too, before his reputation elevated him and finally almost literally stifled him.

"It wasn't radio that made Gilbert: he was there already," is Snagge's view. "He was a Regency period character, throughout, and

[1] The best account is *Master of None* (Putnam 1958).

his rudeness was studied: not merely vulgar abuse. At one time he was talking to my father, and a man came up and patted him on the shoulder. Gilbert turned, and didn't say anything like 'Go away, I'm busy' or 'Why the hell d'you interrupt?' He just looked at the man and said 'What emporium of so-called education does that tie come from?'

"Gilbert had a first-class brain and enjoyed first-class company—and wanted others to share it. He once said to me, as we met when leaving Broadcasting House, 'Come with me.' I followed him into a chauffeur-driven car, and we were driven to the Savile Club. There, talking in a group, were Compton Mackenzie, Lord Birkett, and Lionel Hale. We joined them and Gilbert ordered a bottle of port. What conversation it was! I don't think I even opened my mouth. His memory was fantastic and his quotations innumerable. He also had the curious gift of being forgiven. If he'd had to leave the table because he was drunk, he would always send flowers or some token afterwards, with a formal apology."

Gilbert left a "trail" behind him at the BBC Monitoring Service, where he spent his early BBC years. His tale of From Workhouse to Broadcasting House has been told many times, and no doubt Cambridge gave to him what Oxford gave to John Betjeman, "Niagaras of splendid talk." And he was a policeman, and could have been a barrister, all under the name of Gilbert Harding. Coleridge at one time despaired of writing, and joined the militia under the name of Silas Tomkyn Comberbatch. But later he wrote *Kubla Khan*, until interrupted by the Person From Porlock. Gilbert's life was always being interrupted, but he always left a long, long trail a-winding behind him. Snagge remembers him as an occasional OB commentator, making one particularly amusing job of describing the Passing-out Parade at Sandhurst, where the pony mounts the steps.

He went to Canada, where he was intensely disliked—"this Englishman who thinks that because half the world is painted red, he owns it"—but they couldn't resist him, and he was invited everywhere, as this curious, Regency character, very different from the ordinary BBC civil-servant representative. Back in England, he job-hunted within the Corporation, but kept members of the BBC Club at a roar with his tales in the evening drinking sessions. Then a producer offered him a job.

Gilbert the professional, in *Twenty Questions*, was one person: Gilbert the eventual actor, was another, and it was then the time when his earlier friends began to avoid him. You could be having a really intelligent conversation alone with him, and then two or three others would turn up, and Gilbert would break off and not exactly give you the brush-off but change into his actor-image.

What a barrister he would have been! He told Snagge he gave it up because he couldn't stand the sight and tales of misery and dirt that were put before him. He hated filth of all kinds with an almost physical loathing. Illness and injury in animals also shocked him. "Parsley" (as Barsley was called—"the man whose father is a not very conspicuous pillar of that breakaway church") recalls a morning in Richmond Park years ago, when walking with young daughters and a dog, which had a bandage over a cankered ear. A large open car came alongside, and a majestic hand from the tonneau waved the chauffeur to halt. Out stepped Gilbert, briefly greeted the family, but immediately went to the dog, whose tail wagged like a metronome. What ailed it? Was Parsley giving it the right treatment? Would all be well? Satisfied, the Regency figure resumed his seat and waved his vehicle on.

But he also showed kindness to humans at all levels. Parsley was once rehearsing a Bank Holiday programme, in which Bernard Braden had agreed to appear with his family as a Canadian reacting to the British holiday scene. The telephone rang in the producer's cubicle. Gilbert Harding wished to speak to Parsley. He said "What time d'you want me along? I'm standing in for Bernie." Parsley was assured he would be given the explanation later. It transpired that Braden had been involved in a car accident earlier that day: not a serious one, but a child had been hurt. It was no fault of Bernie's, but it had upset him. He had rung for Gilbert's advice, and Gilbert had insisted on taking his place. "You see, Parsley," he explained in the studio, "I have genuinely enjoyed my Bank Holiday, explaining British habits to my two young Indian friends [he indicated them] and I shall have much pleasure in conveying as much to your listeners." What can one say to that, except to thank one's lucky stars for a man like Gilbert Harding?

JOYCE GRENFELL

Stephen Potter, whose word "gamesmanship" (derived, so he elaborately claims, from a game of tennis once played with C.E.M. Joad) is already in the Penguin Dictionary, was a "Third Programme" character long before the Third Programme began, and it is

Jack Payne
He called Savoy Hill
"the chummy place"

Radio Times Hulton Picture Library

Henry Hall says goodbye (September 1937)
"The only man who got everything he wanted out of the BBC"

Radio Times Hulton Picture Library

Richard Dimbleby training with the BBC War Reporting Unit, 1944. "Richard brought a permanence to our impermanent professions. . . . We knew him as a simple man, a good man, and in the end a very brave man."

Wynford Vaughan Thomas

Radio Times Hulton Picture Library

Alistair Cooke
To Britain with love, in a "Letter from America" (1955)

BBC Copyright Photograph

Franklin Engelmann in *Brains of Britain*
The one and only "Jingle." He was not allowed to read the wartime news, because of his "German" name

BBC Copyright Photograph

"Tommy" Woodrooffe: He sailed through disaster

Radio Times Hulton Picture Library

"Thank you for the fruit!"

Marjorie Anderson, whose programme *Thank You For Your Letters* was a worldwide wartime favourite, gets an unrationed gift from some of her most fervent admirers, the crew of HMS *Roebuck* in 1945.

PA/Reuter

The man who launched the Archers

An early wartime photo of Godfrey Baseley in the series *At Longford's Farm*. (1943)

BBC Copyright Photograph

Two commentators and a Captain
Left to right: Godfrey Talbot, the late Captain Beach, of Cross Channel Steamers and Wynford Vaughan Thomas (1941)

Radio Times Hulton Picture Library

"Ten seconds from—now"
Michael Barsley at the production panel

"That'll sound better."
Bernard Braden goes through the script of his *Bedtime with Braden* show (1953)

Radio Times Hulton Picture Library

The Quickest Voice in the Business

Stewart Macpherson, Canadian who made his name as Ice-Hockey and Boxing Commentator (1947)

BBC Copyright Photograph

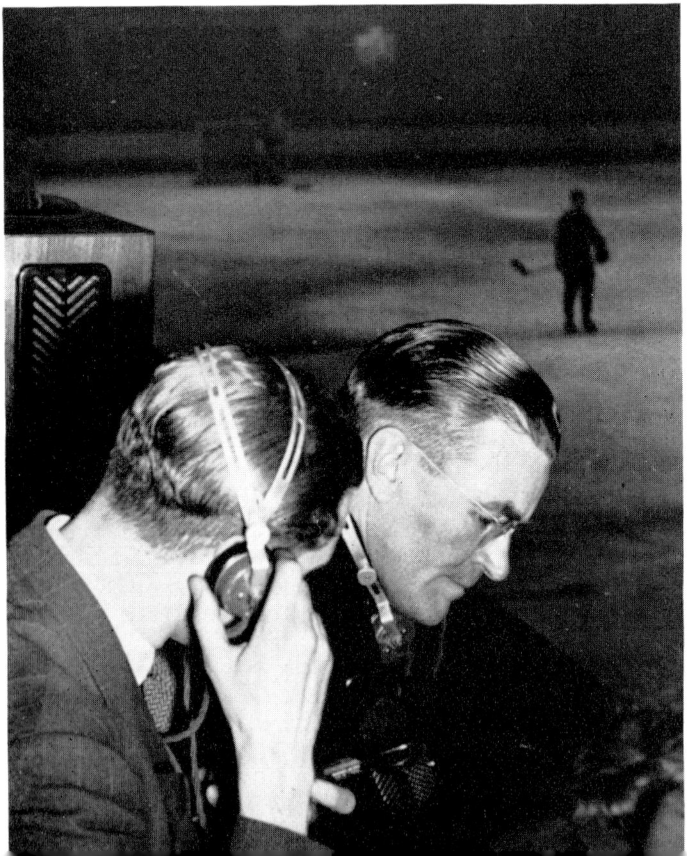

significant, as Joyce Grenfell points out, that the first programme to go out on the new service was one of their "How" series. But there was another side to Potter, as we can now explain.

"Stephen had begun a serious group of programmes called 'How,' about, for instance, how an Orchestra is assembled and run, and another about how 'Intercom.' works. This was during the war. But he wanted some light relief, and he asked me, 'Would you be amused to write a piece about—how to sell a hat, shall we say?' So I did a funny 'How *Not* to Sell a Hat,' and that was the beginning. Stephen abandoned the serious thing entirely, and the formula of the 'How' was that, in the first two minutes, you told how—satirically but straight—then the whole of the rest of the programme was How Not To. I wrote quite a lot of it independently, but a great deal was mutually improvised. But in those days, no tape. We used to have these marvellous speedwriters from the BBC, who'd come in and take down our impromptu conversation, which was all typed up, and from that we got a script.

"It was hair-raising working with Stephen, because he was a last-minute man, and the whole thing was held together with safety-pins and a bit of glue and we got the damp scripts as we went into the studio."

This was usually "The Grafton," as it was known in BBC circles, a rather gloomy one-time theatre in Grafton Street, near Warren Street tube station. But at least it was isolated, and not part of the busy main building. Potter, like Louis MacNeice, was nearly always his own producer, and a very meticulous one, however last-minute the preparations had been.

"This was strange," Joyce Grenfell went on, "because in his own life he seemed to be so disorganized. But his productions were of very high quality. He was great to work with, and we sort of sparked each other off. The cast was small and select—the regulars were Carleton Hobbs, Gladys Young, Betty Hardy, Deryck Guyler, Ronnie Simpson, and quite often Roy Plomley. Celia Johnson did one on "How to Listen to Music." Stephen wrote a superb, very moving script for her. But I think things were at their best when he himself took part, because he was a natural broadcaster."

The "How" series was often imitated but never equalled. By more recent standards of satire on the BBC, perhaps the shafts were not quite sharp enough, perhaps the attitude had more kindness and less cruelty, but the Potter-Grenfell approach was considered very daring at the time, and at first needed all the support of Laurence Gilliam to guide it past the Authorities, who later loved it. "Perhaps," she says, "we were the manure from which *Beyond the Fringe* and the other satires grew and it's not a bad thing to be manure."

Miss Grenfell regards the opening of the Third Programme as a mark of distinction for Stephen Potter and "How to Broadcast" (she is too modest to add herself), and the Third itself she thinks of as a great awakener and bringer of freedom to broadcasting. Her own career since the days of "How" has given her a position unique in the theatre.

It is a mistake to call her "The English Ruth Draper," because her monologues are much more varied, as is her repertoire, including the songs, ridiculous or waif-like. But her solo performance is appreciated all over the world, and her approach to it is the simplest and most honest you could find anywhere, and founded on sympathy rather than sarcasm. Much of this she says she owes to her broadcasting experience during the vintage years (the bouquet of *Château Comment* is light and dry) and she is a firm believer in radio.

She agrees with the award to radio for imagination, as opposed to television:

"I think you can do something pretty intimate on television and I quite enjoy doing it in a way, because of the colour—I think I enjoy all the media—but of course the one to write for is radio. And you make friends through radio: I think I won my public, such as it is, through the friends I've made on radio. Some of them have grandchildren by now—after all, I've been at it since 1939!"

Joyce is one of those people who are convinced that radio is on its way back in popularity. She will say "Look what it's done for music," which is of course undeniable, but in general she can point to people who say "I simply couldn't be without my radio." She cites one friend with a large garden which she runs herself, but often with a portable beside her—not just as a background, but to add to the pleasure of what she's doing. It's important to make this last distinction, since "transistoritis," as we might call the addiction which demands the presence of the little bakelite box, usually yacking away with pop, is a modern disease—or at least, affectation, a symptom which psychiatrists could easily explain. A. E. Housman wrote:

"Ale, man, ale's the stuff to drink,
For fellows whom it hurts to think."

One might substitute transistors for alcohol. We make honourable exception for those in solitary jobs who can't be reached by any *Music While You Work*. Barsley has even found an Arab shepherd in the fields where shepherds watch'd near Bethlehem, his transistor, wailing, on a cord round his neck. But Joyce Grenfell was not thinking of that use for the medium. It does, of course, make an undemanding background, which the telly can never do.

MALCOLM MUGGERIDGE

The reputation of Malcolm Muggeridge, with the wider public, largely began with his television appearances, but he was by then no stranger to the microphone. He has had an unspectacular but varied career, and it surprises his friends to know that he spent his childhood in, of all places, Croydon, went to a mere borough secondary school, and found life at Cambridge boring and tedious. (This is one of Malcolm's favourite words, and he pronounces it "teejus.") It had, he said in a TV talk, "the rank stench of a decaying class in a society which was in the last stages of decomposition." Odd that another personality of radio and TV, Gilbert Harding, found his Cambridge full of delightful talk but ultimately of no value. So John Betjeman, also in this class, summoned by bells to Oxford but failed his degree in Theology.

Lecturer at Cairo University, wanderer in India: it is no wonder that Muggeridge was restless. When asked about his war service, he simply replies "I was a spy," which is in fact true, and his high decoration from the French Government proves it. His friendship with Sidney and Beatrice Webb got him to Moscow, and his first BBC talk was on the subject of the Webbs.

"The broadcasting scene remains unforgettable—the airless, sultry studio; the little red light indicating that one is on the air . . . the inexorable moving hand of the noiseless clock; the figures behind the glass partition, so near and yet so remote; the glass of water always brackish to the taste; the sense of being far, far away from everyone and everything, in total isolation. How can I ever forget it?"[1]

An invitation to join *The Critics* followed, after a long period. This experience Malcolm found faintly ludicrous, and when, some ten years later, as Editor of *Punch*, he was planning a parody on the team, under the title "The Pundits," he found the task beyond him.

---

[1] *Muggeridge Through the Microphone* (BBC Publications, 1967).

Examination of the scripts proved them impossible to lampoon, in his opinion. They were already parodies. It is obvious that, from this stage on, the name Muggeridge was received in BBC Establishment circles with a certain diffidence, and at one time sheer distaste, which later turned to adulation. It is impossible, really, to say that "The BBC," as such, has any consistent attitude towards anybody, but Muggeridge has always been a marked man in some way, a distinction on which we are sure he prides himself.

"Being on *The Critics*," he wrote afterwards, "involved going to a film and a play, reading a book, listening to a radio programme and visiting some sort of art show. It was one of those experiences which, though not particularly momentous in itself, yet stamps itself like stigmata upon one; the more so in my case because I have always had a rooted objection to being entertained or culturally uplifted."

He was fortunate in having, as his producer, his old colleague Donald Boyd, whom he remembered from *Manchester Guardian* days. "I vividly recall his brooding, ironic presence, conveying a sense—to me, most sympathetic—that human beings are always ridiculous, and never more so than when they clothe themselves in the magisterial garments of literary and artistic punditry.... We each had an allotted role, mine being that of an ageing and already grizzled *enfant terrible*.... After lunch, we went upstairs to our studio and recorded the programme. It was a talking marathon. Out of the babble of talk occasional shrill cries would emerge, like the cries of sea-birds when waves are breaking on a silent shore. I can still hear a female voice shrilly proclaiming: 'I *liked* it!' and a male one in a deeper key, but equally insistent: '*I don't like* Raphael!' By five o'clock we were finished, and emerged into Portland Place, breathing in the air greedily after our incarceration...."

Sessions of *The Brains Trust* he found equally traumatic, if we are to believe him. Only in *Any Questions* did he seem to find any congenial radio company. But Muggeridge was still not cast in that inexorable role which he apparently feared—"poor Gilbert Harding for ever imprisoned in his irascibility, a Dimbleby in his pomposity, a Frost in his jocularity."

"Ah, but what of a label for Muggeridge?" asked Barsley, who, with Andrew Miller-Jones, first introduced him as a television interviewer in the early series of *Panorama* in 1954.

"He defies analysis. He is either liked or loathed. The mannerisms of Muggeridge are such as to make some people—particularly women—seethe with anger. They are the people who look without listening, and that means the majority of television-viewers. Critics, too. When the *Sunday Express* printed the headline THE MOST UNPOPULAR MAN ON TV, with a photo of Malcolm's maddeningly benign smile, they added 'Do You Want to Look at this Face for Another Two Years?' thus giving the game away. On that occasion, he rang me up and said 'Dear boy, do you want me to resign or something?' I replied that I was, on the contrary, delighted at the publicity. 'Oh good, so am I,' he said. 'I think we ought to celebrate.' And as a typical afterthought, 'I wonder what poor old Gilbert's going to say....' We had a splendid lunch, that Monday, at Boulestin's. I had known Muggeridge as a journalist before the war. Occasionally we appeared in the same issue of *Time and Tide* under Lady Rhondda's capable editorship, my poetry of disillusion beside his prose of disapprobation. His book on The Thirties is a masterpiece of concise journalism, and later made the basis of an acid television programme with Andrew Miller-Jones."

Muggeridge's replies in *Any Questions* were, and still are, witty and devastating. He is a man who has been everywhere and knows everyone. He has worked in Cairo, India, Moscow and Washington. He has been singled out by the sort of man who says "That's the fellah that attacked the Queen. Ought to be cut at his club." In fact, Muggs never attacked the monarch at all, but only the conception of monarchy, as presented by the Court circle of the time, and his remarks, unnoticed when printed in the *New Statesman*, only achieved notoriety because they were reprinted by the *Saturday Evening Post* on the eve of a royal tour of the United States. The subsequent "humanizing" of the House of Windsor after the pattern of the House of Orange vindicated Muggeridge's point, although, with malice ahindsight instead of aforethought, he probably deplores the "chummy" royal family image just as much.

The Muggeridge television career may not at first seem to have any connection with the heyday of radio, but on reflection it does. He is above all a man of words. "If this telly business were to conk out tomorrow," he once said, "I wouldn't feel a pang—though it might cost me a penny or two. I'd much rather have the printed word, or the spoken word. Those committed wholly to television get consumed by it, and it's all made into a sort of entertainment."

When the heaven-sent chance of interviewing Lord Reith seemed possible, it was Muggeridge who was given the monumental task—

one of the landmarks of BBC television, in which the pictures, for once, were as fascinating as the words. His radio exchanges with Bertrand Russell, some on the Overseas Service, are equally worth reading.

Let us hope that Muggeridge long remains a man of words—and a man of his word, as far as the all-consuming telly is concerned. Come back, Malcolm, all is forgiven.

WYNFORD VAUGHAN THOMAS

"My first big broadcast was at the 1937 Coronation—and it was in Welsh! I was in a state of absolute paralysed nerves and my first words, I know, were a sensation, so many people didn't know what the language was. I think they must have thought we'd got lines crossed with Peru or somewhere." (Curiously enough the first announcement of the fall of Rome, where Wynford was at the time, also came through in a Welsh news bulletin, and nobody in London caught it properly at first, or could understand what had happened.)

"The spirit of Reith brooded over Broadcasting House in those days. It was a strange experience to walk in for the first time into that hall, with its inscriptions. It was like entering a temple: no doubt about it. You moved about the corridors with awe and reverence, and you felt as if you had been admitted into a High Church, and you were taking Holy Orders.

"But I never got heavily involved in that more restricted side, I'm glad to say. I was never a tangled-up man: I dodged all the memos and all the restrictions, and found in Outside Broadcasts an exhilarating feeling of freedom. We were priests of the BBC Church, if you like, and with 'Lobby' and Tommy Woodrooffe and the others, we were an exclusive order—but we were working priests, working in the vestry. Every day there was a new adventure, some new technique to be tried, some new sport to be reviewed. Those early days were the most exciting of the lot. The principles of good commentary were being hammered out, and I was very lucky to be there at that stage. Moreover, you were judged by your peers, people working with you."

Wynford admits to having been dubious about commentating, even when he'd had some experience of it, and a good deal of thought and preparation were necessary.

"You can't just pick up a microphone and just flannel along. Lobby wouldn't have it. He worked on principles: he almost believed

Some Radio Personalities 215

in a ritual of commentary. You often hear this word 'homework' used; knowing the background. Well, it's true. You had to do it, to make a really effective broadcast, and this is surely what made BBC commentary far superior, during that period, to any other way of reporting.

"Almost unconsciously," he admits, "You absorbed the BBC's code of honour, the general feeling that this was the way the BBC looked at things, this is the way the BBC did things, and you took it in automatically. But that didn't mean you had to become a typical BBC man. I'm not: I was an escapee, a hoverer on the edge. One thing I did learn, however, was the importance of order. A Welshman prefers chaos. We're not a nation—we're a conspiracy, as you probably know, and we're always slightly agin it, and we don't take kindly to the arrangement of life according to a pattern. Well, I was for the first time in an organization which insisted on a certain amount of order, of people being in the right place at the right time. It was a discipline I needed, and I've always been grateful to the BBC for it. If this sounds very solemn, may I also say that what I enjoyed above all things was the gaiety that went with the job. The sense of fun behind the scenes.

"I think I'd say, looking back, that I did equally appreciate the big occasions and ceremonies—the growth of them under one's own description, gradually unfolding the procession that wound itself into a great climax, or the elaborate ceremony ending in a glorious burst of singing and colour—or the launching of a big ship, again a climax. You had to be there, to catch the moment of it, and the emotion."

(By contrast Wynford can quote an early television experience of a ship launching and the difficulties of following the director's choice of pictures, culminating in his cry: "There she is, the whole vast bulk of her!" just as a close-up of a Royal Personage appeared on the screen.)

Stewart Macpherson, the quick-talking, metallic-voiced Canadian who came over as a sports-commentator, taught Stuart Hibberd how to describe ice-hockey, chaired *Twenty Questions* and *Ignorance is Bliss* after a spectacular spell as a War Report correspondent, went in the early days to the City of London, to try his rapid-fire questions on the natives of the Square Mile. His companions were Wynford and Gilbert Harding, to whom he'd conveyed the opinion that BBC interviewers were very mealy-mouthed.

"We took him down to the City, to hear what we ought to do. Stewie leapt from the car with his microphone and stopped an immaculate City gent coming along, sticks the mike under his nose, and said 'I've got a surprise for you, brother—you're on the air!' The gent paused, and giving him a very kindly smile, replied, 'Brother—if after such a short period of acquaintance I can address you by such a familiar term—I have a surprise for you—you can go to hell!'—and moved on.

"Then Gilbert got out. Now Gilbert was a freak-attracter. If you put him in the middle of a crowd, he'd meet the one person who thought the earth was flat, and on this occasion, he picked the one man in the City who was wearing riding breeches and a cloth cap and a hacking jacket. Gilbert—whose technique of interview was hardly the most skilful; there was no come-on talk, you collided with Gilbert, and he stunned you with the microphone—Gilbert boomed at this chap 'Stop!' The man, naturally, looked startled. 'What d'you do?' Gilbert demanded. The man then replied 'Well, if it's any business of yours, I'm a gentleman farmer.' Gilbert boomed back: 'The tone of your reply, sir, means you are neither!'

One of Wynford Vaughan Thomas's friends, from their schooldays together in Swansea, was another Thomas—Dylan Thomas. His father taught Wynford English.

"Perhaps the thing which first impressed you about Dylan was his voice. It was as rich and deep as an organ, and spoke poetry beautifully, classical as well as his own. But you couldn't tie him down to anything—that was the trouble."

Laurence Gilliam was the first Head of a Department to take note of him, and became the instigator, if not the parent, of *Under Milk Wood*. It was Douglas Cleverdon, a BBC producer in Bristol and thereafter at Features in London, who took on the monumental task of keeping Dylan at it, giving radio a chance of acquiring the finest broadcast material in its history.

"Dylan was willing to try radio," says Wynford, "but the mechanics of the thing—the locations—he never understood. On one occasion he was due to appear at a studio in Swansea, but turned up at the right time, but in the wrong place, (in London) rather the worse for wear. To him The Studio was The Studio: no matter where. It was any room with a microphone in it." Seeing that the poet needed to cool off, Wynford and a friend took him to the nearest railway station. "Where did trains go to from here? There was Darlington, home of railways. All right, Darlington it should be. We got him a ticket, put it in his pocket, hung a string round his neck with a label saying 'Wake me up at Darlington' and put him in a carriage. No one saw him for two weeks. Then came a letter—rather like G. K. Chesterton's telegram: 'I am in Market Harborough. Where ought I to be?' In it Dylan asked plaintively 'Why did you get me to go to Darlington?' adding a graphic description of the town, and giving cogent reasons why he would never visit Darlington again."

There are many more stories about Dylan, both inside and outside the BBC. Like many scriptwriters, he used to look things up in Reference Library, and the present Librarian, Joan Houlgate, who was then an assistant, remembers that he was sometimes given a room near the library, for writing. His producer would sometimes lock him in, if it was during pub hours. But once a young secretary found the door unlocked, looked in, and asked brightly and helpfully, "Would you like a cup of tea, Mr Thomas?"

It is impossible to talk with Wynford for long without wanting to hear some of his war stories. Though we in *War Report* knew he was a splendid "straight" reporter, cheerfulness kept breaking in during his despatches, and at intervals, and after VE Day, we heard some of the tales behind the scenes. He had been in the fighting on the doomed and tragic beach at Anzio, about which he wrote a book, which was made into a film by Dino de Laurentiis.[1]

"I arrived at a time when the Army was in the doldrums. They'd been through Salerno, and Anzio lay ahead, and Monty was about to leave us. I went to one of his conferences, and he gave us a rousing talk, ending 'Well, gentlemen, I want to say one thing, and one thing only. [There we were, in pouring rain, stuck in the mountains of Italy.] The Army has got its tails well up. Tails well up!' An American behind me murmured 'Up what?' I never saw Monty again."

The landing in the South of France was quite different.

"This was a great moment, the beginning of what the Americans called 'The Champagne Campaign,' as we found when we jumped from our craft, under a barrage, into warm water. It was my birthday—15th August—and the place, St Tropez. We advanced through the drifting smoke, prepared to sell our lives dearly, when the group with me saw, as the smoke cleared, a gentleman standing holding a tray on which there was, in fact, champagne—excellent champagne, vintage Krug. We crowded round him, and he said 'Soyez les bienvenus,

[1] *Anzio!* (Pan Books Ltd).

messieurs. If I may venture a little criticism, you are, perhaps, somewhat late. . . .'"

Wynford is a *chevalier de tâte-vin*, a high honour in France, and he was later to combine with André Simon in a radio Feature *Growth of a Vintage*. But in 1944, he had to move too quickly through places with famous vineyard names.

"We liberated Tavel, swept through Châteauneuf du Pape, went up through l'Hermitage, then there was a pause, before we reached Dijon, and the Americans couldn't understand why this was occurring. I looked at the map, and to me it seemed quite clear. The French had reached Chalon-sur-Saône, and ahead lay Burgundy, with all its glories. So I went across to French HQ, and there they were, General de Lattre de Tassigny, General Monsabert, and the others. There, also, was a large map of the vineyards of France, on which the German positions had been carefully marked, and with emotion General Monsabert said to me, 'We're coming up to the great vineyards, the Golden Slope. In matters of wine, I am a man of the Left! It's impossible to imagine trampling the vineyards of *La France*—they'd never forgive us—they're the property of the whole nation.'

"Then suddenly, the whole atmosphere changed. A young *sous-lieutenant* entered and saluted smartly, and said '*Courage, mes Généraux!* We have found the weak spot in the German defences. Every one of them is on a vineyard of inferior quality!' So there was an epic decision. *Attaquez!* For several days I was underground. We moved from cellar to cellar, and I'll never forget emerging from time to time, to find I was in Meursault, and then in Beaune, and so I floated gently through the *Côte d'Or*, through the *Côte de Nuits*, until we came near to the Americans, who were trying to outflank the Germans. A charming Frenchman who was with me suggested we take a gift to the American General Patch, so we loaded up the jeep with some of the finest wines I have ever seen, and eventually handed them over. The General thanked us, and said he'd invite the French over for a *vin d'honneur*. Meanwhile, said an aide, 'Leave it to the doc—he knows all about this *chambré* stuff.' Glorious wines, La Tâche of unbelievable age, Clos du Roi—a whole roll-call of names they represented.

"So, in an eighteenth-century hotel nearby, there took place this noble occasion, the Americans awaiting the French with pomp and ceremony. They arrived, and the wine appeared. It had been *chambré'd* all right—it was almost bubbling! The American host added,

'We're in luck—the Doc's hotted it up with medical alcohol!' Never have I admired the French powers of restraint more. The French general lifted his glass, then put it down, and said quietly to me 'Liberation, Liberation—what crimes are committed in thy name!' "

Wynford Vaughan Thomas is another BBC man who "went over" (they still use that phrase within the Corporation, as if to join ITV were to change your religion. But at one time the phrase meant a man who deserted sound radio for BBC Television, just as Low Churchmen in the C of E sometimes hate High Churchmen more than Roman Catholics). Wynford, probably one of the most zestful, restless, rip-roaring correspondents in the BBC, never made a success of similar excursions into television. The medium somehow didn't suit him: he always sounded right, but didn't look the part. Perhaps he was too impatient and discursive a man for the cameras. Instead, he became a desk man who was never at his desk, but always fixing up some new idea. He is certainly the most unlikely tycoon in a business which does not often harbour humorists.

His own stories, over the years, are legion. A whole book could be compiled from them, and we hope he will do it himself, or find his own Boswell. They range from his Hymn to Haley to his account of the exploits of a legendary US War correspondent called Sammy Goldstein. He describes how Sammy accompanied him to the Vatican, where the press was to meet His Holiness. They paused in front of a famous painting of a woman, and Sammy said, "Jeez, how d'ya like to lay a cow like that?" The audience began when the tiny white figure appeared—or rather, the pressmen broke ranks and surged forward. Left behind in the rush was Sammy, crying, as the Benediction was made, "Hold it, Your Highness, till I get ya in focus!"

The time came for Papal presentations. Each man received a red book (of prayers) and a rosary. Wynford was asked "Americano?" and replied "Church of England." He received his little book, and *two* rosaries. As the Pope passed on, Sammy whispered to Wynford: "Give ya five bucks for dat one," and still on his favourite subject, "with dat I could lay any Catholic chambermaid in the Bronx!"

There are few things Wynford hasn't attempted. There were the times when he saved the day on public occasions by keeping Dylan Thomas out of alcoholic trouble. Once, he confesses, he missed out. Dylan was to appear at Swansea Town Hall for some civic award, and

Wynford guaranteed to put him on a train which he knew ran nonstop to Swansea station, where he would be met by friends. Time passed. No word of confirmation from Swansea that all was well. Finally came a despairing telephone call. Wynford had forgotten that it was Friday, and that on Fridays, the train made one stop. One had been enough, and the scene in the hall after the poet had arrived will long remain in the city's memory.

Besides being a prodigious traveller—in 1949 he made a round-the-world radio trip in eight days—Wynford is a man of culture and taste. As already indicated, the taste extends particularly to wines: he has been a colleague of André Simon and Cyril Ray (Cyril was a fellow war-correspondent for the BBC in the vintage series *War Report*). As for culture, he claimed at one time that the style of his commentaries was based on the Sermons of John Donne. And as for exuberance, we called him "the human alka-seltzer."

Apart from enjoying his role in contemporary radio, Wynford would have enjoyed the earlier pre-war days perhaps even more. He had a fine phrase for that era:

"I for one look back with regret to this *Elizabethan Age* of the BBC."

This is his conclusion after he has said: "Modern broadcasting is a specialists' business. The time has long gone by when one man could tackle the whole range of broadcasting work in the course of a single day. But the old pioneers still thrill newcomers with their stories of how they used to arrive at their offices to write a few scripts in the morning, and spend the evening announcing, acting, producing, radiating goodwill as radio 'uncles' and conducting the station choir if they had a few minutes to spare."

Specialization had to come, however, and standards of performance rose as a result. "But something of the old zest and adventure of the early days is still needed in our programmes." Wynford, we feel, would have been very much at home in Savoy Hill.

MARJORIE ANDERSON

Writers who produce books on the BBC are sometimes accused of neglecting women broadcasters and producers, and there is probably some truth in it, though they probably set out with no such idea—indeed, with a chivalry which somehow fades away. We ourselves do not echo Bob Hope's remark "You women are all alike—sensational!" But neither do we overlook the warning "Never underestimate the power of a woman." In our office at one time there was a postcard over the secretary's desk which read: "Behind every successful man there's a woman telling him he's wrong." Who in the BBC, faced with a list of female names famous in radio history, could overlook a Mary Somerville, a Hilda Matheson, a Mary Adams, a Freda Lingstrom, or a Grace Wyndham-Goldie, or even a power in the land and a Governor, Lady Violet Bonham-Carter, or such publicly unknown powers behind the scenes in programme-planning, Joanna Spicer and Clare Lawson Dick?

But there have been, and are, women in the BBC whose names mean something quite different, and who have no desire for power or position—who are, indeed, almost embarrassed and certainly puzzled at their own immense popularity.

One such person is Marjorie Anderson. Like many a BBC personality we have quoted in this book, she got into the BBC largely by chance. At the beginning of the war, Marjorie had been turned down by the Wrens, because she apparently showed signs of catarrh. The advertisement for a BBC announcer in the *Morning Post* was one for which she wasn't fitted—it said "over thirty-five" for one thing, presumably because of people being called up. But her mother persuaded her, and in due course she got an answer. She remembers having typed her letter, and hearing later that there'd been about 3000 applications for the job, she puts this fact down as partly responsible for her being short-listed.

"I remember the interview before John Snagge and Elizabeth Cowell very clearly. It was early spring, and I wore a tweed suit of lime green—rather a daring colour in those days, but I must have been feeling pleased with myself, although overawed by the whole business. Mr Snagge asked me if I was a good mixer, and I boldly said I was—I'd recently been in pantomime, anyhow. Could I read at sight? I said I could. I'd never have courage like that now," she added in her own disarming way. Marjorie didn't in fact get the job advertised, for the Home Service, but months later was recommended for the Overseas Service (then called the Empire Service). So that is how one of radio's most popular favourites began her microphone life, with Georgie Henschel, whom she'd met at the first interview. She was so excited at getting the job, she left her car standing outside the BBC afterwards.

Today Marjorie Anderson is associated with *Woman's Hour*, but she didn't in fact take on that particular task until near the end of our Vintage period. To many thousands of service men and women she was the Voice which read the *Thank You For Your Letters* series, a tribute as great as anything that could be paid, and a job done in her spare time. When asked for the secret of her success in "TYFYL" as they called it, she won't at first admit to any particular quality, but if pressed she will admit that her voice must have had something to do with it, as well as her ability to interpret the feelings, and sometimes carry out the wishes of those who wrote to her, mainly from India and South East Asia Command. These were her "expeditions." For instance, one writer might ask if she'd ever been to that hidden-away spot in the heart of London, Shepherd Market? She had, but she went again, and reported back to one Leslie Hubble in Italy, even trying out the "tankard of foaming ale" he used to enjoy, although she was no beer-drinker, "In fact I'm only just learning to swallow the stuff without making faces, but I did want to carry out your imaginary walk to the letter."

This is typical Marjorie. One of her constant admirers was the crew of HMS *Roebuck*, somewhere at sea. At one time her Commander, Trevor Lean, asked whether children were still able to have holidays by the sea. She went down to Middleton-on-Sea, in Sussex, and found they were. At the end of the war, one of the *Roebuck* company's greatest pleasures was in meeting her, with gifts of rare goodies like bananas and grapes. It's interesting to look at the scripts of these "letters" today, stamped and signed by Admin. as "Passed for Policy and Passed for Security." They were a moving episode in radio. Marjorie's style is romantic but realistic in exactly the right blend. She should have made a book of them.

"The whole thing was terribly exciting during the war. The BBC has never been the same since. That was *the* time." Even the exile to Evesham, which began by annoying her (when she had to announce "This is London," she felt it was cheating, because she wasn't in London, sharing the war dangers), became, in its way, pleasant, since the "studio" was the comfortable room of a country-house, where they brewed tea in time for the morning broadcast, and where she could watch the dawn come up over Bredon Hill.

ROY PLOMLEY

There are some programme ideas which remain apparently for ever welcome on the BBC books, because they are simple, friendly, and popular. The *Desert Island Discs* series, with Roy Plomley, has come as a boon and a blessing to the BBC—particularly planners. It has run for thirty years, and should continue as long as the supply of discs and celebrities continues. Of the continuation of the urbane Roy Plomley, never ruffled, never riled, concealing his boredom when faced with a dull or self-opinionated castaway, rejoicing in the company of one imbued with integrity and blessed with intelligence, there can be no doubt. His introduction, following *Sleepy Lagoon* and that plague of seagulls, is as familiar and comfortable as a favourite pair of shoes.

An important point, as he agrees, is that the copyright is his, and in recent years, the words "in a programme devised by him" have followed the title. The BBC has on several occasions been known to purloin such an idea, or repeat it after the originator has died or otherwise departed, in the same way as many of us know, after foolishly submitting an idea on the telephone, the bland reply "Yes, we were thinking of something along those lines ourselves. . . ." The BBC is not immune from this kind of shoplifting. Jimmy Edwards protects himself in a similar way over his crazy quiz show *Does the Team Think?*

Roy, who lives in a little-known but interesting road near the railway bridge at Putney, where writers write and artists have studios, told us about the prosaic origin of the record programme which has itself set a record:

"I was going to bed one night at the end of 1941. I was, in fact, already in pyjamas. And then the idea suddenly struck me. I'd been on the look-out, as a freelance for the BBC—I've never been on the staff—for something which might sustain a series of programmes. So I sat down there and then, and typed out a letter to Leslie Perowne, whom I'd never met."

Radio was not a new thing to Roy. Before the war, there was as much talk about Radio Luxembourg and Radio Normandie as there is today about "pirate" stations. (One might think that, since one of his ancestors, Francis Plomley, was a surgeon's mate in the eighteenth-century navy, that there might be something of the pirate in him, but the Plomley family, although hailing from Devon, have always been connected with medicine.) Roy became one of the announcers and disc-jockeys, not in Luxembourg but at Fécamp, Normandy. The programmes might run from seven in the morning till one o'clock at night, with all the popular stars on recordings, Tommy Handley,

George Formby, Leonard Henry, Jack Warner, Reginald Foort and so on, under the energetic leadership of the so rightly-named Captain Plugge, Conservative MP for Chatham—the Reith of this radio. Barsley comments: "Luxembourg and Normandie were far less of an idiot-programme than the present BBC Radio One, which plunges deeper and deeper into the swamp of popular drool, with disc-jockeys gibbering like monkeys, and scripts far more witless, if I may say so, than the pre-war stuff I wrote for Radio Luxembourg in the late 1930s. A showman like Sir Thomas Beecham was not too proud to conduct in aid of the family pills, worth a Guinea a Box. We even had the Communists on our side: Luxembourg programmes were listed in the *Daily Worker*."

But *Desert Island Discs* rapidly climbed to a favourite position within the BBC fold.

"After the series had been accepted," Plomley continues, "we chose names of the time, like James Agate and Frances Day. By 'we' I mean myself and tireless Monica Chapman, who produced about seven hundred castaways. Vic Oliver was our first. We've always kept a standby list of two or three hundred names, but there've always been people coming into the news, chaps who sail round the world, actresses who win Oscars, boxers like Henry Cooper who floors Cassius; people who suddenly pop up, and seem far more exciting to us than the regular list of you-know-who's.

"The second stage, after the choice of a Castaway is made, is sitting in the BBC Record Library with him and well over three-quarters of a million discs to choose from. The selection reveals a lot about his or her interests and personality. That's where the background homework comes in, the most important part of the interview, which is, thank God, unscripted. Now you begin to find out what sort of person the castaway is; whether he's introspective; whether he's nervous or relaxed, placid or inquisitive, honest and independent, or just sent by his agent. I expect the Castaway to do his share too. I remember Ninette de Valois saying, 'When I took up the idea, I thought it was all rather a joke. The more I went on, the more serious it seemed to become.'"

Plomley allows complete freedom of choice. It would be to debase the golden hoard of his currency if his Castaways were influenced by him. One of them chose eight overtures. Another, all records made by herself. Well, if that's what the lady wants, she shall have them. But what, we asked, if there's a really bad choice?—"I see what you mean. Yes, sometimes I have to talk someone out of a disc which would be, for any of a variety of reasons, completely out of place. My formula is simply to take the Castaway out for a drink—'Let's break off,' if you like—and the chances are he'll come back saying, 'There's one disc I'd like to leave out, or change. . . .' And it's nearly always *that* one. One point I do make: their choice must be their own honest individual one, made without thinking of pleasing the listeners.

"As can be imagined, Castaways fall into two categories: those who are generally interested in the situation, and really try to imagine themselves in it, and those who tend to regard it as a self-advertising gimmick, like those interviews so often given for nothing, provided the plug is given for the show, or the book, or what have you.

"Very occasionally I get someone like that, someone who's on the make, trying to show off, or who's insincere. That always seems to me to stick out a mile, when I hear the programme played back. I'm never actually ordered from on high in the BBC to put anyone in. They—whoever they are—may draw the producer's attention to someone special, but the chances are I've already got the person in mind myself. I *have* had difficulties, but of a different kind. One Castaway was chosen without his knowledge, while he was abroad. He turned up without knowing the programme would consist of choosing music—and he turned out to be entirely tone-deaf! So Monica and I, for the first and only time, constructed the story for him. We found out what school he'd been to, and put in the school song. Since he'd been in the Army, we then chose his regimental march. After that, we rang up his wife, and asked if they had a joint favourite from years back, and she had, a dance tune, 'our' tune. Bit by bit, we pieced his selection together. We've had scoops, too. 'Our Enery' was recorded before his fight with Cassius Clay, so although a commercial firm had banned all words from him, we were in the clear—on the day of the fight. For the start of the World Cup in football, we had Sir Stanley Rous—who else? Lord Harewood was our first Royal Castaway."

The surprising, unpredictable choices by famous figures are Roy's pride and joy to recount.

"Take Gordon Harker, for instance. You'd expect things like *Knock 'em in the Old Kent Road*, demanded in sepulchral cockney. Not a bit of it. It was mostly Wagner. Gordon turned out to know the *Ring* cycle inside out. James Robertson Justice chose six different movements from Beethoven Quartets. It was superb—and he topped them off with a bird-song, and the bagpipes. I didn't expect Stokowski to call for Dixieland jazz and tango, but he did. Dame Flora Robson chose some 'pop' music, because she said it cheered her up, and so on."

To be invited to be a Castaway is still a privilege, not a concession or a chore. Devilishly simple in its devising, the idea is endlessly interesting and revealing, except perhaps when Plomley, to those who have followed him, is really fed up with the speaker before him, who has, in fact, probably been "planted." Finally, we were reminded that the luxury permitted to the Castaway had to be an inanimate object. "We had so many requests for people from the opposite sex."

What perhaps gives DID (shall we call it, in the initial manner?) additional interest is that its originator is not just a radio or TV man. His main pleasure in life is writing plays for the legitimate stage. They don't often get a London showing, but the provinces know him.

TOM CHALMERS

Tom Chalmers was known in the BBC as the man who openly declared he'd get chamber music played on the Light Programme. "We got hold of a rather bright young man from the Music Department—he's since gone to other and much higher spheres in music—and we said 'We want a chamber-music series, and it's going to be scheduled opposite *ITMA*. We shan't try to rival *ITMA*'s listening figures of course, but let's see if we can offer something different, of a prestige nature—a sort of chamber-music-while-you-work, though we won't call it that.' Well, the bright young man was Basil Douglas: his programme, *Music in Miniature*. You can have £150 per programme, we said—and that was big money in those days."

One secret of the programme was that the titles were not revealed until the end. *Music in Miniature* proved that there was indeed a public for this kind of thing, and a surprisingly large public too.

"We did the same thing for poetry on the Light," went on Chalmers. "You may remember Wilfred Pickles introducing *The Pleasure's Mine*. It had fantastic audiences, and proved the point that you could interest the hitherto unwilling listener if you knew how to put your idea across. *Mirror of the Month* was a good example of the light topical radio magazine." He agreed that it was almost the radio equivalent of *Lilliput* magazine, popular in that day. But the Light Programme had, in his opinion, far more to it than the present Radio 2 programme. "It had guts to it. It could present the very popular *Focus* series, Progress Report and so on, and experts like Sir Adrian Boult would come on, explaining, say, how a symphony was constructed, and he was such a good broadcaster I told him that if ever he was out of a job, I'd get him one as an announcer!" The men running the Light found wonderful material in the Regions: Chalmers cites *The Archers*, from the Midlands, *Have a Go!* from the North, and *Any Questions* from the West Region.

The fertile brain of Norman Collins was behind many of the best Light Programme ideas, and Collins, if anybody, personified the programme he founded. It is not often that a successful, best-seller author can turn his hand to being top executive in both radio and television—and continue to write best-sellers. *Dick Barton* was one of Norman Collins's brain-children, and equally, the Diary of Mrs Dale, and *Down Your Way*, which first brought Dimbleby into a regular, popular postwar series with Arthur Phillips. *Radio Newsreel*, with its famous signature tune, began during the war, and the title is still used. The technique of the short excerpt and the on-the-spot interview arose from a combination of experiment in the Outside Broadcast Department and Features, and the experience of the War Reports.

Talk of Norman Collins and Maurice Gorham brought a reminder that both these two had played a notable part in the External Services —which meant broadcasting overseas. To them, says Chalmers, must be added the name of the late John Grenfell Williams, a remarkable, modest, immensely likeable South African, who came to England to train as a medical missionary, but was lured into the BBC, partly because he spoke perfect Afrikaans, and partly out of the sense of adventure in broadcasting to the Africa he loved so much—the black Africa. From running the BBC African Service, he rose to join the Collins-Gorham hierarchy and contributed greatly to it.

"Grenfell Williams's enthusiasm for Africa was so great," said Tom Chalmers, "that it persuaded me to go out there myself, to Nigeria—and that changed my whole life. It was at one of our Saturday lunch-time Guinness sessions. We would meet—Gorham, Williams, Collins and myself—at any pub which served draught Guinness, not easy to get during the war. The pub also had to be near a bomb-site, because Norman Collins was collecting material for his novel *London Belongs to Me*."

At such meetings in pubs, BBC careers are indeed often made, or changed—or sometimes ruined. With Tom Chalmers, who has now left the BBC for commercial radio, anything could happen.

These Radio Personalities of ours have not been chosen at random, or out of favouritism, or because they're representative. Many more could have been added. But each of these people presents a facet of life in the BBC in those days, and each brought personality to a job which can otherwise be as humdrum as that of the business executive.

11

The BBC's Jubilee

THE BBC can be said to have won its Silver Medal by the Twenty-fifth Anniversary, November 1947. The occasion brought forth a large number of special programmes and reminiscences. A Royal visit to the Concert Hall at Broadcasting House culminated in a Jubilee edition of *ITMA*: Sir Adrian Boult and Sir John Barbirolli shared a Jubilee Concert: Robert Donat presented a grandiose documentary, produced by D. G. Bridson: Vera Lynn sang in a Leslie Mitchell show, *Alhambra of the Air*: Alistair Cooke, Gracie Fields, Jack Payne, Eric Barker, Alec Guinness, Wilfred Pickles, were all in evidence: on the newly-fledged Third Programme Stephen Potter and Joyce Grenfell mounted one of their inimitable "How" programmes: life inside the BBC itself was covered by Peter Eton's wry, occasionally debunking survey, and *The Programme was Recorded* covered most of the appropriate Departments. Noel Johnson played the heroic Dick Barton, Roy Rich compèred *Housewive's Choice*, and the voice of the Radio Doctor could be heard in the land, rumbling on about collywobbles and bile.

Even television, scarcely a teenager, chipped in. Robert Barr compiled a pictorial history of the Corporation, Joan Gilbert introduced a special *Picture Page*, Macdonald Hobley was in charge of *Kaleidoscope*, Fred Streeter chatted about gardens, the Drama Department put on a performance of *Murder in the Cathedral*, with Eric Fawcett producing a take-off called *Funny Thing, this Wireless!* Quite a week.

For many, the highlight was on the anniversary itself, a round-the-table revival of recordings and reminiscences (there was certainly an "r" in the month) introduced by John Snagge, with a Barsley-Worsley production called *Do You Remember?* The broadcast took place in a studio rebuilt after the famous bomb explosion in 1940—an event in itself to be remembered, as Snagge pointed out. Taking part in the programme, with their personal choice ranging over twenty-five years, were Sir Harold Nicolson, Mabel Constanduros, Stuart Hibberd, Ted Kavanagh and Wynford Vaughan Thomas. Our own working title for the programme was "Underneath the Archives."

Snagge began with the words "Tonight we are in reminiscent mood," a sentiment which is no doubt appropriate for the BBC's Golden Jubilee in 1972. That mood was kept, unashamedly, throughout, and in a wide variety of ways. As we might have expected, one request, by Ted Kavanagh, was for Bruce Belfrage's recorded account of what happened over the bomb, which exploded as he was beginning to read the news. Bruce denied all the remarks attributed to him. A voice was dimly heard saying "It's all right," believed to be that of Lord Lloyd, due to speak later, but with ceiling plaster like confetti on his large domed head, Bruce went on with the news like a good naval type, and made no reference to the incident.

Our guests' reminiscences may have been thought to be old hat by telly enthusiasts, but there's no hat like an old hat, particularly if it is worn at a slightly rakish angle. That night, we had one ace up our sleeve, which no listener and hardly any of the staff knew about. This time Ted Kavanagh had asked to hear a re-play of Tommy Woodrooffe's commentary on "The Illumination of the Fleet" at the Spithead Review after the Coronation, ten years earlier.[1] There had been agonizing conferences about repeating this, with its memorable opening lines "At the present moment the Fleet's lit up, and when I say the Fleet's lit up, I mean it's all lit up with little lamps...." The recording was not to be played out of any denigration of that magnificent pioneer of commentaries, and to prove it, we would follow it with a subsequent, typical Woodrooffe broadcast from a Cup Final.

The production team supported the idea. Higher and Higher went the plea for a decision, until it reached Director-General level. Sir William Haley—to our enormous relief, we felt—agreed, provided we received Woodrooffe's approval, and that there was no advance publicity. Both provisions we naturally kept, and we had, of course, already got Tommy's agreement. One newspaper quoted him afterwards as being very annoyed about it: in fact, he was in the studio during the programme, and at the party afterwards, was to be seen talking with Haley, who was drinking gin-and-tonic to Tommy's black coffee! Following the item, in addition to the football commentary, came a composite description of the telephone reaction, including a call from Sweden, expressing boundless admiration for the "joyous spirit of the BBC."

When Harold Nicolson began his reminiscences, the figure of Haley was seen to move quietly into the producer's cubicle, evoking a

---

[1] See page 67.

momentary feeling of panic among the producers, who knew that Nicolson, once a BBC Governor, had voted against his appointment. However, though Nicolson was live, his script had been read beforehand—indeed, the script had been the cause of a crisis before transmission. The original was mislaid during rehearsals. Nicolson refused a duplicate: his own copy must be found. Eventually, the production secretary, a cheerful Scots-Irish girl whom we called "Thumper," because she reminded us of Disney's helpful rabbit, unearthed it ("Is this the one? It's got squiggles all over it!"). Nicolson, a fastidious writer with a very felicitous turn of phrase, had an equally engaging manner of speaking, with hesitations and the feeling of searching for the exact word or emphasis. All this was considered carefully in advance: hence the guide-lines of his own particular squiggles. Many notable broadcasters do this, and for them there is only *one* script they must have when the green light glows, and they are on the air.

Sir Harold's main theme was Reith, but he began "One is startled to discover that this elderly, nay this venerable institution is a mere stripling of twenty-five. The undergraduate has suddenly become a don...." Of Reith he said "Stark and solitary, he took his meals in his own cabin. We all wanted to go on wonderful journeys to the Hesperides, but were much more likely to find ourselves confined to Dundee." In tribute, he added "It was Reith who, with his high ideals, gave the BBC its sense of responsibility."

Sir William Haley retreated silently from the cubicle, and everybody breathed again. Nicolson chose recordings by Marconi, G. K. Chesterton, and Mr Middleton the immortal gardener. Stuart Hibberd recalled Stanton Jefferies, first BBC Director of Music (when the C stood for "Company"): Dame Nellie Melba's final farewell, and a recording of Lillian Harrison as Nurse Edith Cavell, following them with two contrasts, the frenzy of the Last Night of the Proms, and the Olympian, cosmic sonority of J. C. Stobart's "Grand Good Night" of Savoy Hill days—days when, as Stuart reminded us, timing was not all-important. He cited the example of a well-known actress making a broadcast appeal. She over-ran by seventeen minutes. A memo reached Hibberd later from on high: it read "She must now be placed on the list of unmanageable old ladies." (There probably was one.)

We all expected Mabel Constanduros[1] to give us one of the

See page 113.

Grandma Buggins episodes, and she did. There followed the original version of Percy Grainger's "Country Gardens," played by the inveterate Cecile Dixon, who was once described as "the girl who sleeps under the piano," so instantly could she be on call. We say original version, since like so many tunes of its kind, it has been translated and travestied for the transistor public. Another favourite was Harry Lauder's "Keep Right On to the End of the Road." He did, too: he was the first artist to get a fee of £1000 from the BBC, for his Seventieth Birthday programme.

"Ah, the happy halcyon days of the Thirties!" Vaughan Thomas began, and immediately doused the halcyon feeling with a talk by J. B. Priestley in 1938, on the horrors of gas-mask drill. This, however, was a reminder that much of Wynford's most memorable broadcasting was done as a war correspondent: we had the barrage at the Battle of Alemein; Howard Marshall's first dispatch, when wet and dripping from the Channel, on D Day; Robert Reid's dramatic account of de Gaulle entering Notre-Dame in Paris under a hail of bullets—a commentary during which Reid was knocked over by the crowd, but his microphone readjusted, went on talking. Finally, a speech by Churchill. Given time, he could perhaps have included the equally sonorous voice of his friend Dylan Thomas.

When his turn came, the massive figure of Ted Kavanagh squirmed uneasily in the tiny, tubular steel chair the BBC provided for speakers in those days (nowadays the chairs are so comfortable you are likely to doze off before the green light glows). Ted had never considered himself much of a speaker—except at the "warm-up" sessions of *ITMA*—but he introduced a winner in Woodrooffe's commentary. He started with a serious broadcast talk on "How to Reduce Weight," given in the same flat voice as the physical-jerks lady's diction on the rhythmical-exercise occasion as famous as "The Fleet's Lit Up," but we would not allow Ted to introduce this one. Gillie Potter followed, talking about Hogsnorton, and Edward Ward, reporting the war. Finally, after Belfrage and the Bomb, there was a quick-fire moment or two from *Mr Murgatroyd and Mr Winterbottom*, in which Tommy Handley and Ronald Frankau were still cheerfully murdering the language every week, plundering it for puns.

Snagge's job was to introduce the speakers and the recordings, but he said privately afterwards that if he had been choosing his own radio remembrances, he would have included the singing of "Abide with Me" before the Cup Final, some personal memories of Reith,

Ed Murrow of "This is London" fame during the war, Richard Dimbleby ("that Caesar of commentators") describing the earthquake at Skopje in Yugoslavia, Roger Bannister running the first four-minute mile on a little-known athletic occasion in Oxford, and the *Vivat Regina* from the Coronation Service of 1953.

So the Silver Jubilee was celebrated. For the Golden Jubilee, the recorded wealth is double, but the early recordings remain immortal. We shall not listen to their like again.

CHARLES CURRAN

1947 was an eventful year for another BBC man who eventually rose to the top job.

Charles Curran, a Cambridge graduate, who had served five years in the Indian Army, joined the BBC soon after his military career ended, a gap of just two years. He confessed to us in an interview that at the time he knew very little about broadcasting, but that in retrospect, three things seemed to stand out. "I doubt if we were aware of them at the time. First, there was a very gentlemanly atmosphere about the whole affair. I was a member of the Home Talks Department, and I was dealing with political and economic talks. There were arguments about what we should do, and about the extent of our critical comment, and I have no doubt that above my head arguments must have been going on with Government about whether we were acting with sufficient respect for the problems of Government. But the tone and range of comment as I recall it was on a comparatively narrow range. One was working in the atmosphere of the traditional *Times* leader—an 'on the one hand, on the other' kind of situation. Indeed, one of my contributors, a most balanced man, was spoken of to me by one of my superiors as being 'good, but didn't I think a little viewy?'"

That's a phrase Charles Curran has heard, in different terms, many times recently, as propounded by those who think they know what BBC views ought to be. But at the time, he continued, "We were working within the censensus, and the consensus was pretty narrow. We were all behaving very properly towards each other and towards the public."

Curran's second characteristic in those days was the very close and very complete system of editorial control.

"I could count five layers of supervision between myself and the

Controller of Talks and they went up, as it seemed to me, in a straight line, and none of them could be missed out if one referred upwards. But reference upwards was much less a matter of discretion for the producer in those days than it is now, because there was a process known as "scrutiny." This meant that the text of every talk had to be seen before transmission by one or other of the five, and comments might be made to the producer which he would then have to seek to impose on the speaker—usually, of course, by persuasion. But I can remember a few awkward moments when I was under a positive instruction to secure certain changes in a script. It was a very difficult position indeed if a contributor was a man of strong views—and indeed many were, because that was how they had established their claim to be respected as political commentators."

Charles Curran resigned from the BBC in 1950, and gives this as one of the reasons. He admits he can't say honestly, here and now, whether or not it was a major reason, but it was certainly in his mind.

"The third fact which I remember," he continued, "is the small awareness which one had of other parts of the BBC. As a post-war recruit one had little knowledge of the External Services—and this was a kind of self-impoverishment in the world in which we were then living—and we were scarcely aware at all of the existence of television. That is perhaps less surprising because it was still on a very small and pioneering scale. I did try to get into television towards the end of my time in Talks, but I had no evidence to offer of visual capacity and I did not succeed. What one was very much aware of was the apparent permanence of those members of the Talks Department staff who had entered the BBC's service during the war and who were still there after it. Those of us who came after the war were often starting on a delayed career and had enjoyed an experience of the world which did not lead us to be naturally patient."

The job Curran took on after his three years with the BBC was certainly to do with patience. He joined the staff of *The Fishing News* and became its Assistant Editor.

"I felt that I needed a craft, that print journalism represented such a craft, and that the production of Talks in radio did not. I think I was wrong, but I knew that I was not satisfied." However, even a year away from the BBC convinced him—"with great certainty," he puts it—that he needed the element of public service in his life if he was to be happy. This has been a lure of the Corporation which has proved strong with many a man. So he asked to come back, and eventually did come back through what he calls "the fortuitous and happily open back door of the Monitoring Service—a re-entry which I have never regretted. I learned a great deal in the Monitoring Service which would have made me a better Talks producer if I had known it in 1947."

This branch of the BBC, with its headquarters at Caversham, has always been a "mystery" part of the Corporation, but many of those who have served there profess great belief in it, particularly as an experience which widens the horizon. It is perhaps characteristic of Charles Curran's outlook that he became the BBC's Canadian Representative from 1956 to 1959, and that eight years later he had become Director of External Services, and thus was in touch with the whole world. Like Hugh Carleton-Greene, he became DG after a thorough working knowledge of the BBC from the inside, and he summed up his attitude to his employers, after his return, in these words:

"The most important fact was that I was back in an organization whose central and only motive was to serve the public interest. Beyond that, as I then knew from experience, nothing else really mattered. I had found a satisfactory mainspring for my life and I knew that the same mainspring worked a machine which meant a great deal to the country. I have never since then found any need to question what was my motive in working—and that is a great debt to acknowledge to any employer."

Those who had the belief that the Corporation, because of its civil-service type of structure, lived in an unrealistic world of its own, welcomed the introduction of a managerial image at the highest level, particularly in the field of radio. "Give me back my legions!" cried the Roman general Cassivelaunus to Caesar after the battle of Cannae. But it was no use the BBC crying "Give us back our legions of listeners!" when those listeners had left them, to become watchers. It was no use pretending that the days of wine and roses were still there; no use bolstering the hydra-headed monster representing the administrative structure in Broadcasting House, and the Regional Headquarters throughout the country. By its actions the BBC found it better, in its debt to the public which paid for its salaries and its programmes, with a tax as compulsory as that of Caesar, to run after the rival ITV, in search of circuses rather than bread, in search of quantity rather than quality.

Reith, we feel, would never have pursued such a course, even in the name of realism. He might have quoted a Latin tag in describing the action of his successors: *video melior proboque: deterior sequor* (I see the better, and approve it: I follow the worse). As for the inevitable wielding of the pruning-hook, no one can have envied the pruners their work, just as no one could imagine that the steady reduction in the power and prestige of radio could be achieved without much loss of face and faintings of heart. In the political sphere, there are nations like Sweden and Denmark which can shrink to a comparatively lowly, unimportant world status without sacrifice of quality or personality. But in its own sphere, BBC radio was probably too big, too complex and too well entrenched to live with its new minority status.

IAN TRETHOWAN

It was in an effort to put its radio house in order that the BBC introduced this managerial role. Ian Trethowan, a former diplomatic correspondent of the late *News Chronicle* and later Assistant Editor of Independent Television News, moved quickly from BBC Television to the job of Managing Director, BBC Radio. He thus followed in the direct line of succession from Sir Lindsay Wellington, first Director of Sound Broadcasting until 1963 and Frank Gillard, who assumed the title Managing Director in 1969. (Trethowan's opposite number, equal in rank as Managing Director, Television, is Huw Wheldon.) A new appointment was made in 1972 of a General Manager representing local radio.

It is perhaps not a bad thing that Trethowan today has had little to do with the Corporation in an administrative way, and can therefore approach BBC radio policy from an untrammelled viewpoint. The interest in the medium is certainly there, as he pointed out to us in a special interview:

"I'm one of the generation that was brought up on radio, just as my children were brought up on television. As a boy before the war, radio was part of my life. During the war, radio was part of the air one breathed."

The egg, in other words, was laid, and eventually, as he put it, "the possibility of moving into radio at a gratifyingly senior level was personally very interesting." Trethowan does not like it to be implied that he undertook to do a rescue-job. "That's being very unfair to my predecessor." He gives, in other words, full credit to

Gillard and his associates for the drastic measures they took in the mid-1960s.

"In 1953, Television 'took off.' Then came commercial TV, and the thing soared. Radio almost wholly lost its basic family evening audience. Some cried "Ichabod! [Trethowan pronounces it "Eyechabod."] The glory has departed. But then, somewhere in these mid-sixties, people began to take stock of television. And they took a realistic look at what radio could do."

All this is common knowledge, and the measures taken are there for all to see, and for all to judge. But Trethowan's present attitude is what matters for the BBC, and he seems able to maintain a sense of optimism as well as recognition of his own role.

"There is a radio bandwaggon which is moving anyway. Whether the BBC get on that bandwaggon and keep a large slice of it will depend on myself and my successors. One has an enormous responsibility over the style of the radio services, and their efficient management. . . . In a phrase, the buck stops here."

Trethowan, however, believes to a large extent in delegating responsibility ("You cannot run a creative broadcasting service with too heavy a hand.") He believes to an equally large extent in local radio. ("I think local radio is something in which broadcasting and the BBC—*and* the BBC," he emphasized, "goes back to the grassroots, where you remember it starting years ago.") It may seem a little difficult, at present, to find much evidence for this last thought.

Presumably the "grass-roots" (whatever that phrase really means) represent the BBC in its early, adventurous days, days which led to the Vintage Years and that heady sense of freedom. We can scarcely believe that BBC local radio stations, in general, represent such a spirit. Surely, the argument goes, the BBC threw in their twenty stations in a great hurry as an effort to forestall the start of commercial radio, always inevitable and now imminent. Trethowan does not agree. "At the moment," he claims, "I think it's not too much to say that there's an affection for the BBC through the local stations, and we want other places like Taunton, Shrewsbury, Warwick, East Anglia, York."

We do not wish to appear discouraging, but the contribution of BBC local stations to radio as a whole has so far been disappointing to many people. From our own experience of the past, the BBC Regional stations were sources of immense vitality and talent, working often in proud autonomy. Think of the contribution made by the BBC West

Region under Gillard's control, or the dramatic splendours of Scottish radio and the comedy of the North of England. The regional legacy has been taken up, not by the BBC, but by Independent Television companies such as Granada and Anglia, and may well be taken up again by commercial radio which, when it comes, may be very different from the preconceived idea a man like Trethowan wants to envisage.

"If you're running a commercial station, there's no problem," he told us. "The object of the exercise is to make money, and so you plan it all with a view to maximizing your profits, and you make such genuflections to culture as you may think politically desirable, but basically the object is to make money." This attitude is as naïve as to pretend that the object of all BBC work is to Do Good. Moreover, in its division into the Goodies and the Baddies, it forgets that, as far as Television is concerned (and that is where the public hackles are raised) it is men like Sir Lew Grade who keep their family programmes free from brutality and sexual titillation.

If BBC radio finds itself confronted by a commercial radio with a real sense of local purpose as well as local talent, what chance has it got?

"Our own local radio will only be partly in competition," Trethowan goes on, "and our competition will only be partly from local radio—there will be more from Radios 1 and 2." It is, of course, understood that the help of these big battalions will make a difference.

On the question of an alternative radio service, we found the views of Howard Thomas invaluable at this transitional stage.

"I believe that commercial radio has arrived too late in the day in Britain. It should have preceded commercial television and not succeeded it. There is no real demand from the public for commercial radio. I am sorry to say that I think it will always be a secondary service. It will be helpful for motorists, fodder for housewives, and pap for teenagers, but in a world which will, I hope, have four television channels, feature films on pay-TV, and visual cassettes, commercial radio must be the poor relation of communications.

"I doubt whether the Vintage Years of Radio can ever be recaptured, because they depended so much on the enthusiasm of gifted people who had found a new outlet for their abilities and energy. Before those days, the Press had been the main market for people like us; then radio gave us all sorts of new opportunities.

"For me, writing for newspapers in Manchester was the path

towards a national outlet. The situation is utterly different today, with so many markets for creative people, writers, producers, directors, musicians, and performers. As well as the BBC's two channels there are five major commercial companies competing for the services of creative people. The theatre is there too, and the film industry will always be the ultimate target, because it is certain to return to its old glories.

"Few of us will want to go back to radio, and the new generation of talented people will not want to be encumbered by the limitation of a 'blind' medium. They will seek success in the more glowing visual world of television and films."

A final question to Howard Thomas: does the BBC deserve to win that Gold Medal in 1972?

"Yes," he replied confidently. "Because with all its faults of civil service attitudes and top-heavy administration, the BBC has been a marvellous training ground for people like us. We were allowed to experiment and to make mistakes, and through the tough process of trial and error so many of us learnt our trade.

"Working there, too, we also made many valuable and delightful associations. Friendship and connections began which have been not only beneficial in career development but have also been the source of some joy of living. The BBC was a fine club to belong to, and most of us have a tremendous affection for the institution. The BBC began a camaraderie for the amusing, dedicated, mad, attractive people with whom we were able to work."

Brave words, and we echo them. But they are not really sufficient to explain either the BBC's glory or the BBC's dilemma.

The nostalgic view is one thing. The know-how view—the cold, clinical appraisal of the BBC's chances in clinging on to its reputation, and eventually its Charter in 1976—is another. Perhaps we may take a third view.

In this collection of reminiscences, we have tried not to take the line "What was good enough for my father is good enough for me." We have never believed in a BBC *status quo*. What we do believe is that, faced with a new situation and a changing world, the BBC may have faltered in its standards, or wasted its time chasing false gods. John Reith has often been quoted as saying that the object was "to give the public what it wants." What he in fact said was "to give the public what it *thinks* it wants"—and there is a world of difference.

We are thinking particularly of radio, because our reminiscences are about radio, and radio in this country is shortly to undergo a great change, as men like Ian Trethowan and Howard Thomas realize. It is impossible to predict the outcome at this stage, but it is equally obvious that, since 1953, which is the last year of our vintage, radio has become the Cinderella of the communication services. It is the Ugly Sisters—BBC TV and ITV—who are invited to the Ball. Cinderella has no Fairy Godmother (in fact, her licence doesn't cost anything any more) and can only remain in her kitchen. Yet she knows that her Sisters will be locked in deadly rivalry for the hand of Prince Charming—who looks very like the impresario Prince Littler. So she smiles to herself, and carries on, and we wish her good luck, and once again congratulate her on her independence from the advances of commerce and politics, and hope that no more politicians like Lord Hill will be appointed as her Chairman.

What is, to us, obviously not to be recommended to her is that she should doll herself up, and follow whatever trend may be popular. At one time the BBC created a trend, or established a taste. It had within its staff men capable of doing this. Today it follows where it should lead. It tries to read the crystal ball of popular opinion (which in itself is created by outside influences, and does not just evolve) and follow whatever forecast may seem favourable. Yet all the time, its unwieldy structure and hidebound hierarchy forbids any sudden, unorthodox move which might capture the imagination—and capture a new public.

A vintage takes time to mature, yet the planting of the vineyard was usually due, in the first instance, to a man of genius, knowing just where to plant his vines and how to nurture them. Too often the radio vintage today is that artificially fortified concoction called tonic wine—a shot in the arm, a frantic effort to be "with it," whatever "it" may be.

The BBC would be the first to honour its own proud history. During 1972, its main object in celebrating its Golden Jubilee has been to recall golden days, when it reigned supreme. Witness the much publicized nostalgia of getting Arthur Askey and Richard Murdoch together again, delving among the archives in Broadcasting House for a repeat of the old flat there, and Mrs Bagwash and Nausea and finding, rather unkindly we feel, John Snagge's moustache cup among the old treasures. Witness the celebrated get-together of the Goons, with no expense spared, at a recorded *reprise* in the old BBC Camden Theatre, with royalty queuing up for seats.

It is perfectly in order for the BBC to be nostalgic, as we have been ourselves. But it is no longer a particular honour or privilege to be asked to write or perform for the BBC as such, and yet BBC people go around still pretending that it is. The assumption is still there, but not the assurance.

If one takes a particular example—that of presentation, of the BBC Voice on the air, whether it be to read the news, or give information about forthcoming programmes—the overall standard seems to us to have declined, and there is no one within the organization to maintain it. Accepted pronunciation no longer matters: we have heard a Head of Presentation recently declare: "We leave it to them." It is a measure of criticism of the BBC at present that there is no one who can recognize that in the slipshod words there is a lowering of the BBC standards as we knew them. It is not a conscious abandonment of BBC standards: it has grown up because no one really cares. A News Bulletin is injected into a popular programme: it is written and spoken objectively and without emphasis, and it may be a catalogue of disasters beginning with an air-crash and ending with widespread floods. But, one feels, there is no one who has foreseen what effect this will have on the listener, and there is no one who cares. Reith may have been hypersensitive about the effect of radio in people's own homes. Today this effect is shrugged off by people with no overall perception of their means of communication. The loser, as always, is the listener.

The BBC World Service, on the other hand, seems to have kept up its standards to a far greater extent, unconscious of the hot breath of competition from television; members of this branch of the BBC have been able to keep to the guide-lines set down years ago, and still valid.

We have attempted, in this combined reminiscence, to recall the best stories and the best examples from what we regard as the BBC's great contribution to radio. Savoy Hill men may claim that the pioneering years were the best of all. Recent attempts to revive an admitted interest in radio may point to a new future for Cinderella. She may never go to the ball, but a buffet-supper or a barbecue may be brought to her. She may learn from the example of the United States, where radio had no vintage, disappeared underground, but is now shooting forth tendrils which may grow. At least the BBC is proud and jealous of its past.

We have also reflected what is true of the BBC and radio world—

that the trivial can appear tremendous to those who work within the medium. The question of a missed cue, or a break in transmission, or even a wrong inflexion which will be heard by millions. These are what rivet the attention of programme staff, and the smoother the result, the easier will the listener think it is to perform the feat.

In these reminiscences, we have sometimes felt like truant schoolboys emptying their pockets of minor items like marbles, or a sticky sweet, or cigarette-cards, or a penknife with a device for getting stones out of horses' hooves. We have also felt, at times, that we realized what the BBC was all about, that we

> "Took upon 's the mystery of things,
> As if we were God's spies."

Does the BBC deserve its Gold Medal for its 50th Anniversary? We say yes, as Howard Thomas says yes, but perhaps for different reasons. We say yes, not only for our own sense of gratitude for working within such an organization for so many years, and feeling this pride in once saying "we're from the BBC," but because we believe that BBC radio can emerge from its next struggle, if not intact, at least with an appreciation of its own particular role.

This, then, is our Anniversary present, not so much to the BBC as to the listeners, who are the people who matter. The great ones in radio played it by ear, and the public listened. We can think of no greater tribute to what we regard as those vintage years of radio.

Index

Abdication, the, 21, 87
Adams, Godfrey, 4
Administration, 13, 26, 120
Agg, Howard, 114
Alan, A. J. (Captain L. H. Lambert), 8
Allen, Frederick, 18, 21
Allison, George, 82
Anderson, Marjorie, 220ff.
Andrews, Eammon, 80
Any Questions? 213
Announcers, anonymity of, 16, 17
Archers, The, 24, 114
Arnhem, 197
Arnold, Doris, 146
Ashbridge, Sir Noel, 56
Askey, Arthur, 147, 149ff.
Auden, W. H., 121
Audience Research, 30
Aylward, Gladys, 117

Babbage, Wilfred, 36
Baily, Leslie, 179
Baird, J. L., 38
Balalaika, 112
Baldwin, Stanley, 88
Balfour, Honor, 169
Band Waggon, 141
Barnes, Sir George, 157, 159
Baseley, Godfrey, 114
Barr, Robert, 201
Bates, Sir Percy, 70
Beecham, Sir Thomas, 39, 129
Beerbohm, Sir Max, 157
Belfrage, Bruce, 33
Benchley, Robert, 28
Bennett, Sir John Wheeler-, 61
Bernhard, HRH Prince, 175
Berryman, Lt-Gen, 100
Black, George, 108

Boat Race, the, 75ff.
Bomb, the BBC, 61
Bonham-Carter, Lady Violet, 54, 159, 194, 222
Boult, Sir Adrian, 43, 46
Bowman, Bob, 81
Boyd, Donald, 193, 212
Braden, Bernard, 78
Brains Trust, The, 162ff.
Brand, Colonel, 1, 2
Bridson, D. G., 117, 118
Briggs, Professor Asa, 60
Brittain, Vera, 128
Britten, Benjamin, 92, 120
Broadcasting House, 10
Brockington, Leonard, 100
Browne, Laidman, 34
Buggins Family, the, 113
Bulpit, Sergeant, 97
Burgess, Alan, 93
Byam, Guy, 197

Campbell, Commander, 164
Carnival, 110
Carpendale, Admiral, 4
Chalmers, Tom, 226
Chapman, Monica, 225
Charles, HRH Prince, 77
Chesterton, G. K., 26
Children's Hour, 45ff.
Christmas Day programme, 85, 92
Churchill, Sir Winston, 25, 99, 105, 157
Clair, René, 29
Clarke, R. T., 183
Cleverdon, Douglas, 102, 158, 163
Coates, Joan, 91
Cock, Gerald, 66, 86, 87
Collins, Norman, 227
Constanduros, Denis, 114

Constanduros, Mabel, 113
Constantine, Lord, 79
Cooke, Alistair, 167
Cooper, Henry, 225
Coronation Day, 1953, 103
Cotterell, Leonard, 14,
Country Magazine, 175
Cox, Sir Geoffrey, 14, 183
Critics, The, 212
Crocombe, Leonard, 6
Crossman, R. H. S., 48
Curran, Charles, 233ff.
Cutforth, Rene, 14, 98

D Day announcement, 188ff.
Daily Express, 16
Dalby, W. Barrington, 82
Dales, The, 114
Dark Tower, The, 119
Davies, Sir Walford, 43
Day, Miss Frances, 72
Dillon, Francis, 13, 175
Dimbleby, Richard, 184, 186ff, 206
Director-General, function of, 53
Down Your Way, 187
Duncan, Peter, 143
Dunstan, Eric, 50
Dupuis, Colonel, 189
Duty Officer, 23

Easter in Europe, 129ff.
Eckersley, Roger, 153
Elizabeth, HRH Princess, 90, 91
Ellison, John, 144
Engelmann, Franklin, 18
Engineers, BBC, 36ff.

Fabricius, Johann, 198
Farjeon, Herbert, 51
Features Department, 171ff.
Felton, Felix, 27, 157
Fielden, Lionel, 2, 38
"Fleet's Lit Up, The," 67
Fleming, Peter, 59
Fletcher, Lynton, 38

Foort, Reginald, 66
Foot, Robert, 53
Forbes, Bernard, 97
Forsyte Saga, The, 34

Gardner, Charles, 180
Genn, Leo, 34, 98
George V, HM King, 19, 86, 92
George VI, HM King, 86, 98, 107
George, Brian, 80
Geraldo (Gerald Bright), 155
Gielgud, Val, 10, 29, 33, 46, 106, 110, 123, 126
Gill, Eric, 10
Gillard, Frank, 62, 75, 91, 177, 196, 200
Gilliam, Laurence, 6, 7, 12, 27, 61, 78, 92, 103, 130, 171-3, 177-8
Girls, BBC, 31
Girls, PBX, 25
Glendenning, Raymond, 83
Glock, Sir William, 43
Glover, C. Gordon, 84, 149
Goldstein, Sammy, 219
Goring, Marius, 110, 120
Gorham, Maurice, 6, 228
Grade, Sir Lew, 152, 239
Graves, Cecil, 10, 53
Graves-Pierce, John, 23
Green, Sir Hugh, 58ff.
Grenfell, Joyce, 208ff.
Grisewood, Freddie, 19
Grisewood, Harmon, 20, 54, 68, 110
Guthrie, Sir Tyrone, 5, 116-18
Guyler, Deryck, 138, 209

Haley, Sir William, 48, 52ff, 98, 107, 189
Hall, Henry, 152ff.
Halton, Matthew, 194
Handley, Tommy, 2, 5, 26, 134ff, 141
Handley's Half Hour, 135
Harding, Gilbert, 26, 44, 206ff.
Harrison, Lillian, 110, 128
Heppenstall, Rayner, 158, 178

Index 245

Herbage, Julian, 44, 129
Hervey, Grizelda, 34, 35
Hibberd, Stuart, 11, 14, 18ff.
Hill, Lord, 48, 204
Hobbs, Carleton, 35
Holland, Prime Minister, 100
Hollis, Christopher, 88
Hopkins, Anthony, 43, 129
Horne, Kenneth, 145
Housewives' Choice, 5, 44
Howland, Alan, 18
Huxley, Julian, 164-5
How programmes, 26, 44, 206-8

In Town Tonight, 143
Inns, George, 5
Instone, Anna, 43, 44, 129
Iremonger, Rev F. A., 20, 122
ITMA, 5, 133ff.
ITN, 14

Joad, Dr Cyril, 164
Johnston, Brian, 82
Jones, John Glyn-, 3, 193

Kavanagh, Ted, 134, 141
King-Hall, Commander, Stephen, 46
Knox, Collie, 152
Koch, Dr Ludwig, 41
Kossoff, David, 115

Ladbrook, Charles, 94, 101
Lane, John, 94
Lang, Archbishop, 88
Laski, Marghanita, 169
Levy, Muriel, 34
Lewis, Cecil, 4
Lidell, Alvar, 14, 16, 18, 22
Lidgett, Dr Scott, 125
Light Programme, 227
Lillie, Beatrice (Lady Peel), 28
Liverpool, 137, 150

Lotbinière, Seymour de, 16, 21, 66, 70, 74, 104, 214
Lorraine, Robert, 38
Lusty, Sir Robert, 48

McAuliffe, General A. C., 201
McCulloch, Derek (Uncle Mac), 45, 165
Macdermot, Robert, 168
McGivern, Cecil, 161
McIntyre, Duncan, 101
Mackay, Angus, 79ff.
McKechnie, James, 34
Mackenzie, Sir Compton, 103, 110
McKie, Dr, 105
Macleod, Joseph, 18, 190
MacNeice, Louis, 7, 80, 118ff, 158, 173
Maconochie, Sir Richard, 156
Macpherson, Stewart, 74, 80, 215
Malan, Group-Captain, 100
Manio, Jack de, 52, 178
Man Born to Be King, the, 53, 211ff.
Marshall, Howard, 66, 74, 92-3, 196
Marson, Lionel, 21
Marvell, Holt, 111
Maschwitz, Eric, 6, 106-112
Matheson, Hilda, 156
Matheson, Muir, 94
Max-Muller, Charles, 73
Maxted, Stanley, 194, 197
Melville, Alan, 202
Michie, Bryan, 5, 44
Miller-Jones, Andrew, 108
Mills Brothers, 108
Mitchell, George, 5
Monday Night at Eight, 147
Monitoring Service, 236
Montgomery, Lord, 199
Moore, Brian, 81
Morris, John, 15
Morris, Johnnie, 46
Muggeridge, Malcolm, 165, 187, 211
Muller, Red, 72
Murdoch, Richard, 147
Murrow, Ed, 109, 179
Music Magazine, 42

246 THOSE VINTAGE YEARS OF RADIO

Nicolls, Sir Basil, 60, 163
Nicolson, Sir Harold, 7, 35, 54, 157
Norden, Muir and, 52

O'Donnell, B. Walton, 22
Ogilivie, F. W., 53
O'Sullivan, Eileen, 25
Outside Broadcasting, 65ff.

Palmer, Rex, 8, 79
Panorama, 187
Parker, Gibson, 190
Payne, Jack, 1
Peach, L. du Garde, 46, 116
Penn, Lord Dawson of, 19
Peoples' Pleasures, 139
Pepper, Harry, S., 146, 153
Phillips, Frank, 3, 14, 206
Pickles, Wilfred, 17, 107
Pidsley, Reginald, 41, 180
Pitt, Percy, 43, 129
Plomley, Roy, 209, 222ff.
"Polish Corridor," the, 106
Pooh, Winnie the, 36
Potter, Stephen, 158, 208
Priestley, J. B., 56
Proms, the, 42

Queen Mary, HM, 102-3
Queen Mary, The, 70
Question Masters, 168

Radio Doctor, the 48, 204
Radio Times, 6, 8
Redgrave, Sir Michael, 38
Reid, Robert, 200
Reith, Lord, 2, 10, 20ff, 29, 35, 38,
   42, 48ff, 58, 84, 106
Repertory Company, 33
Robertson, Alec, 44, 129
Rodgers, W. R., 118, 131
Rose, Howard, 115
Rowley, Elizabeth, 159

Russell, Audrey, 169
Ryan, A. P., 58, 193

Sargent, Sir Malcolm, 43
Sayers, Dorothy L., 122ff.
Shaw, G. B., 170
Shelley, Norman, 33, 35, 47
Shuter, John, 13
Siepmann, Charles, 156
Sieveking, Lance, 5, 107
Silent Minute, the 59
Silver Jubilee, BBC, 50
Silvey, R. J., 19, 30
Smart, Billy, 139ff.
Smith, R. D., 158
Somerville, Mary, 156, 222
Speaight, Robert, 120, 125
Sports Report, 79
Squirrel's Cage, The, 5, 117ff.
Standing, Michael, 73
Stewart, Andrew, 64, 159
Stobart, J. C., 6
Stone, Christopher, 62, 108

Talbot, Godfrey, 91, 182
Talks, Dept, 156ff.
Tape-recorders, 39, 174
Thalben-Ball, Dr George, 43, 129
Third Programme, 157
Thomas, Dylan, 119, 216, 220
Thomas, Howard, 27, 52, 161, 238
Thomas, Wynford Vaughan, 40, 74,
   91, 93, 99, 193, 214ff.
Top of the Form, 168
Train, Jack, 142
Trethowan, Ian, 236ff

Under Milk Wood, 159, 217

Vizard, John, 40

Wakelam, Captain, H. B. T., 79
Waldman, Ronnie, 41, 134, 145

War Report, 191ff.
Watt, John, 27, 48, 72, 136, 145ff. 164
Welch, Rev. J., 122
Wellington, Sir Lindsay, 63ff.
Westbury, Marjorie, 33, 34
Williams, John Grenfell, 228
Wilmot, Chester, 196ff.
Wimsey, Lord Peter, 122
Windsor, Duke of, 57
Wincott, Geoffrey, 35
Wood, Sir Henry, 4, 3

Wood, Sir Kingsley, 21
Wood, R. H., 86
Woodrooffe, Tommy, 67, 104, 105, 214
Word, Director of the Spoken, 157
Worsley, Francis, 134, 142
Wynn, Hon. R. B. T., 37

Young, Filson, 110
Young, Gladys, 34, 92, 120, 128, 209

OHIO UNIVERSITY LIBRARY

ease return this book as soon as you have
it. In order to avoid